CW01651161

Fluency in Number Facts
Teacher's Guide

Years 3 & 4

Peter Clarke

William Collins' dream of knowledge for all began with the publication of his first book in 1819. A self-educated mill worker, he not only enriched millions of lives, but also founded a flourishing publishing house. Today, staying true to this spirit, Collins books are packed with inspiration, innovation and practical expertise. They place you at the centre of a world of possibility and give you exactly what you need to explore it.

Collins. Freedom to teach.

Published by Collins

An imprint of HarperCollins*Publishers*
77 – 85 Fulham Palace Road
Hammersmith
London
W6 8JB

Browse the complete Collins catalogue at
www.collins.co.uk

© HarperCollins*Publishers* Limited 2013

10 9 8 7 6 5 4 3 2 1

ISBN-978-0-00-753128-8

The authors assert their moral rights to be identified as the authors of this work

All rights reserved. No part of this publication may be reproduced, stored in a retrieval system, or transmitted in any form or by any means, electronic, mechanical, photocopying, recording or otherwise, without the prior written permission of the Publisher or a licence permitting restricted copying in the United Kingdom issued by the Copyright Licensing Agency Ltd., 90 Tottenham Court Road, London W1T 4LP.

British Library Cataloguing in Publication Data
A Catalogue record for this publication is available from the British Library

Edited by Gaynor Spry
Cover design by Nikki Kenwood
Cover artwork by Gwyneth Williams
Internal design by Nikki Kenwood
Illustrations by Ilias Arahovitis and Jouve
Typeset by Jouve

Printed by Martins the Printers Ltd, Berwick upon Tweed

Acknowledgement
The author wishes to thank Brian Molyneaux for his valuable contribution to this publication.

Contents

Introduction

The first aim of The National Curriculum for Mathematics (2014) is to ensure that all pupils:

> *'become **fluent** in the fundamentals of mathematics, including through varied and frequent practice with increasingly complex problems over time, so that pupils have conceptual understanding and are able to recall and apply their knowledge rapidly and accurately to problems'.*

Mathematical fluency involves being able to reason mathematically and calculate accurately, efficiently and flexibly.

It is acquired by mastering the following knowledge and skills:

- a thorough conceptual understanding of number, including place value, addition, subtraction, multiplication and division
- the ability to identify patterns and relationships
- the development of strategic approaches to recall and derive number facts.

Essential to mastering these is:

- purposeful dialogue in pairs and as a group
- effective activities to practise and consolidate numerical skills and the recall of number facts
- meaningful and informative assessment, including self-assessment.

Fluency in Number Facts aims to support conceptual understanding, and the development of mental fluency, in basic numerical skills through whole-class, paired and individual games and activities, and assessment.

The series is divided into Key Stage 1 (Years 1 and 2), Lower Key Stage 2 (Years 3 and 4) and Upper Key Stage 2 (Years 5 and 6). It consists of three *Teacher's Guides*, accompanying *Facts and Games* books and *CD-ROMs* containing all of the resources needed for the games and activities in downloadable form.

Teacher's Guide

Containing Teacher's Notes on:
- whole-class games and activities
- paired games and activities
- individual activities

Facts and Games book

Containing:
- Maths Facts
- paired games

CD-ROM

Containing:
- Maths Facts from the *Facts and Games* books
- resources for the whole-class games and activities, including PowerPoint slides
- paired games from the *Facts and Games* books as well as additional paired activities
- individual activities
- Mental fluency challenges
- number cards
- assessment and record-keeping formats

Each *Teacher's Guide* and *Facts and Games* book covers three Key domains of becoming fluent in number, and are based on the expectations of The National Curriculum for Mathematics (2014).

- Number and place value
- Addition and subtraction facts
- Multiplication and division facts

How to use *Fluency in Number Facts*

Fluency in Number Facts is a flexible 'dip in' resource that is designed to be used in many different ways to meet the needs of individual children, and different classroom and school organisational arrangements.

Each of the games and activities is intended to be used for approximately 10 minutes as a way of sharpening children's memory and recall of the basic number facts. Use them either at the start or end of a mathematics lesson or as a quick filler activity at any time throughout the day – a '10 minutes memory maths' session.

The following is a suggested approach to choosing a suitable game or activity:

Decide which Key domain you want to develop fluency in:
- Number and place value
- Addition and subtraction facts
- Multiplication and division facts

Refer to the *Fluency in Number Facts: Teacher's Guide*

↓

Decide whether you want the children to practise and consolidate their fluency in this Key domain:
as a whole class   in pairs   individually

Refer to the *Fluency in Number Facts: Teacher's Guide*

↓

Choose an appropriate game or activity.

Refer to the *Fluency in Number Facts: Teacher's Guide*

↓

Locate the necessary resources.

Refer to the *Fluency in Number Facts: Facts and Games books and/or the accompanying CD-ROM*

Curriculum information

The games and activities in this pack practise and consolidate the following Lower Key Stage 2 (Years 3 and 4) National Curriculum for Mathematics (2014) Programme of Study:

Year 3

Number and place value

Pupils should be taught to:

- count from 0 in multiples of 4, 8, 50 and 100; finding 10 or 100 more or less than a given number
- recognise the place value of each digit in a 3-digit number (hundreds, tens, ones)
- compare and order numbers up to 1000
- identify, represent and estimate numbers using different representations
- read and write numbers to at least 1000 in numerals and in words
- solve number problems and practical problems involving these ideas.

Addition and subtraction

Pupils should be taught to:

- add and subtract numbers mentally, including:
  - a 3-digit number and ones
  - a 3-digit number and tens
  - a 3-digit number and hundreds
- estimate the answer to a calculation and use inverse operations to check answers
- solve problems, including missing number problems, using number facts, place value, and more complex addition and subtraction.

Multiplication and division

Pupils should be taught to:

- recall and use multiplication and division facts for the 3, 4 and 8 multiplication tables
- write and calculate mathematical statements for multiplication and division using the multiplication tables that they know, including for 2-digit numbers times 1-digit numbers, using mental [and progressing to formal written] methods
- solve problems, including missing number problems, involving multiplication and division, including positive integer scaling problems and correspondence problems in which n objects are connected to m objects.

Year 4

Number and place value

Pupils should be taught to:

- count in multiples of 6, 7, 9, 25 and 1000
- find 1000 more or less than a given number
- count backwards through zero to include negative numbers
- recognise the place value of each digit in a 4-digit number (thousands, hundreds, tens, and ones)
- order and compare numbers beyond 1000
- identify, represent and estimate numbers using different representations
- round any number to the nearest 10, 100 or 1000
- solve number and practical problems that involve all of the above and with increasingly large positive numbers.

Addition and subtraction

Pupils should be taught to:

- estimate and use inverse operations to check answers to a calculation
- pupils continue to practise both mental methods [and columnar] addition and subtraction with increasingly large numbers to aid fluency

Notes and guidance (non-statutory):

- solve addition and subtraction two-stop problems in contexts, deciding which operations and methods to use and why.

Multiplication and division

Pupils should be taught to:

- recall multiplication and division facts for multiplication tables up to 12 ×12
- use place value, known and derived facts to multiply and divide mentally
- recognise and use factor pairs and commutativity in mental calculations
- multiply 2-digit and 3-digit numbers by a 1-digit number [using formal written layout]
- solve problems involving multiplying and adding, including using the distributive law to multiply two digit numbers by one digit, integer scaling problems and harder correspondence problems such as n objects are connected to m objects.

Notes and guidance (non statutory):

- Pupil continue to practice recalling and using multiplication tables and related division facts to aid fluency
- Pupils practice mental methods and exctend this to 3-digit numbers to derive facts (for example, 600 ÷ 3 = 200 can be derived from 2 x 3 = 6).

Fractions (including decimals)

Pupils should be taught to:

- compare numbers with the same number of decimal places up to two decimal places
- solve simple measure and money problems involving [fractions and] decimals to two decimal places.

Features of the *Fluency in Number Facts: Teacher's Guide*

The games and activities in the *Fluency in Number Facts: Teacher's Guide* are arranged according to the three Key domains. Within each of these Key domains the games and activities are further organised into whole-class, paired or individual games and activities. They are all designed to be used at any time throughout Years 3 & 4.

Whole-class games and activities

This section provides a series of teacher-led games and activities aimed at ensuring the whole class practise and consolidate their fluency in each of the three Key domains.

Each game and activity includes a list of the teacher and pupil resources required as well as instructions and, where appropriate, any variations.

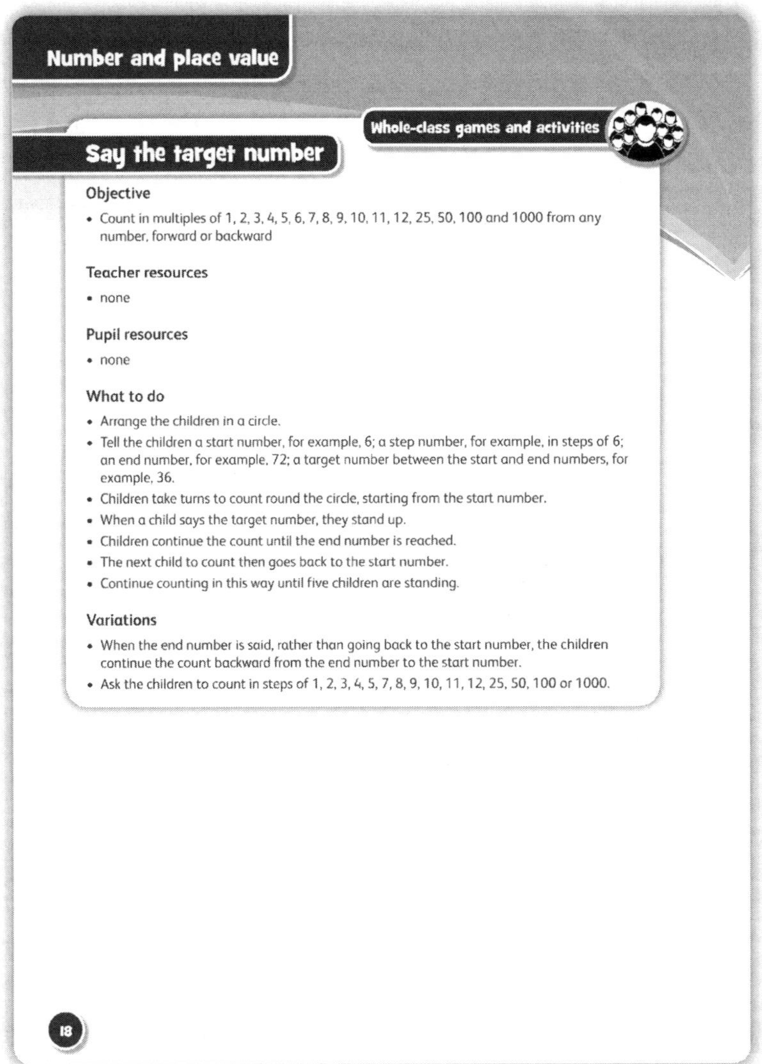

Number and place value

Whole-class games and activities

Say the target number

Objective

- Count in multiples of 1, 2, 3, 4, 5, 6, 7, 8, 9, 10, 11, 12, 25, 50, 100 and 1000 from any number, forward or backward

Teacher resources

- none

Pupil resources

- none

What to do

- Arrange the children in a circle.
- Tell the children a start number, for example, 6; a step number, for example, in steps of 6; an end number, for example, 72; a target number between the start and end numbers, for example, 36.
- Children take turns to count round the circle, starting from the start number.
- When a child says the target number, they stand up.
- Children continue the count until the end number is reached.
- The next child to count then goes back to the start number.
- Continue counting in this way until five children are standing.

Variations

- When the end number is said, rather than going back to the start number, the children continue the count backward from the end number to the start number.
- Ask the children to count in steps of 1, 2, 3, 4, 5, 7, 8, 9, 10, 11, 12, 25, 50, 100 or 1000.

18

PowerPoint slides required for some of the whole-class games and activities are located on the accompanying CD-ROM.

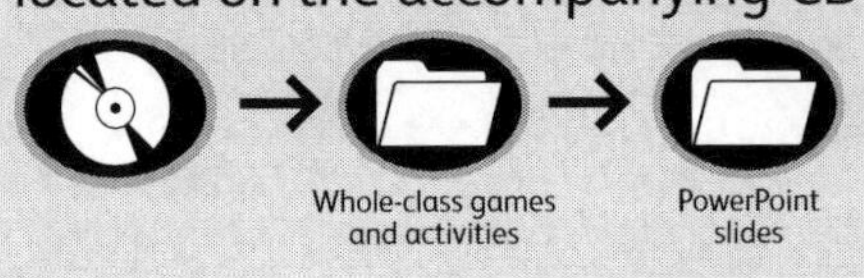

PDF files required for some of the whole-class games and activities are located on the accompanying CD-ROM.

Paired games and activities

Games and activities are provided which children undertake in pairs to practise and consolidate their fluency in each of the three Key domains.

Each game and activity includes a list of the resources required as well as instructions and, where appropriate, any variations.

PDF files required for some of the paired games and activities are located on the accompanying CD-ROM.

→ Paired games and activities

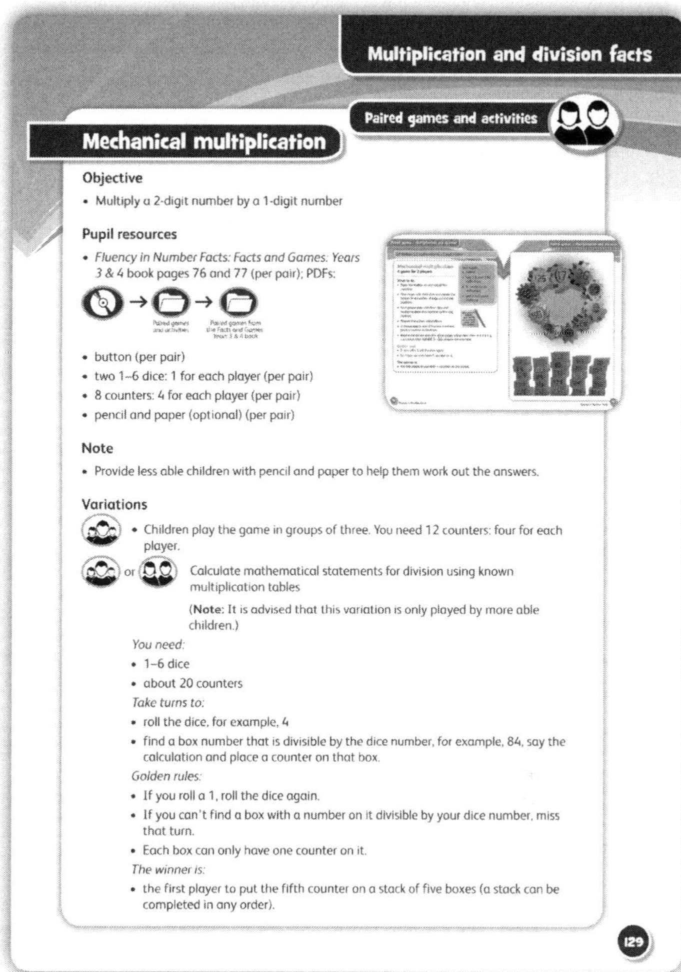
Multiplication and division facts

Paired games and activities

Mechanical multiplication

Objective
- Multiply a 2-digit number by a 1-digit number

Pupil resources
- *Fluency in Number Facts: Facts and Games: Years 3 & 4* book pages 76 and 77 (per pair); PDFs:
  → Paired games and activities → Paired games from the Facts and Games: Years 3 & 4 book
- button (per pair)
- two 1–6 dice: 1 for each player (per pair)
- 8 counters: 4 for each player (per pair)
- pencil and paper (optional) (per pair)

Note
- Provide less able children with pencil and paper to help them work out the answers.

Variations
- Children play the game in groups of three. You need 12 counters: four for each player.

or Calculate mathematical statements for division using known multiplication tables

(**Note:** It is advised that this variation is only played by more able children.)

You need:
- 1–6 dice
- about 20 counters

Take turns to:
- roll the dice, for example, 4
- find a box number that is divisible by the dice number, for example, 84, say the calculation and place a counter on that box.

Golden rules:
- If you roll a 1, roll the dice again.
- If you can't find a box with a number on it divisible by your dice number, miss that turn.
- Each box can only have one counter on it.

The winner is:
- the first player to put the fifth counter on a stack of five boxes (a stack can be completed in any order).

129

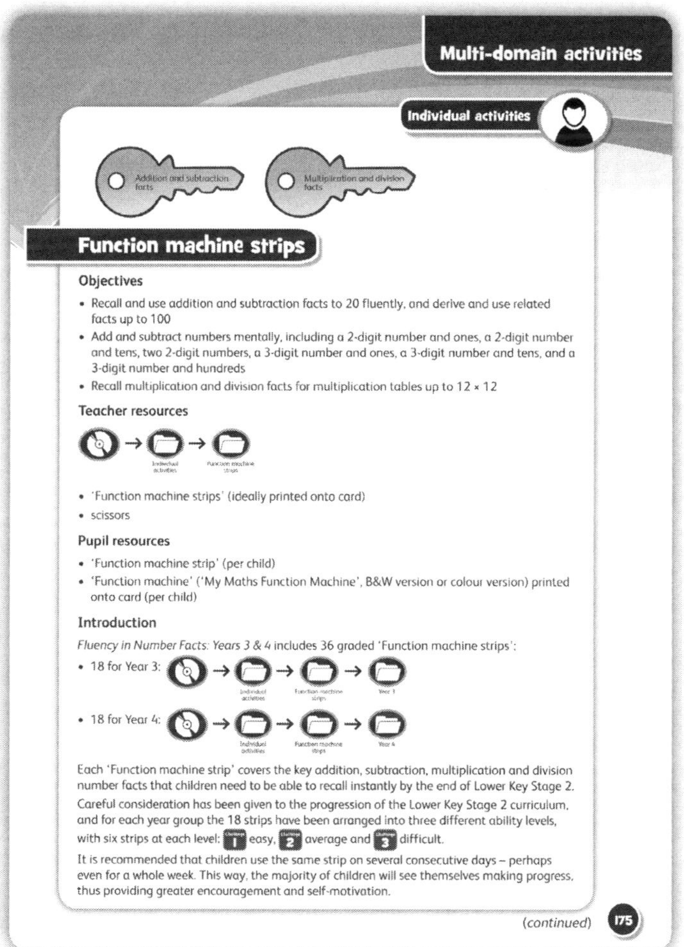
Multi-domain activities

Individual activities

Addition and subtraction facts

Multiplication and division facts

Function machine strips

Objectives
- Recall and use addition and subtraction facts to 20 fluently, and derive and use related facts up to 100
- Add and subtract numbers mentally, including a 2-digit number and ones, a 2-digit number and tens, two 2-digit numbers, a 3-digit number and ones, a 3-digit number and tens, and a 3-digit number and hundreds
- Recall multiplication and division facts for multiplication tables up to 12 × 12

Teacher resources

→ Individual activities → Function machine strips

- 'Function machine strips' (ideally printed onto card)
- scissors

Pupil resources
- 'Function machine strip' (per child)
- 'Function machine' ('My Maths Function Machine', B&W version or colour version) printed onto card (per child)

Introduction

Fluency in Number Facts: Years 3 & 4 includes 36 graded 'Function machine strips':
- 18 for Year 3: → Individual activities → Function machine strips → Year 3
- 18 for Year 4: → Individual activities → Function machine strips → Year 4

Each 'Function machine strip' covers the key addition, subtraction, multiplication and division number facts that children need to be able to recall instantly by the end of Lower Key Stage 2. Careful consideration has been given to the progression of the Lower Key Stage 2 curriculum, and for each year group the 18 strips have been arranged into three different ability levels, with six strips at each level: 1 easy, 2 average and 3 difficult.

It is recommended that children use the same strip on several consecutive days – perhaps even for a whole week. This way, the majority of children will see themselves making progress, thus providing greater encouragement and self-motivation.

(continued) 175

Individual activities

Individual activities are provided which children use, as and when required, to practise and consolidate their fluency in the Key domains of Addition and subtraction, and Multiplication and division.

PDF files required for the individual activities are located on the accompanying CD-ROM.

→ Individual activities

Features of the *Fluency in Number Facts: Facts and Games* book

Maths Facts

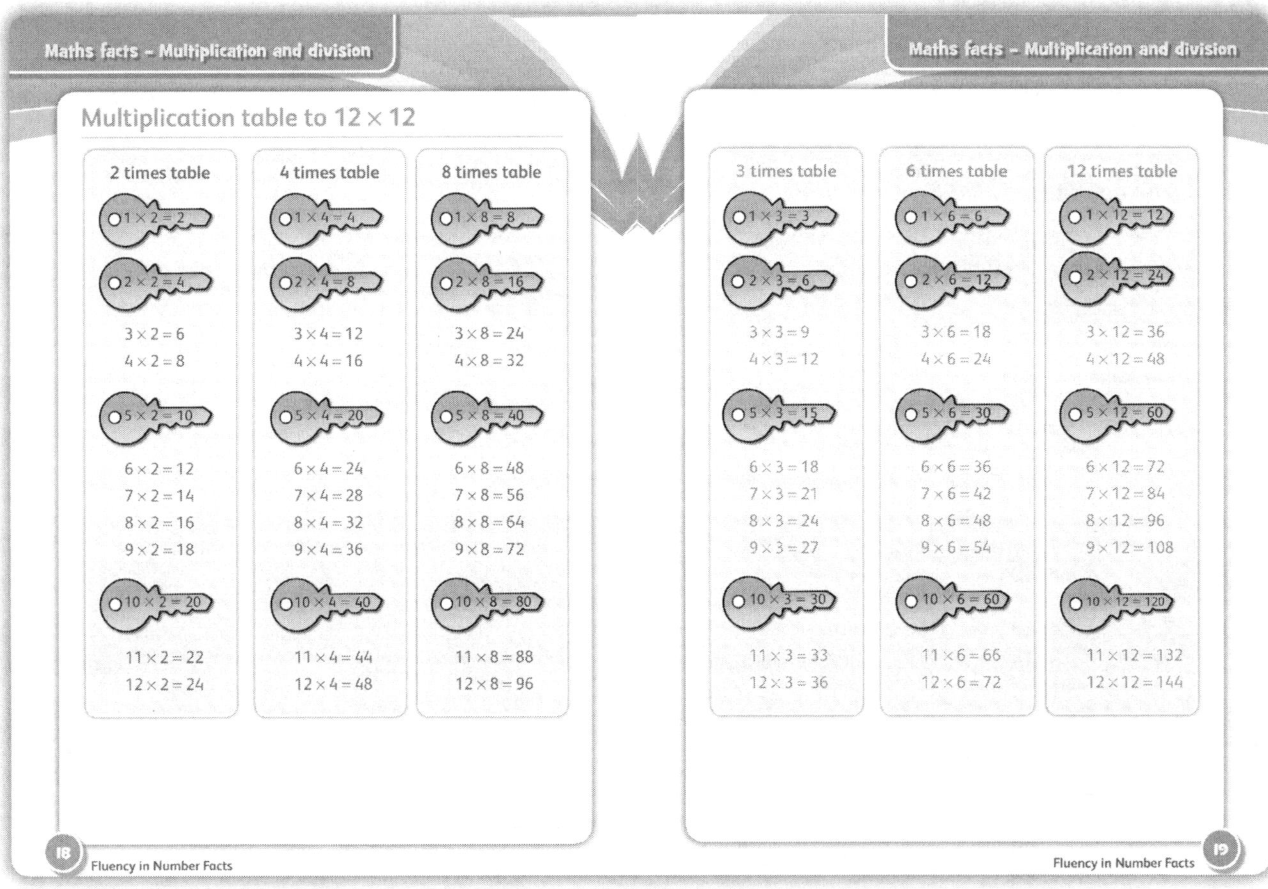
Maths facts – Multiplication and division

Multiplication table to 12 × 12

2 times table	4 times table	8 times table
1 × 2 = 2	1 × 4 = 4	1 × 8 = 8
2 × 2 = 4	2 × 4 = 8	2 × 8 = 16
3 × 2 = 6	3 × 4 = 12	3 × 8 = 24
4 × 2 = 8	4 × 4 = 16	4 × 8 = 32
5 × 2 = 10	5 × 4 = 20	5 × 8 = 40
6 × 2 = 12	6 × 4 = 24	6 × 8 = 48
7 × 2 = 14	7 × 4 = 28	7 × 8 = 56
8 × 2 = 16	8 × 4 = 32	8 × 8 = 64
9 × 2 = 18	9 × 4 = 36	9 × 8 = 72
10 × 2 = 20	10 × 4 = 40	10 × 8 = 80
11 × 2 = 22	11 × 4 = 44	11 × 8 = 88
12 × 2 = 24	12 × 4 = 48	12 × 8 = 96

18 Fluency in Number Facts

Maths facts – Multiplication and division

3 times table	6 times table	12 times table
1 × 3 = 3	1 × 6 = 6	1 × 12 = 12
2 × 3 = 6	2 × 6 = 12	2 × 12 = 24
3 × 3 = 9	3 × 6 = 18	3 × 12 = 36
4 × 3 = 12	4 × 6 = 24	4 × 12 = 48
5 × 3 = 15	5 × 6 = 30	5 × 12 = 60
6 × 3 = 18	6 × 6 = 36	6 × 12 = 72
7 × 3 = 21	7 × 6 = 42	7 × 12 = 84
8 × 3 = 24	8 × 6 = 48	8 × 12 = 96
9 × 3 = 27	9 × 6 = 54	9 × 12 = 108
10 × 3 = 30	10 × 6 = 60	10 × 12 = 120
11 × 3 = 33	11 × 6 = 66	11 × 12 = 132
12 × 3 = 36	12 × 6 = 72	12 × 12 = 144

Fluency in Number Facts 19

Each *Fluency in Number Facts: Facts and Games* book contains lists of the key addition, subtraction, multiplication and division number facts that children need to be able to recall instantly. These facts are presented in different ways to assist children in developing a deeper understanding, and quick recall, of the facts.

Suggested activities are provided in the *Fluency in Number Facts: Teacher's Guide* which suggests how best to make use of these Maths Facts.

PDF files of the Maths Facts pages from the *Fluency in Number Facts: Facts and Games: Years 3 & 4* book can also be found on the accompanying CD-ROM.

Paired games

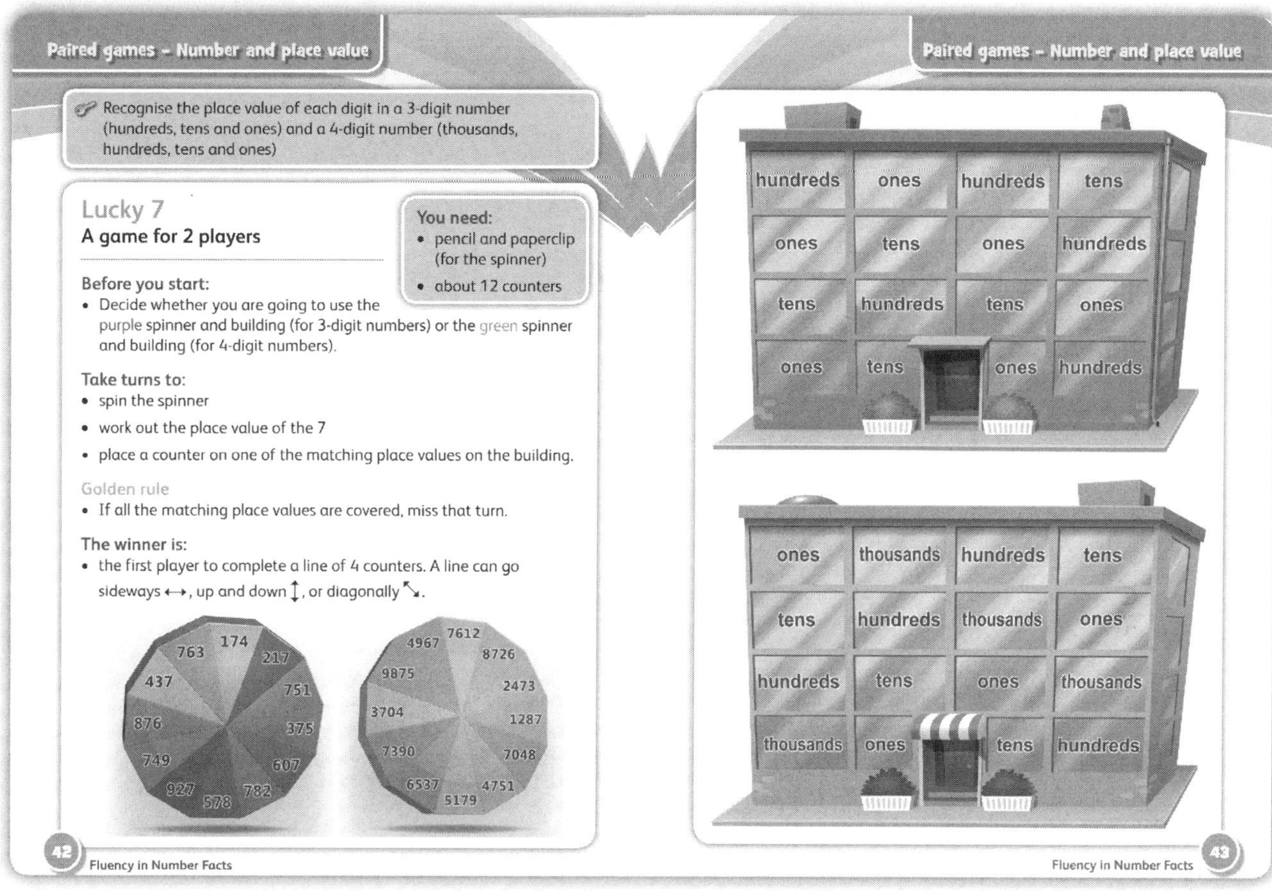
Paired games – Number and place value

Recognise the place value of each digit in a 3-digit number (hundreds, tens and ones) and a 4-digit number (thousands, hundreds, tens and ones)

Lucky 7

A game for 2 players

You need:
- pencil and paperclip (for the spinner)
- about 12 counters

Before you start:
- Decide whether you are going to use the purple spinner and building (for 3-digit numbers) or the green spinner and building (for 4-digit numbers).

Take turns to:
- spin the spinner
- work out the place value of the 7
- place a counter on one of the matching place values on the building.

Golden rule
- If all the matching place values are covered, miss that turn.

The winner is:
- the first player to complete a line of 4 counters. A line can go sideways ⟷, up and down ↕, or diagonally ⤡.

42 Fluency in Number Facts

Paired games – Number and place value

hundreds	ones	hundreds	tens
ones	tens	ones	hundreds
tens	hundreds	tens	ones
ones	tens	ones	hundreds

ones	thousands	hundreds	tens
tens	hundreds	thousands	ones
hundreds	tens	ones	thousands
thousands	ones	tens	hundreds

Fluency in Number Facts 43

Each *Fluency in Number Facts: Facts and Games* book also includes a bank of paired games to help children become fluent in each of the three Key domains.

The games are organised according to the three Key domains and include a list of the resources required as well as instructions and, where appropriate, any variations.

Additional guidance on how to play the games, along with further variations, can be found in the *Fluency in Number Facts: Teacher's Guide*.

Each game is designed to last approximately ten minutes.

PDF files of the paired games from the *Fluency in Number Facts: Facts and Games: Years 3 & 4* book can also be found on the accompanying CD-ROM.

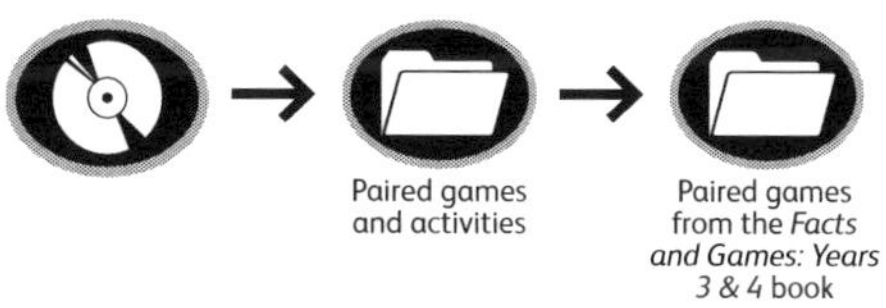

Features of the *Fluency in Number Facts*: CD-ROM

The following resources are available to download from the accompanying CD-ROM.

Maths Facts

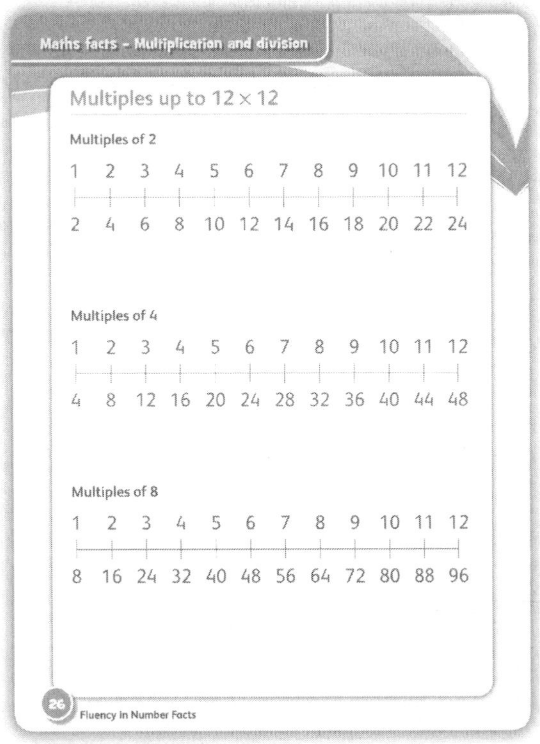
Maths facts – Multiplication and division

Multiples up to 12 × 12

Multiples of 2

1	2	3	4	5	6	7	8	9	10	11	12
2	4	6	8	10	12	14	16	18	20	22	24

Multiples of 4

1	2	3	4	5	6	7	8	9	10	11	12
4	8	12	16	20	24	28	32	36	40	44	48

Multiples of 8

1	2	3	4	5	6	7	8	9	10	11	12
8	16	24	32	40	48	56	64	72	80	88	96

26 Fluency in Number Facts

PDF files of the *Fluency in Number Facts: Facts and Games: Years 3 & 4* book Maths Facts pages.

Whole-class games and activities

PowerPoint slides required for some of the whole-class games and activities. The slides are also provided as PDF files.

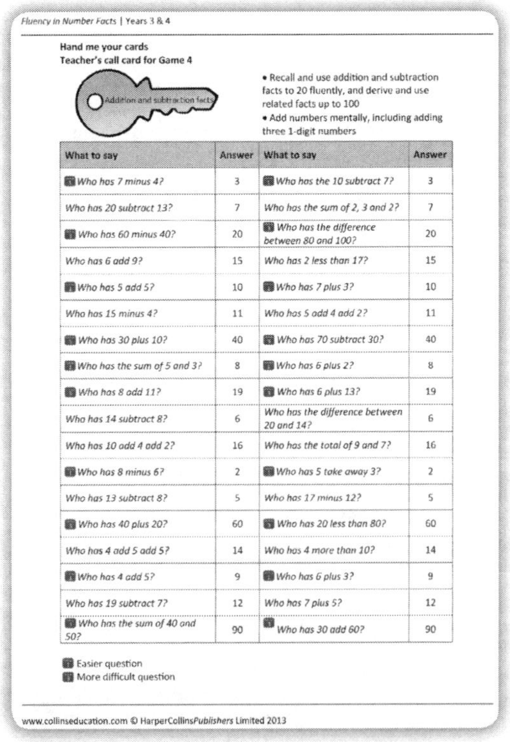
Fluency in Number Facts | Years 3 & 4

Hand me your cards
Teacher's call card for Game 4

Addition and subtraction facts

- Recall and use addition and subtraction facts to 20 fluently, and derive and use related facts up to 100
- Add numbers mentally, including adding three 1-digit numbers

What to say	Answer	What to say	Answer
Who has 7 minus 4?	3	*Who has the 10 subtract 7?*	3
Who has 20 subtract 13?	7	*Who has the sum of 2, 3 and 2?*	7
Who has 60 minus 40?	20	*Who has the difference between 80 and 100?*	20
Who has 6 add 9?	15	*Who has 2 less than 17?*	15
Who has 5 add 5?	10	*Who has 7 plus 3?*	10
Who has 15 minus 4?	11	*Who has 5 add 4 add 2?*	11
Who has 30 plus 10?	40	*Who has 70 subtract 30?*	40
Who has the sum of 5 and 3?	8	*Who has 6 plus 2?*	8
Who has 8 add 11?	19	*Who has 6 plus 13?*	19
Who has 14 subtract 8?	6	*Who has the difference between 20 and 14?*	6
Who has 10 add 4 add 2?	16	*Who has the total of 9 and 7?*	16
Who has 8 minus 6?	2	*Who has 5 take away 3?*	2
Who has 13 subtract 8?	5	*Who has 17 minus 12?*	5
Who has 40 plus 20?	60	*Who has 20 less than 80?*	60
Who has 4 add 5 add 5?	14	*Who has 4 more than 10?*	14
Who has 4 add 5?	9	*Who has 6 plus 3?*	9
Who has 19 subtract 7?	12	*Who has 7 plus 5?*	12
Who has the sum of 40 and 50?	90	*Who has 30 add 60?*	90

Easier question
More difficult question

www.collinseducation.com © HarperCollins*Publishers* Limited 2013

PDF files required for some of the whole-class games and activities.

Paired games and activities

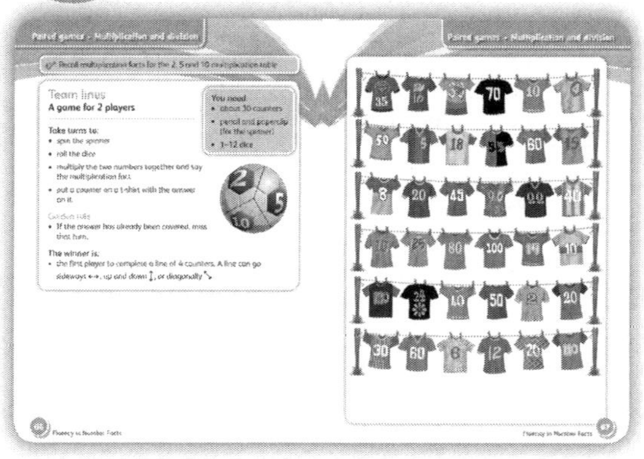

PDF files of the *Fluency in Number Facts: Facts and Games: Years 3 & 4* book paired games.

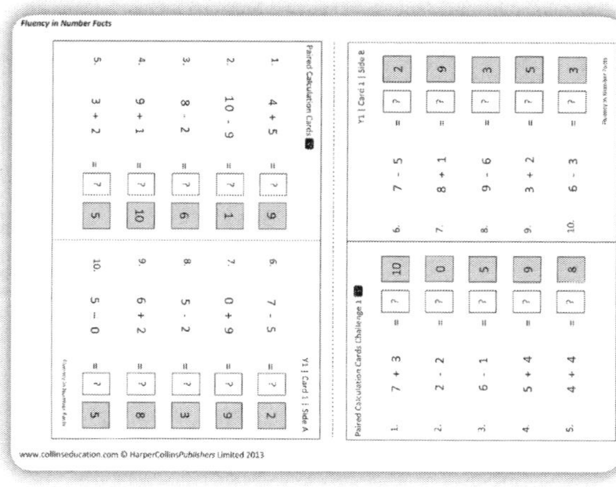

PDF files required for some of the paired games and activities.

Individual activities

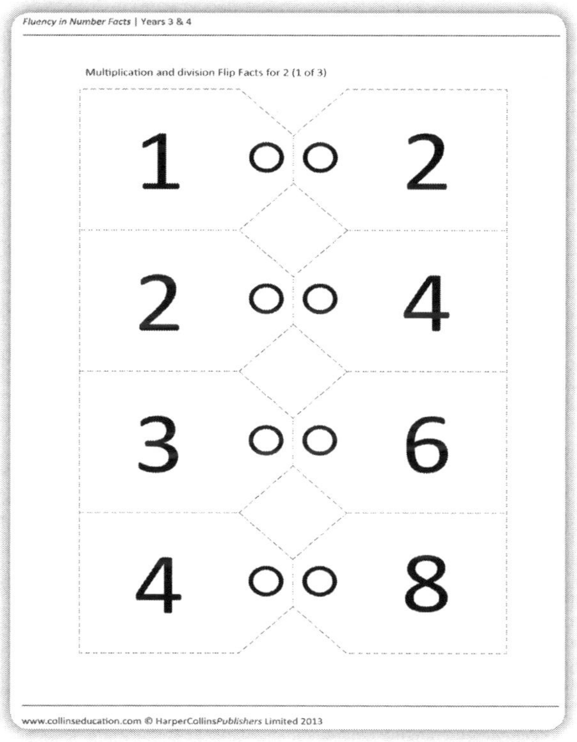

Fluency in Number Facts | Years 3 & 4

Multiplication and division Flip Facts for 2 (1 of 3)

1 ○○ 2

2 ○○ 4

3 ○○ 6

4 ○○ 8

www.collinseducation.com © HarperCollinsPublishers Limited 2013

PDF files required for some of the individual activities.

Written activities

Refer to pages 148–169 of the *Fluency in Number Facts: Teacher's Guide: Years 3 & 4* book for an explanation as to how to use each of the written activities.

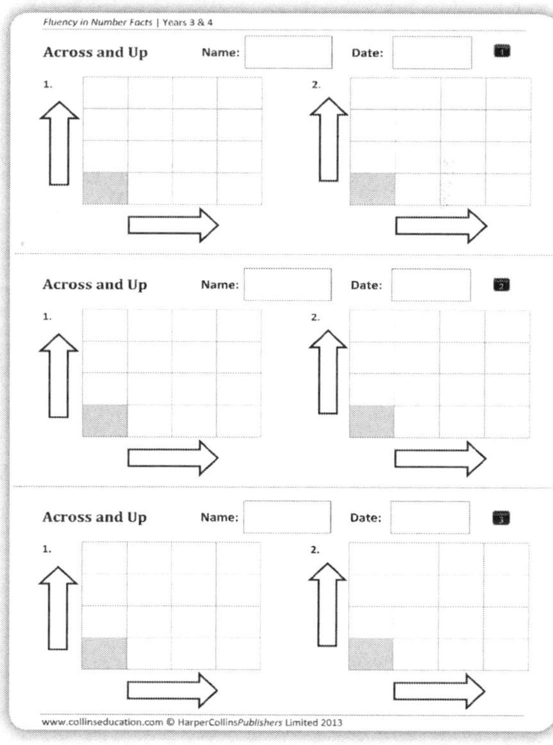

Fluency in Number Facts | Years 3 & 4

Across and Up Name: Date:

1. 2.

Across and Up Name: Date:

1. 2.

Across and Up Name: Date:

1. 2.

www.collinseducation.com © HarperCollinsPublishers Limited 2013

WORD files required for the written activities.

Mental fluency challenges

Fluency in Number Facts: Facts and Games: Years 3 & 4 includes 36 graded Mental fluency challenges (18 for Year 3, and 18 for Year 4).

These challenges are aimed at providing children with further practice and consolidation and also at offering teachers a means of assessing individual children's proficiency in the mental recall of number facts.

Each challenge covers the key addition, subtraction, multiplication and division number facts that children need to be able to recall instantly by the end of Lower Key Stage 2.

Careful consideration has been given to the progression of the Lower Key Stage 2 curriculum, and for each year group the 18 challenges have been arranged into three different ability levels, with six exercises at each level: easy, Challenge 1 average Challenge 2 and challenging Challenge 3.

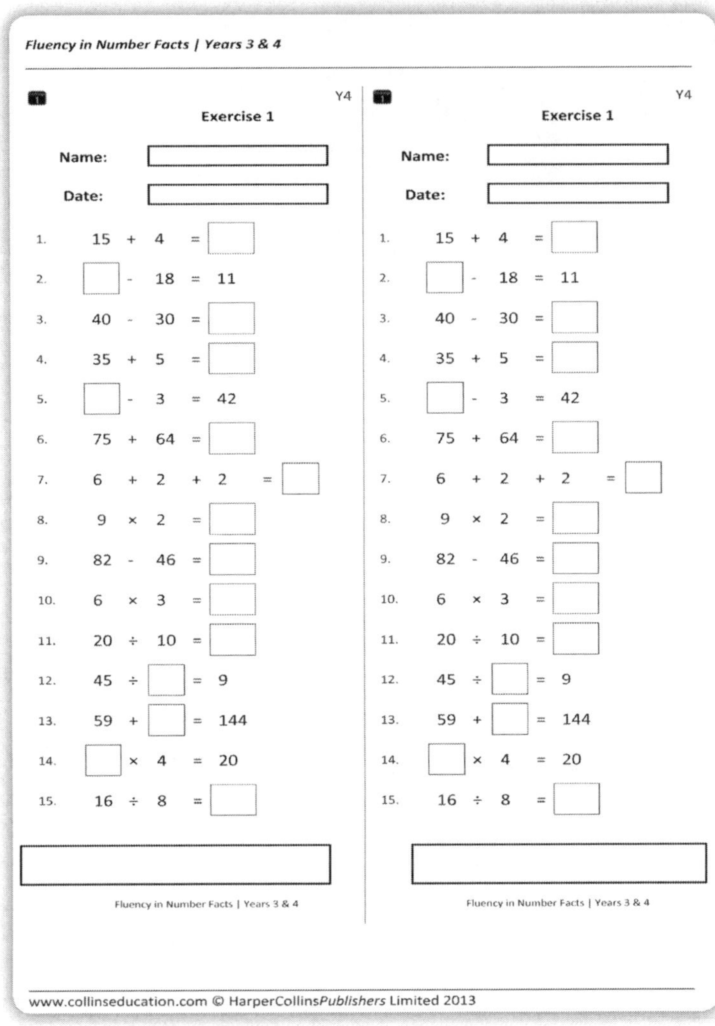

Fluency in Number Facts | Years 3 & 4

Y4

Exercise 1

Name:

Date:

1.	15	+	4	=	☐		
2.	☐	-	18	=	11		
3.	40	-	30	=	☐		
4.	35	+	5	=	☐		
5.	☐	-	3	=	42		
6.	75	+	64	=	☐		
7.	6	+	2	+	2	=	☐
8.	9	×	2	=	☐		
9.	82	-	46	=	☐		
10.	6	×	3	=	☐		
11.	20	÷	10	=	☐		
12.	45	÷	☐	=	9		
13.	59	+	☐	=	144		
14.	☐	×	4	=	20		
15.	16	÷	8	=	☐		

Fluency in Number Facts | Years 3 & 4

Y4

Exercise 1

Name:

Date:

1. 15 + 4 = ☐
2. ☐ - 18 = 11
3. 40 - 30 = ☐
4. 35 + 5 = ☐
5. ☐ - 3 = 42
6. 75 + 64 = ☐
7. 6 + 2 + 2 = ☐
8. 9 × 2 = ☐
9. 82 - 46 = ☐
10. 6 × 3 = ☐
11. 20 ÷ 10 = ☐
12. 45 ÷ ☐ = 9
13. 59 + ☐ = 144
14. ☐ × 4 = 20
15. 16 ÷ 8 = ☐

Fluency in Number Facts | Years 3 & 4

www.collinseducation.com © HarperCollins*Publishers* Limited 2013

It is recommended that children do the same exercise on two or three consecutive days. This way, the majority of children will see themselves making progress over the two or three days, thus providing greater encouragement and self-motivation.

It is envisaged that these exercises could be given to the children either where they take as long as they need to answer all ten questions, or as a timed activity (for example: I want you to answer as many of these questions as you can in eight minutes. Ready? Go!). Alternatively, to encourage speed and recall, set the children to work and as they finish the exercise they raise their hand and you tell them how long it took them to complete it.

Both PDF and WORD versions of the Mental fluency challenges are provided.

The WORD version is provided so that individual schools or classes can, if they perceive it necessary, modify the content of the challenges to better suit the needs of their children. However, it is important to be aware that if changes are made to the content, that the continuity and progression of the challenges will be affected.

As well as the WORD and PDF versions of the Mental fluency challenges, there is also an audio file of each exercise.

A Mental fluency challenge answer sheet is also provided for children to use to record their answers when using the auditory version of the challenges.

Refer to pages 170–172 of the *Fluency in Number Facts: Teacher's Guide: Years 3 & 4* book for a more detailed explanation as to how to use the Mental fluency challenges.

Number cards

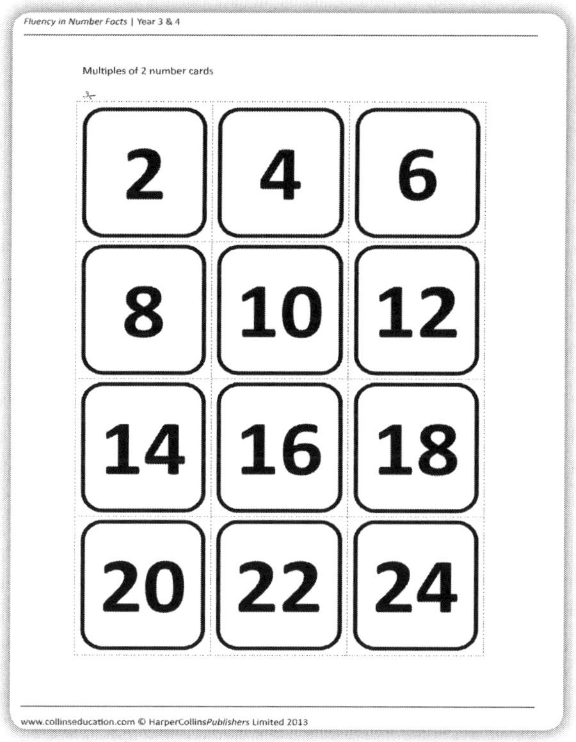
Fluency in Number Facts | Year 3 & 4

Multiples of 2 number cards

2	4	6
8	10	12
14	16	18
20	22	24

www.collinseducation.com © HarperCollinsPublishers Limited 2013

PDF files of the number cards required for some of the games and activities.

Assessment and record-keeping formats

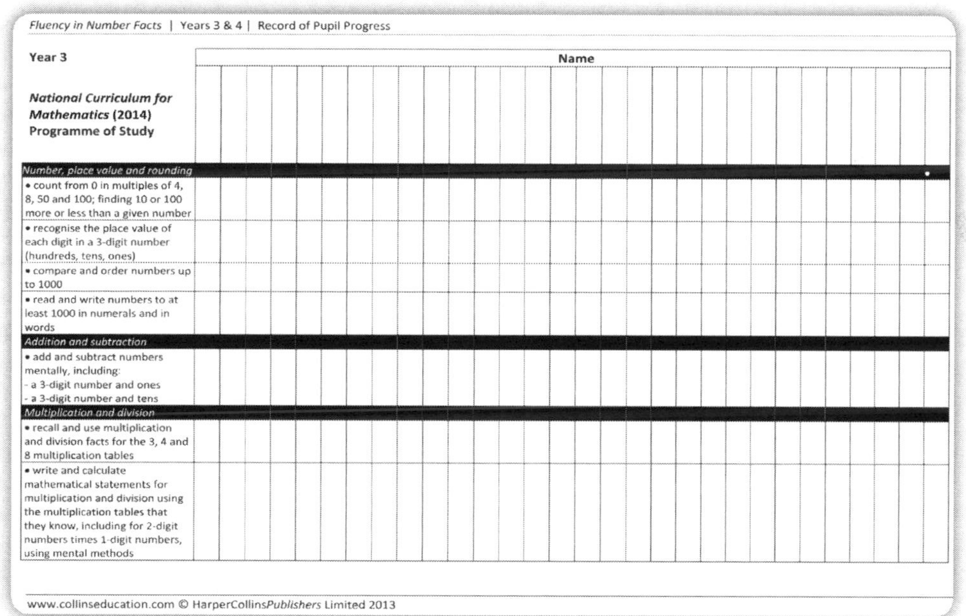
Fluency in Number Facts | Years 3 & 4 | Record of Pupil Progress

Year 3 ***National Curriculum for Mathematics* (2014) Programme of Study**	Name
Number, place value and rounding	
• count from 0 in multiples of 4, 8, 50 and 100; finding 10 or 100 more or less than a given number	
• recognise the place value of each digit in a 3-digit number (hundreds, tens, ones)	
• compare and order numbers up to 1000	
• read and write numbers to at least 1000 in numerals and in words	
Addition and subtraction	
• add and subtract numbers mentally, including: - a 3-digit number and ones - a 3-digit number and tens	
Multiplication and division	
• recall and use multiplication and division facts for the 3, 4 and 8 multiplication tables	
• write and calculate mathematical statements for multiplication and division using the multiplication tables that they know, including for 2-digit numbers times 1-digit numbers, using mental methods	

www.collinseducation.com © HarperCollins*Publishers* Limited 2013

WORD files are provided for each of the following assessment and record-keeping formats:

- Record of Pupil Progress
  - Year 3
  - Year 4

These charts are designed to enable teachers to keep a record of the level of mastery that individual children have achieved in the Number and place value, Addition and subtraction, and Multiplication and division National Curriculum for Mathematics (2014) Programme of Study. The assessment criteria provided on each chart can be modified to better suit the requirements of individual schools and classes.

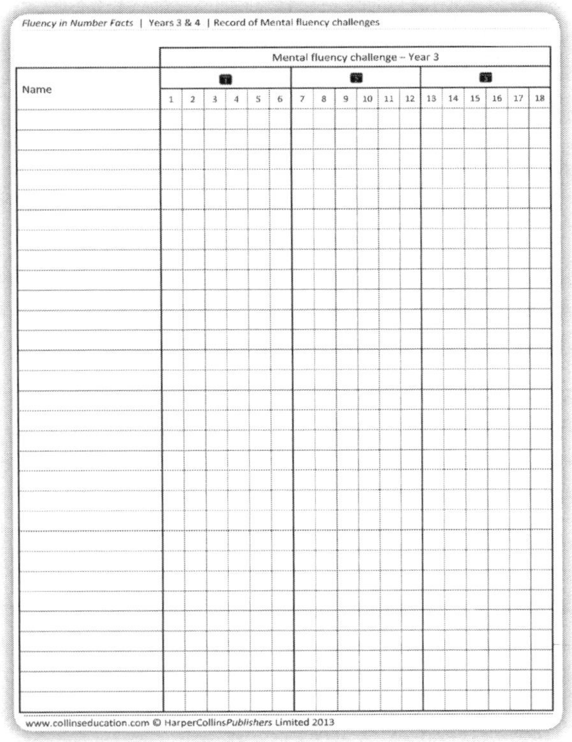
Fluency in Number Facts | Years 3 & 4 | Record of Mental fluency challenges

Name	Mental fluency challenge – Year 3																	
	1	2	3	4	5	6	7	8	9	10	11	12	13	14	15	16	17	18

www.collinseducation.com © HarperCollins*Publishers* Limited 2013

- Record of Mental fluency challenges:
  – Year 3
  – Year 4
- Record of Function machine strips:
  – Year 3
  – Year 4
- Record of Paired calculations cards:
  – Year 3
  – Year 4

These charts are designed to enable teachers to keep a record of which activity individual children have completed.

'Record of Mental fluency challenges' can also be used to record children's scores.

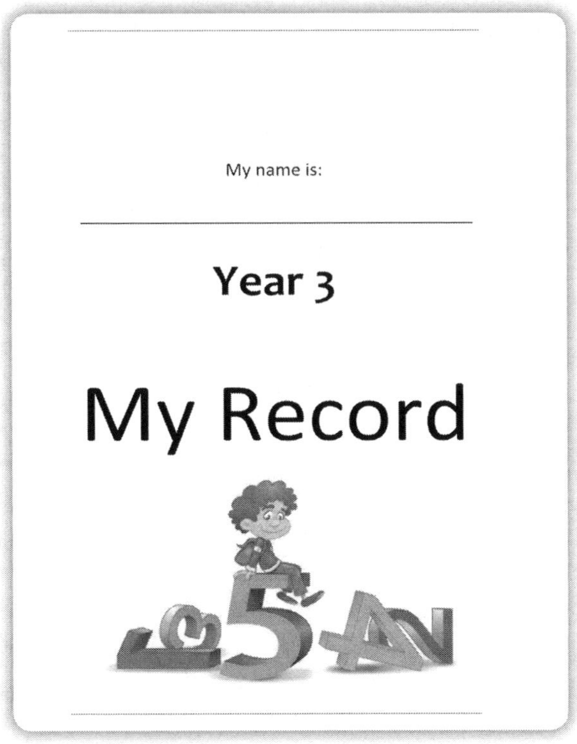
My name is:

Year 3

My Record

- Pupil self-assessment booklet:
  – Year 3
  – Year 4

These booklets are designed to be completed by individual children at the end of each term to assist them in gauging their own level of proficiency in each of the three Key domains. The assessment criteria provided on each booklet can be modified to better suit the requirements of individual classes and children. Also make sure that you print the Word files as a booklet as shown.

CD-ROM flowchart

The flowchart below has been included to assist teachers in locating the resources found on the accompanying *Fluency in Number Facts*: CD-ROM.

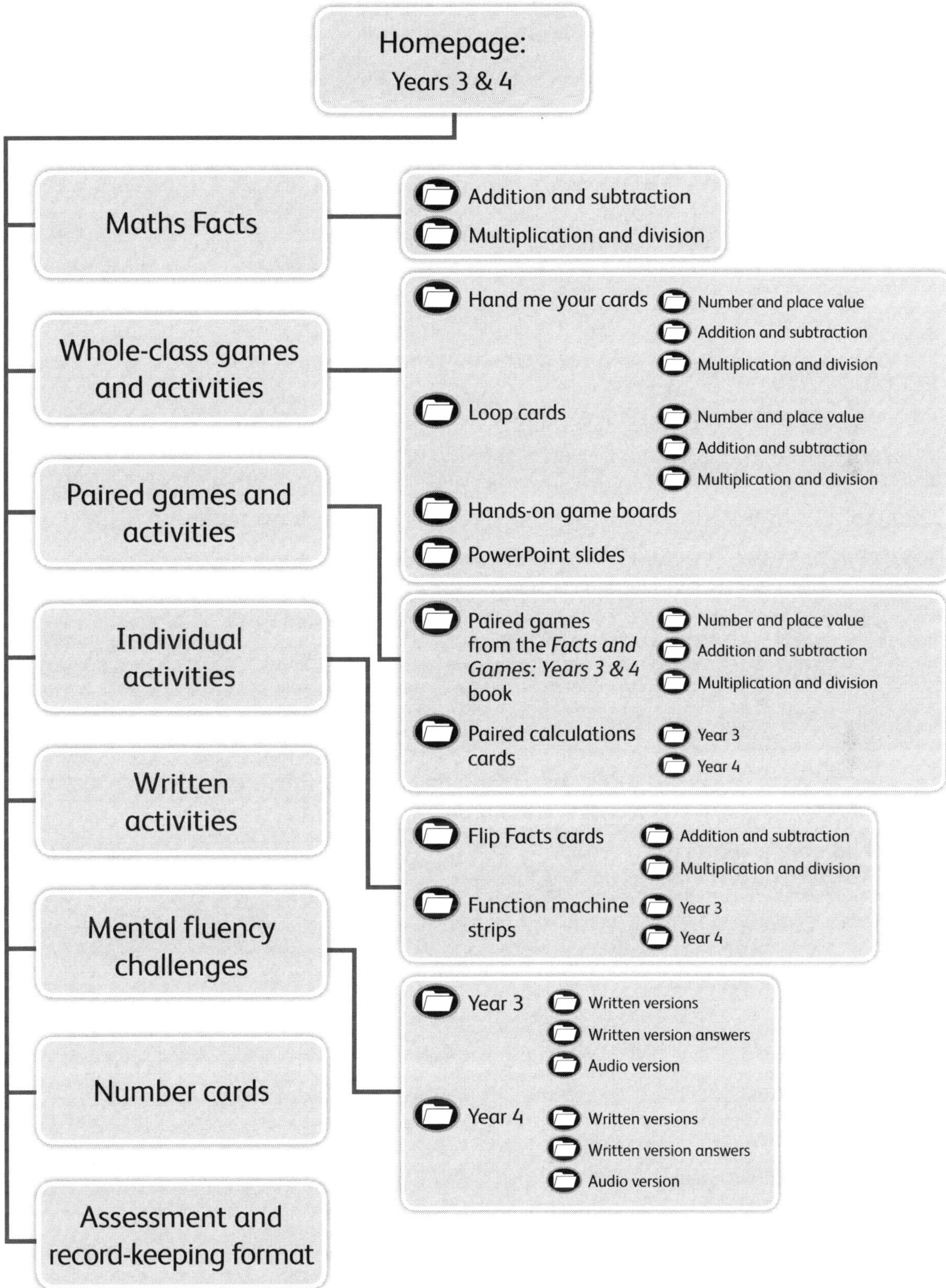

Say the target number

Objective

- Count in multiples of 1, 2, 3, 4, 5, 6, 7, 8, 9, 10, 11, 12, 25, 50, 100 and 1000 from any number, forward or backward

Teacher resources

- none

Pupil resources

- none

What to do

- Arrange the children in a circle.
- Tell the children a start number, for example, 6; a step number, for example, in steps of 6; an end number, for example, 72; a target number between the start and end numbers, for example, 36.
- Children take turns to count round the circle, starting from the start number.
- When a child says the target number, they stand up.
- Children continue the count until the end number is reached.
- The next child to count then goes back to the start number.
- Continue counting in this way until five children are standing.

Variations

- When the end number is said, rather than going back to the start number, the children continue the count backward from the end number to the start number.
- Ask the children to count in steps of 1, 2, 3, 4, 5, 7, 8, 9, 10, 11, 12, 25, 50, 100 or 1000.

Whole-class games and activities

And the winner is...

Objective

- Count in multiples of 1, 2, 3, 4, 5, 6, 7, 8, 9, 10, 11, 12, 25, 50, 100 and 1000 from any number, forward or backward

Teacher resources

- 'And the winner is…'

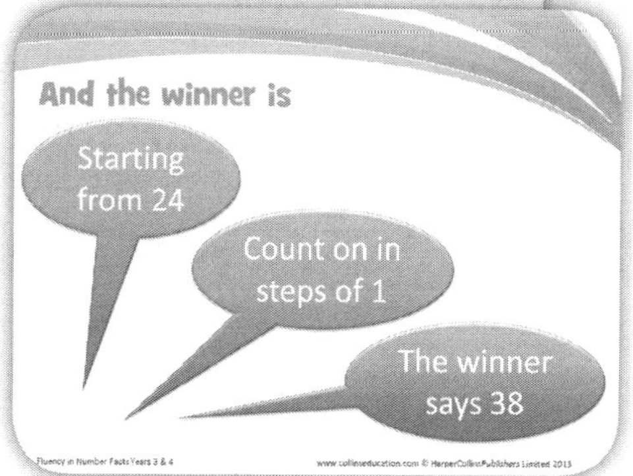

Pupil resources

- none

(**Note:** This is the whole-class version of the paired game described on pages 48 and 49 of the *Fluency in Number Facts: Facts and Games: Years 3 & 4* book.)

What to do

- Arrange the children into pairs.
- Display one of the 'And the winner is…' slides.
- Demonstrate with a child how to play the game:
  - decide who will start the count at the 'Starting from…' number, for example, 'Starting from 24'
  - take turns to count in the steps shown, for example, 'Count on in steps of 1'
  - the winner is the player that says the winning number, i.e. 38.
- Children play the games in pairs.
- Use other 'And the winner is…' slides, to play several rounds.

Variation

- Change the start number, step and winning number on the slides.

Counting stick

Objective

- Count in multiples of 1, 2, 3, 4, 5, 6, 7, 8, 9, 10, 11, 12, 25, 50, 100 and 1000 from any number, forward or backward

Teacher resources

- counting stick, i.e. a stick ideally 1 metre in length, marked off in ten equal divisions. If possible, add pieces of Velcro at each divider in order to attach labels to the stick.

- small labels showing numbers 0–10, multiples of 2, 3, 4, 5, 6, 7, 8, 9, 10, 11, 12, 25, 50, 100 and 1000 to the 10th multiple (if appropriate). Alternatively, use Post-it Notes for the labels.

Pupil resources

- none

What to do

- Decide which multiples you want the children to practise, i.e. count in multiples of 1 from any number, forward or backward.
- Name one end of the stick 0 and the other 10. Count in steps of 1 forward and when confident, backward.
- Randomly point to divisions and ask questions such as: *Which number belongs here?* If appropriate, stick the corresponding label on the stick.
- When confident, name one end of the stick a number other than 0, for example, 14. Children count on from this number.

Variation

- Count in multiples of 2, 3, 4, 5, 6, 7, 8, 9, 10, 11, 12, 25, 50, 100 or 1000 from any number, forward or backward. Name one end of the stick 0 and the other end the 10th multiple. When confident, name one end of the stick a multiple other than 0.

Fizz / Fizz Buzz

Objective

- Count in multiples of 2, 3, 4, 5, 6, 7, 8, 9, 10, 11 and 12 from any number, forward or backward

Teacher resources

- none

Pupil resources

- none

What to do

- Decide which multiples you want the children to practise, i.e. multiples of 3.
- Recite the multiples of 3 from 3 to 36 with the class, i.e. 3, 6, 9, 12…
- Ask the children to stand.
- Count forward round the class in steps of 1, from 1 to at least 36.
- When a multiple of 3 is reached instead of saying the number the child says *Fizz*, i.e. 1st child says *1*, 2nd child says *2*, 3rd child says *Fizz*, 4th child says *4*, 5th child says *5*, 6th child says *Fizz…*
- Continue counting round the class for as long as is appropriate.

Variations

- Play 'Fizz' for the multiples of 2, 4, 5, 6, 7, 8, 9, 10, 11 or 12 counting forward to the 12th multiple.
- Play 'Fizz' for the multiples of 2, 3, 4, 5, 6, 7, 8, 9, 10, 11 or 12 counting backward from the 12th multiple.
- Play 'Fizz Buzz'. For example, for any multiple of 3 say *Fizz* and for any multiple of 5 say *Buzz*. If the number is a multiple of both 3 and 5, for example, 15, say *Fizz Buzz*.

Say it and you're out

Objective

- Count in multiples of 1, 2, 3, 4, 5, 6, 7, 8, 9, 10, 11, 12, 25, 50, 100 and 1000 from any number, forward or backward

Teacher resources

- none

Pupil resources

- none

What to do

- Decide which multiples you want the children to practise, i.e. multiples of 4.
- Recite the multiples of 4 from 4 to 48 with the class, i.e. *4, 8, 12, 16…*
- Write any three of these multiples of 4 on the board, for example, 8, 20 and 36.
- Ask the children to stand.
- Count forward round the class reciting the multiples of 4 from 4 to 48, i.e. 1st child says *4*, 2nd child says *8*, 3rd child says *12…* (the 13th child starts from 4 again).
- When a child says one of the multiples of 4 written on the board, that child has to sit down and is out.
- Continue counting round the class until one child is left standing. This child is the winner.

Variations

- Count forward and backward round the class reciting the multiples of 4 from 4 to 48, i.e. 1st child says *4*, 2nd child says *8*, 3rd child says *12…* 12th child says *48*, 13th child says *44*, 14th child says 40…
- When there are only four or five children left standing, ask the rest of the class if they can work out who will be the winner.
- Play 'Say it and you're out' counting in multiples of 1, 2, 3, 5, 6, 7, 8, 9, 10, 11, 12, 25, 50, 100 and 1000.

Remember the numbers

Objectives

- Read numbers to at least 1000 in numerals
- Recognise the place value of each digit in a 3-digit and 4-digit number
- Order and compare numbers beyond 1000
- Round any number to the nearest 10, 100 or 1000
- Recognise the place value of each digit in a number with up to two decimal places
- Order and compare numbers with up to two decimal places

Teacher resources

- 'Remember the numbers'

Pupil resources

- none

What to do

- Say: *I'm going to show you a slide with some numbers on it. I'm then going to hide the numbers and ask you some questions about them. You need to try and remember the numbers before I hide them. Ready?*
- Display one of the 'Remember the numbers' slides for about ten seconds.
- Hide the slide, then ask questions similar to the following:
  - *What is the largest (smallest) number?*
  - *Which numbers are odd (even)?*
  - *Which number has 3 tens?*
  - *Which number has 6 ones (units)?*
  - *Which numbers are less than (greater than) 50?*
  - *Which number rounds to 60?*

Variations

- Repeat using other 'Remember the numbers' slides.
- Change the numbers on the 'Remember the numbers' slides

Whole-class games and activities

Point to it

Objectives

- Recognise the place value of each digit in a 3-digit and 4-digit number
- Recognise the place value of each digit in a number with up to two decimal places

Teacher resources

Whole-class games and activities → PowerPoint slides

- 'Point to it'

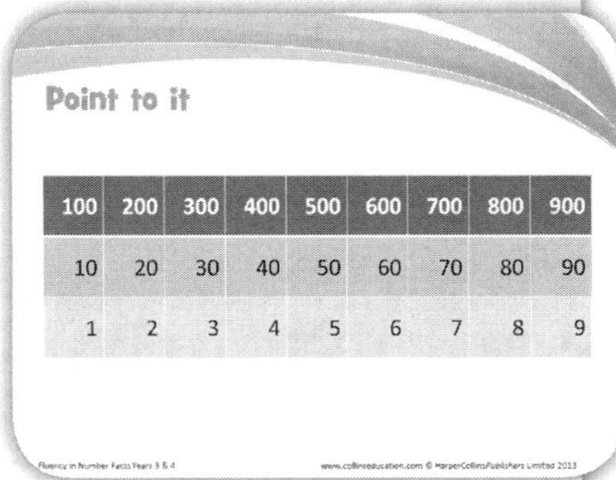

100	200	300	400	500	600	700	800	900
10	20	30	40	50	60	70	80	90
1	2	3	4	5	6	7	8	9

Pupil resources

- pencil and paper (per child)

What to do

- Decide which range of numbers you want the children to use and choose the appropriate slide.
- If using the second slide for example, ask each child to write down three 3-digit numbers, for example, 486, 837, 168.
- Display the second slide and point to a number on the slide for example, 80.
- If a child has a number with the same place value, they cross it out, i.e. ~~486~~.
- If they don't, they do nothing.
- The winner is the first child to cross out all nine digits in their three numbers.

(**Note:** Be sure to keep a record of the numbers pointed to for checking purposes.)

Variations

- Display the first slide and ask each child to write down three 2-digit numbers, for example, 98, 14, 72.
- Display the third slide and ask each child to write down three 4-digit numbers, for example, 5821, 2657, 3279.
- Display the fourth slide and ask each child to write down three decimal numbers, each with three digits, to one decimal place, for example, 53·4, 36·9, 17·2.
- Display the fifth slide and ask each child to write down three decimal numbers, each with three digits, to two decimal places, for example, 7·28, 8·39, 2·54.

Guess the number

Objectives

- Read numbers to at least 1000 in numerals
- Recognise the place value of each digit in a 3-digit and 4-digit number
- Order and compare numbers beyond 1000
- Round any number to the nearest 10, 100 or 1000
- Recognise the place value of each digit in a number with up to two decimal places
- Order and compare numbers with up to two decimal places

Teacher resources

- small pieces of paper or card
- hat
- something to fasten the paper or card onto the hat (for example, a paperclip)

Pupil resources

- none

What to do

- Write a 3-digit number on a small piece of paper or card, for example, 582, and fasten it to the hat.
- Ask a child to come to the front and, keeping the number a secret from this child, put the hat on them.
- This child then asks questions to the rest of the class to find out the number on the hat. However, she or he can only ask questions that will give a 'yes' or 'no' response, for example: *Is it a 3-digit number? Is the number less than 500?*
- Repeat using different numbers with other children.
- Who can guess the secret number asking the fewest questions?

Variations

- Write a 2- or 4-digit number on a small piece of paper or card.
- Write a decimal number on a small piece of paper or card.

Place value bingo

Objectives

- Read numbers to at least 1000 in numerals
- Recognise the place value of each digit in a 3-digit and 4-digit number
- Recognise the place value of each digit in a number with up to two decimal places

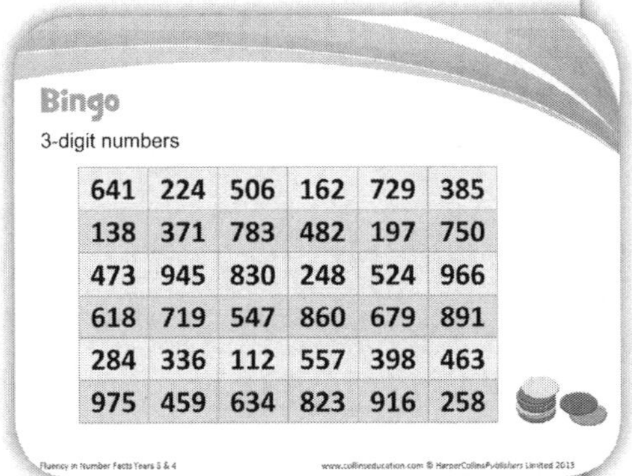

641	224	506	162	729	385
138	371	783	482	197	750
473	945	830	248	524	966
618	719	547	860	679	891
284	336	112	557	398	463
975	459	634	823	916	258

Teacher resources

- 'Bingo'

Pupil resources

- pencil and paper or small individual whiteboard and pen (per child)

What to do

- Decide which range of numbers you want the children to use and choose the appropriate slide.
- Ask each child to write down any five numbers from the slide.
- If using the 'Bingo 3-digit numbers' slide for example, say statements similar to the following:
  - *Cross out any number that has 4 tens.*
  - *Cross out any number that has 9 ones.*
  - *Cross out any number that has 5 hundreds.*
  - *Cross out the number that has 6 hundreds, 1 ten and 8 units.*
  - *Cross out the number that has 3 ones, 6 tens and 4 hundreds.*
  - *Cross out the number that has 8 tens, 5 units and 3 hundreds.*
- Children see if any of their five numbers match the description.
- If a child has a match, they cross out that number.
- The winner is the first child to cross out all five of their numbers and call out 'Bingo!'

(**Note:** Be sure to keep a record of the numbers for checking purposes.)

Variations

- Ask the children to write down more or fewer than five numbers from the slide.
- Use the 'Bingo: 2-digit numbers', 'Bingo: 4-digit numbers', 'Bingo: Tenths' and the 'Bingo: Hundredths' slides.

Higher or lower?

Objectives

- Count in multiples of 1, 2, 3, 4, 5, 6, 7, 8, 9, 10, 11, 12, 25, 50, 100 and 1000 from any number, forward or backward
- Read numbers to at least 1000 in numerals
- Recognise the place value of each digit in a 3-digit and 4-digit number
- Order and compare numbers beyond 1000
- Order and compare numbers with up to two decimal places

Teacher resources

- 'Higher or lower?'

Pupil resources

- none

What to do

- Decide which range of numbers you want the children to use and choose the appropriate set of slides.
- Display the first slide. If using the 'Higher or Lower: 3-digit numbers' for example, the number 427.
- Tell the children that there are ten slides altogether, and that each slide has a 3-digit number on it.
- Ask the children to decide whether they think the next number will be higher or lower than the current number, i.e. 427.
- If they think the number is going to be larger, they put their hands in the air.
- If they think the number is going to be smaller, they put their hands on their head.
- Display the second slide, i.e. 614.
- Keep going until all ten slides are revealed.

(**Note:** The question mark at the side of the second last slide is to indicate that the next slide is the last slide.)

Variations

- Use the 'Higher or Lower: 1–10', 'Higher or Lower: 1–20', 'Higher or Lower: 2-digit numbers', 'Higher or Lower: 4-digit numbers' set of slides.
- Use the 'Higher or Lower: Tenths' set of slides (tell the children that there are 11 slides in the range 1 to 2).
- Use the 'Higher or Lower: Hundredths' set of slides: tell the children that there are 11 slides in the range 1·1 to 1·2.
- Use the 'Higher or Lower: Multiples of…' set of slides, telling the children that there are 12 slides. The default version is set for multiples of 4. However these can be changed to include the 12 multiples of any multiplication table up to 12 × 12.
- Re-arrange the order of the slides. Ensure that the second last slide has the question mark on it and that the last slide has a 'glow' around the number.
- Change the numbers on the slides.

Gladiators

Objectives

- Read numbers to at least 1000 in numerals
- Count in multiples of 1, 2, 3, 4, 5, 6, 7, 8, 9, 10, 11 and 12 forward or backward
- Recognise the place value of each digit in a 3-digit and 4-digit number
- Order and compare numbers beyond 1000
- Find 10 or 100 more or less than a given number
- Round any number to the nearest 10, 100 or 1000
- Recognise the place value of each digit in a number with up to two decimal places
- Order and compare numbers with up to two decimal places

Teacher resources

- 'Gladiators'

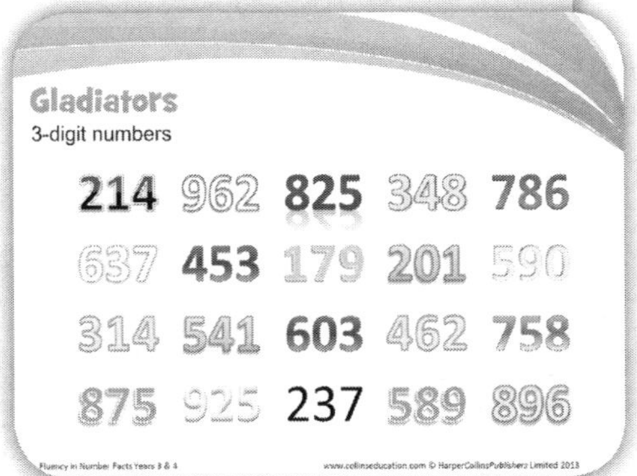

Pupil resources

- 2 × rulers or 'swords'

What to do

- Decide which range of numbers you want the children to use.
- Display the appropriate slide.
- Ask two children to stand either side of the numbers.
- If using the 'Gladiators: 3-digit numbers' slide for example, say statements similar to the following:
  - *Point to the number 541.*
  - *Point to the number that has 5 hundreds, 8 tens and 9 units.*
  - *Point to the number that has 6 tens, 2 ones and 9 hundreds.*
  - *Point to any number greater than 700.*
  - *Point to the odd number between 635 and 638.*
  - *Point to the number that is 1 less than 180.*
  - *Point to the number that is 10 more than 191.*
  - *Point to the number that is 100 less than 562.*
  - *Point to a number that rounds to 600.*
  - *Point to a number that rounds to 830.*
- The first child to point to the correct number stays in. The other child sits down.
- Quickly choose another child to come and take the place of the child that just sat down.
- Continue as above.
- Which child can stay in the longest?

Variations

- The children sitting down ask the two children standing by the numbers a question where the answer is on the slide.
- To quicken the game, have two children standing either side of the numbers, one behind the other. When a child loses and has to sit down, there is an immediate replacement.
- Use the 'Gladiators: Numbers 1–10', 'Gladiators: Numbers 1–20', 'Gladiators: 2-digit numbers' or 'Gladiators: 4-digit numbers' slide.
- Use the 'Gladiators: 2 times table' slide. Say statements similar to the following:
  - *Point to the next number in this pattern: 0, 2, 4, 6.*
  - *Point to the next number in this pattern: 18, 16, 14, 12.*
- Use the following slides in a similar way: 'Gladiators: 3 times table', 'Gladiators: 4 times table', 'Gladiators: 5 times table', 'Gladiators: 6 times table', 'Gladiators: 7 times table', 'Gladiators: 8 times table', 'Gladiators: 9 times table', 'Gladiators: 10 times table', 'Gladiators: 11 times table' and 'Gladiators: 12 times table'.
- To consolidate children's understanding use the 'Gladiators: 2, 5 and 10 times tables' slide, and say statements similar to the following:
  - *Point to the next number in this pattern: 0, 5, 10, 15.*
  - *Point to the next number in this pattern: 20, 18, 16, 14.*
  - *Point to the next number in this pattern: 20, 30, 40, 50.*
- Use the following slides in a similar way: 'Gladiators: 3, 4 and 8 times tables' and 'Gladiators: 6, 7, 9, 11 and 12 times tables'.
- To reinforce the relationship between different multiplication tables, use 'Gladiators: 2, 4 and 8 times tables' and 'Gladiators: 3, 6 and 12 times tables'.
- Use the 'Gladiators: Multiples of 10 and 100' slide. Ask questions similar to the following:
  - *What is 37 rounded to the nearest multiple of 10?*
  - *What is 549 rounded to the nearest multiple of 100?*
- Use the 'Gladiators: Tenths' slide. Say statements similar to the following:
  - *Point to the number that has 9 tenths.*
  - *Point to the number that is between 6·5 and 7·2.*
- Use the 'Gladiators: Hundredths' slide. Say statements similar to the following:
  - *Point to the number that has 7 tenths.*
  - *Point to the number that has 4 hundredths*
  - *Point to the number that is between 7·8 and 8·2.*

Whole-class games and activities

Hands-on

Objectives

- Read numbers to at least 1000 in numerals
- Count in multiples of 1, 2, 3, 4, 5, 6, 7, 8, 9, 10, 11 and 12 forward or backward
- Recognise the place value of each digit in a 3-digit and 4-digit number
- Order and compare numbers beyond 1000
- Find 10 or 100 more or less than a given number
- Round any number to the nearest 10 or 100
- Recognise the place value of each digit in a number with up to two decimal places
- Order and compare numbers with up to two decimal places

Teacher resources

- none

Pupil resources

- 'Hands-on' game board (per pair)

What to do

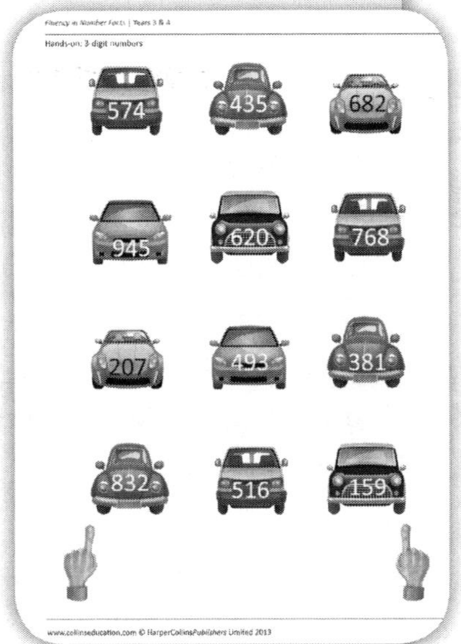

- Decide which range of numbers you want the children to use.
- Arrange the children into pairs and provide each pair with a copy of the appropriate Hands-on game board.
- Tell the children to put the game board between them and each child to put their index finger on a hand at the bottom of the game board.
- If using the 'Hands-on: 3-digit numbers' game board for example, say statements similar to the following:
  - *Point to the number 620.*
  - *Point to any number larger than 381.*
  - *Point to the odd number between 381 and 516.*
  - *Point to the number that is 1 less than 160.*
  - *Point to the number that is 10 more than 564.*
  - *Point to the number that is 100 less than 535.*
  - *Point to the number that has 3 hundreds, 8 tens and 1 unit.*
  - *Point to the number that has 5 units, 3 tens and 4 hundreds.*
  - *Point to the number that rounds to 380.*
  - *Point to the number that rounds to 600.*
- The first child to point to the correct number wins.
- Children keep count of how many rounds they win.
- Play for as long as is appropriate.
- The winner in each pair is the child who wins more rounds.

Variations

- Provide each pair with a pile of counters. As a child wins a game they take a counter. The winner in each pair is the child who wins more counters.
- Use the 'Hands-on: Numbers 1–10', ' Hands-on: Numbers 1–12', 'Hands-on: Numbers 1–20', 'Hands-on: 2-digit numbers', or 'Hands-on: 4-digit numbers' game boards.
- Use the 'Hands-on: Multiples of 2' game board. Say statements similar to the following:
  - *Point to the next number in this pattern: 2, 4, 6, 8.*
  - *Point to the next number in this pattern: 14, 12, 10, 8.*
- Use the following 'Hands-on' game boards in a similar way: 'Hands-on: Multiples of 3', 'Hands-on: Multiples of 4', 'Hands-on: Multiples of 5', 'Hands-on: Multiples of 6', 'Hands-on: Multiples of 7', 'Hands-on: Multiples of 8', 'Hands-on: Multiples of 9', 'Hands-on: Multiples of 10', 'Hands-on: Multiples of 11' and 'Hands-on: Multiples of 12'.
- Use the 'Hands-on: Tenths' game board. Say statements similar to the following:
  - *Point to the decimal number 9·4.*
  - *Point to any decimal number smaller than 4·2.*
  - *Point to the number between 1·5 and 2·5.*
  - *Point to any decimal with 6 tenths.*
- Use the 'Hands-on: Hundredths' game board in a similar way.
- Use the 'Hands-on: Multiples of 10 and 100' game board to practise and consolidate rounding to the nearest 10 or 100. Ask questions similar to the following:
  - *What is 83 rounded to the nearest multiple of 10?*
  - *What is 786 rounded to the nearest multiple of 100?*

Whole-class games and activities

Who's left standing?

Objectives

- Read numbers to at least 1000 in numerals
- Count in multiples of 1, 2, 3, 4, 5, 6, 7, 8, 9, 10, 11 and 12 forward or backward
- Recognise the place value of each digit in a 2-digit, 3-digit and 4-digit number
- Order and compare numbers beyond 1000
- Find 10 or 100 more or less than a given number
- Recognise the place value of each digit in a number with up to two decimal places
- Order and compare numbers with up to two decimal places

Teacher resources

- none

Pupil resources

Number cards

- '1–20 number cards' or '2-digit number cards' or '3-digit number cards' or '4-digit number cards' or 'Tenths number card' or 'Hundredths number card' (one card per child)

What to do

Game 1: Count in multiples of 1, 2, 3, 4, 5, 6, 7, 8, 9, 10, 11 and 12 forward or backward

- Provide each child with a 1–20 number card.
- Say: *Everyone stand up. Look at the number on your card. Sit down if the number on your card is the next number in the pattern:*
  - *42, 35, 28, 21…* (14)
  - *41, 31, 21, 11…* (1)
  - *6, 9, 12, 15…* (18)
  - *15, 12, 9, 6…* (3)
  - *11, 10, 9, 8…* (7)
  - *10, 8, 6, 4…* (2)
  - *60, 50, 40, 30…* (20)
  - *45, 35, 25, 15…* (5)
  - *45, 36, 27, 18…* (9)
  - *0, 2, 4, 6…* (8)
  - *13, 14, 15, 16…* (17)
  - *0, 4, 8, 12…* (16)
  - *20, 16, 12, 8…* (4)
  - *11, 13, 15, 17…* (19)
  - *55, 44, 33, 22…* (11)
  - *50, 40, 30, 20…*(10)
  - *35, 30, 25, 20…* (15)
  - *60, 48, 36, 24…* (12)
  - *30, 24, 18, 12…* (6)

The winners are the children still standing with 13 on their cards.

Game 2: Order and compare 2-digit numbers

- Provide each child with a 2-digit number card. (**Note:** Ensure you use the 12 '2-digit number cards' provided on the CD-ROM.)
- Say: *Everyone stand up. Look at the number on your card. Sit down if the number on your card is:*
  - *between 51 and 56* (53)
  - *between 35 and 40* (37)
  - *more than 90* (92)
  - *between 55 and 60* (59)
  - *between 23 and 27* (24)
  - *between 45 and 52* (46)
  - *between 70 and 80* (75)
  - *between 31 and 35* (32)
  - *between 40 and 45* (41)
  - *between 26 and 30* (28)
  - *between 82 and 87* (84)

The winners are the children still standing with 60 on their cards.

Who's left standing?

(continued)

Game 3: Order and compare 3-digit numbers

- Provide each child with a 3-digit number card. (**Note:** Ensure you use the 12 '3-digit number cards' provided on the CD-ROM.)
- Say: *Everyone stand up. Look at the number on your card. Sit down if the number on your card is:*
  - *between 250 and 300* (268)
  - *between 642 and 691* (680)
  - *between 736 and 849* (776)
  - *between 399 and 499* (409)
  - *between 355 and 405* (357)
  - *between 126 and 241* (135)
  - *between 487 and 625* (512)
  - *between 924 and 999* (937)
  - *between 699 and 728* (724)
  - *between 338 and 352* (341)
  - *between 792 and 929* (862)

The winners are the children still standing with 693 on their cards.

Game 4: Order and compare 4-digit numbers

- Provide each child with a 4-digit number card. (**Note:** Ensure you use the 12 '4-digit number cards' provided on the CD-ROM.)
- Say: *Everyone stand up. Look at the number on your card. Sit down if the number on your card is:*
  - *between 2591 and 2963* (2718)
  - *between 3936 and 4602* (4573)
  - *between 1948 and 2641* (2086)
  - *between 5220 and 6174* (5934)
  - *between 6894 and 7632* (7502)
  - *between 1256 and 1738* (1357)
  - *more than 9100 (9283)*
  - *between 7693 and 8596* (7861)
  - *between 7999 and 8999* (8745)
  - *between 4755 and 5314* (5149)
  - *between 2995 and 3698* (3495)

The winners are the children still standing with 6210 on their cards.

Game 5: Recognise the place value of each digit in a 2-digit number (tens, ones)

- Provide each child with a 2-digit number card. (**Note:** Ensure you use the 12 '2-digit number cards' provided on the CD-ROM.)
- Say: *Everyone stand up. Look at the number on your card. Sit down if the number on your card has:*
  - *6 tens* (60)
  - *8 ones (or units)* (28)
  - *2 ones (or units)* (32, 92)
  - *7 ones (or units)* (37)
  - *7 tens* (75)
  - *4 tens* (41, 46)
  - *3 ones (or units)* (53)
  - *4 ones (or units)* (24, 84)

The winners are the children still standing with 59 on their cards.

Game 6: Recognise the place value of each digit in a 3-digit number (hundreds, tens and ones)

- Provide each child with a 3-digit number card. (**Note:** Ensure you use the 12 '3-digit number cards' provided on the CD-ROM.)
- Say: *Everyone stand up. Look at the number on your card. Sit down if the number on your card has:*
  - *8 tens* (680)
  - *4 hundreds* (409)
  - *7 tens* (776)
  - *3 tens* (135, 937)
  - *8 ones (or units)* (268)
  - *9 tens* (693)
  - *8 hundreds* (862)
  - *5 tens* (357)
  - *5 hundreds* (512)
  - *4 ones (or units)* (724)

The winners are the children still standing with 341 on their cards.

(continued)

Whole-class games and activities

Who's left standing?

(continued)

Game 7: Recognise the place value of each digit in a 4-digit number (thousands, hundreds, tens and ones)

- Provide each child with a 4-digit number card. (**Note:** Ensure you use the 12 '4-digit number cards' provided on the CD-ROM.)
- Say: *Everyone stand up. Look at the number on your card. Sit down if the number on your card has:*
  - *6 tens* (7861)
  - *5 tens* (1357)
  - *7 tens* (4573)
  - *7 hundreds* (2718, 8745)
  - *6 thousands* (6210)
  - *3 thousands* (3495)
  - *9 thousands* (9283)
  - *2 ones (or units)* (7502)
  - *9 hundreds* (5934)
  - *6 ones (or units)* (2086)

The winners are the children still standing with 5149 on their cards.

Game 8: Find 10 or 100 more or less than a given number

- Provide each child with a 3-digit number card. (**Note:** Ensure you use the 12 '3-digit number cards' provided on the CD-ROM.)
- Say: *Everyone stand up. Look at the number on your card. Sit down if the number on your card is:*
  - *10 more than 331* (341)
  - *100 less than 612* (512)
  - *100 more than 257* (357)
  - *100 more than 580* (680)
  - *10 less than 145* (135)
  - *100 less than 962* (862)
  - *10 less than 786* (776)
  - *10 less than 734* (724)
  - *10 more than 399* (409)
  - *100 more than 837* (937)
  - *100 less than 368* (268)

The winners are the children still standing with 693 on their cards.

Game 9: Find 10 or 100 more or less than a given number

- Provide each child with a 4-digit number card. (**Note:** Ensure you use the 12 '4-digit number cards' provided on the CD-ROM.)
- Say: *Everyone stand up. Look at the number on your card. Sit down if the number on your card is:*
  - *10 more than 4563* (4573)
  - *100 less than 6034* (5934)
  - *100 less than 9383* (9283)
  - *100 more than 5049* (5149)
  - *100 less than 1457* (1357)
  - *10 less than 3505* (3495)
  - *10 more than 7492* (7502)
  - *10 more than 2708* (2718)
  - *100 more than 1986* (2086)
  - *100 more than 7761* (7861)
  - *10 less than 6220* (6210)

The winners are the children still standing with 8745 on their cards.

Who's left standing?

(continued)

Game 10: Compare numbers with one decimal place (tenths)

Recognise the place value of each digit in a number with one decimal place (tenths)

- Provide each child with a tenths number card. (**Note:** Ensure you use the 12 'Tenths number cards' provided on the CD-ROM.)
- Say: *Everyone stand up. Look at the number on your card. Sit down if the number on your card:*
  - *is between 3·8 and 5·1* (4·1)
  - *has 8 tenths* (2·8)
  - *is between 4·8 and 5·4* (5·2, 5·3)
  - *is between 9·1 and 9·5* (9·3)
  - *is between 1·5 and 1·9* (1·7)
  - *has 6 tenths* (3·6)
  - *is between 7·2 and 8·2* (7·5)
  - *is between 7·6 and 9·1* (8·9)
  - *has 4 tenths* (1·4)
  - *is between 2·3 and 2·7* (2·5)

The winners are the children still standing with 6·9 on their cards.

Game 11: Compare numbers with two decimal places (hundredths)

Recognise the place value of each digit in a number with two decimal places (hundredths)

- Provide each child with a hundredths number card. (**Note:** Ensure you use the 12 'Hundredths number cards' provided on the CD-ROM.)
- Say: *Everyone stand up. Look at the number on your card. Sit down if the number on your card:*
  - *is between 2·4 and 2·6* (2·58)
  - *has 6 hundredths* (6·16)
  - *is between 1·2 and 1·5* (1·34)
  - *is between 8·9 and 9·9* (9·38)
  - *has 2 hundredths* (5·02)
  - *is between 2·9 and 4·7* (3·71)
  - *has 9 tenths* (4·95)
  - *is between 6·72 and 7·58* (7·43)
  - *has 2 tenths* (5·27)
  - *is between 7·89 and 9·16* (8·84)
  - *has 9 hundredths* (1·69)

The winners are the children still standing with 2·73 on their cards.

Forming groups

Objectives

- Read numbers to at least 1000 in numerals
- Recognise the place value of each digit in a 2-digit, 3-digit or 4-digit number
- Order and compare numbers beyond 1000
- Recognise the place value of each digit in a number with up to two decimal places
- Order and compare numbers with up to two decimal places

Teacher resources

- none

Pupil resources

→ Number cards

- '1–12 number cards' (but only use the 1–9 number cards)' , or '2-digit number cards, or '3-digit number cards', or '4-digit number cards', or 'tenths numbers cards', or 'hundredths number cards' (one card per child)

What to do

Game 1: Recognise the place value of each digit in a 2-digit, 3-digit or 4-digit number

- Using the 2-digit, 3-digit and 4-digit number cards, provide each child with one card. Ensure that every child has a different number card. (**Note:** It is recommended that you use the '2-digit number cards', '3-digit number cards' and '4-digit number cards' provided on the CD-ROM.)
- Point and say: *Everyone stand up. Look at the number on your card. When I say 'Go!' I want everyone with 7 tens to move to this side of the room. Everyone with 3 ones to move to this side of the room, and everyone else to move to the back of the room. Ready? Go!*
- Once the three groups have been formed, ask the members of each group in turn to call out their number.

Variation

- Use different criteria to sort the numbers, for example: 8 tens / 4 units / *neither* 8 tens *nor* 4 units; 2-digit number / 3-digit number / 4-digit number.

Forming groups

(continued)

Game 2: Order and compare numbers beyond 1000

- Using the 2-digit, 3-digit and 4-digit number cards, provide each child with one card. Ensure that every child has a different number card. (**Note**: It is recommended that you use the '2-digit number cards', '3-digit number cards' and '4-digit number cards' provided on the CD-ROM.)
- Point and say: *Everyone stand up. Look at the number on your card. When I say 'Go!' I want everyone with a number less than 500 to move to this side of the room, and everyone with a number that is more than 500 to move to this side of the room. Ready? Go!*
- Once the two groups have been formed, ask the members of each group in turn to call out their number. Point and say: *Everyone hold up your number card. This group, starting with Trevor, call out your numbers. Now this group, starting with Alex, tell us your numbers.*
- Then say: *As quick as you can, I want each group to put yourselves in order, smallest number to largest number. Ready? Go!*
- Once the two groups have ordered their cards, ask the members of each group in turn to call out their number, starting with the smallest number.

Variation

- Use different criteria to order and compare the numbers, for example:

  Three groups: – less than 370
  – between 375 and 3500
  – more than 3500

  Four groups: – less than 70
  – between 70 and 400
  – between 400 and 5000
  – more than 5000

Game 3: Recognise the place value of each digit in a number with up to two decimal places

- Using the tenths and hundredths number cards, provide each child with one card. (**Note**: It is recommended that you use the 'Tenths number cards' and 'Hundredths number cards' provided on the CD-ROM.)
- Point and say: *Everyone stand up. Look at the number on your card. When I say 'Go!' I want everyone with 7 tenths to move to this side of the room. Everyone with 3 tenths to move to this side of the room, and everyone else to move to the back of the room. Ready? Go!*
- Once the three groups have been formed, ask the members of each group in turn to call out their number.

Variations

- Use just the tenths or the hundredths number cards.
- Use different criteria to sort the numbers, for example: 2 tenths / 9 tenths / *neither* 2 tenths *nor* 9 tenths; tenths number / hundredths number.

(*continued*)

Forming groups

(continued)

Game 4: Order and compare numbers with up to two decimal places

- Using the 'Tenths number cards', 'Hundredths number cards' and '1–9 number cards', provide each child with one card. Use all the tenths and hundredths number cards and supplement these with the 1–9 number cards to ensure that every child has a different number card. (**Note:** It is recommended that you use the 'Tenths number cards' and 'Hundredths number cards' provided on the CD-ROM.)
- Point and say: *Everyone stand up. Look at the number on your card. When I say 'Go!' I want everyone with a number less than 5 to move to this side of the room, and everyone with a number that is 5 or more to move to this side of the room. Ready? Go!*
- Once the two groups have been formed, ask the members of each group in turn to call out their number. Point and say: *Everyone hold up your number card. This group, starting with Sarah, call out your numbers. Now this group, starting with Garry, tell us your numbers.*
- Then say: *As quick as you can I want each group to put yourselves in order, smallest number to largest number. Ready? Go!*
- Once the two groups have ordered their cards, ask the members of each group in turn to call out their number, starting with the smallest number.

Variation

- Use different criteria to order and compare the numbers, for example:

Whole numbers: – 3 or less	Tenths: – 3·7 or less
– between 3 and 5	– between 3·7 and 6·5
– 5 or more	– more than 6·5

Lucky 7

Objective

- Recognise the place value of each digit in a 3-digit number (hundreds, tens and ones) and a 4-digit number (thousands, hundreds, tens and ones)

Pupil resources

- *Fluency in Number Facts: Facts and Games: Years 3 & 4* book pages 42 and 43 (per pair); PDFs:

Paired games and activities → Paired games from the *Facts and Games: Years 3 & 4* book

- pencil and paperclip (for the spinner) (per pair)
- about 12 counters (per pair)

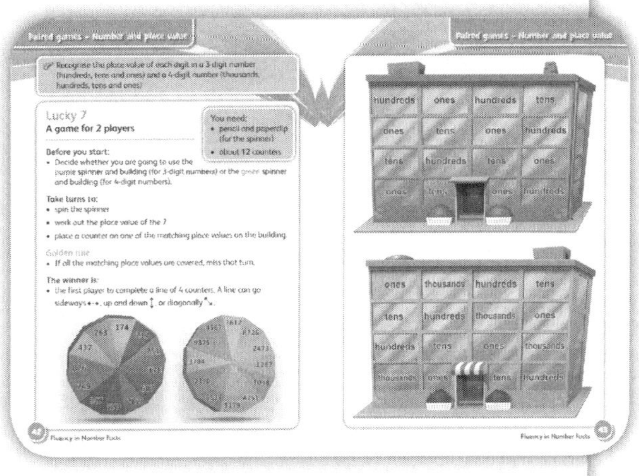

Notes

- Before the children play the game, ensure that they are familiar with how to use the spinners (see *Facts and Games: Years 3 & 4* book page 80).
- The purple spinner is used to practise and consolidate place value of each digit in a 3-digit number (hundreds, tens and ones), and the green spinner to practise and consolidate place value of each digit in a 4-digit number (thousands, hundreds, tens and ones). Instruct children to play the version of the game that is most appropriate to their needs.

Variations

- Children play the game in groups of three.
- Children play the game individually. How few spins of the spinner do they take to complete a line of four counters?

Carpet comparisons

3-digit numbers
4-digit numbers

Objectives

- Read numbers to at least 1000 in numerals
- Recognise the place value of each digit in a 3-digit number (hundreds, tens and ones) and a 4-digit number (thousands, hundreds, tens and ones)
- Order and compare numbers up to, and beyond, 1000

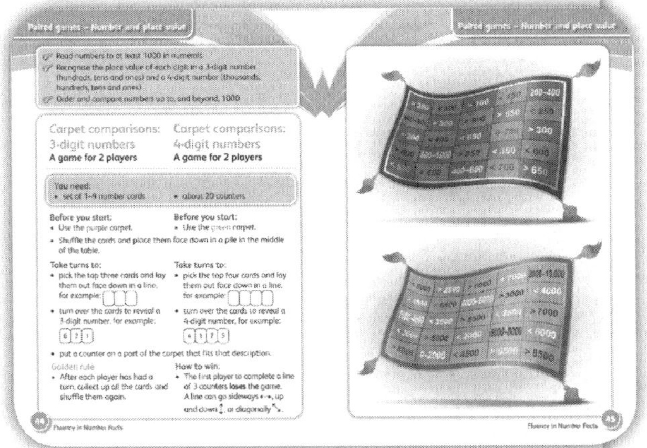

Pupil resources

- *Fluency in Number Facts: Facts and Games: Years 3 & 4* book pages 44 and 45 (per pair); PDFs:

→ Paired games and activities → Paired games from the *Facts and Games: Years 3 & 4* book

- set of 1–9 number cards (per pair)
- about 20 counters (per pair)

Notes

- The purple carpet is used to practise and consolidate place value and comparing 3-digit numbers, and the green carpet to practise and consolidate place value and comparing 4-digit numbers. Instruct children to play the version of the game that is most appropriate to their needs.

Variations

- Children play the game in groups of three.
- Once a player has turned over the cards to reveal their 3-digit or 4-digit number they are allowed to swap two cards. (or)
- The first player to complete a line of 3 counters *wins* the game. (or)
- Begin the game by placing one counter on each of the 25 sections of the carpet, making sure not to cover the descriptions. Each time the children make a number using the number cards they remove a counter from a section of the carpet that describes the number. If the counter has already been removed from that section, they don't collect a counter on that turn. The winner is the first player to collect eight counters. (or)
- Children play the game individually. How few turns do they take to complete a line of three counters?

More or less bubbles

Objective

- Find 10 or 100 more or less than a given number

Pupil resources

- *Fluency in Number Facts: Facts and Games: Years 3 & 4* book pages 46 and 47 (per pair); PDFs:

Paired games and activities → Paired games from the *Facts and Games: Years 3 & 4* book

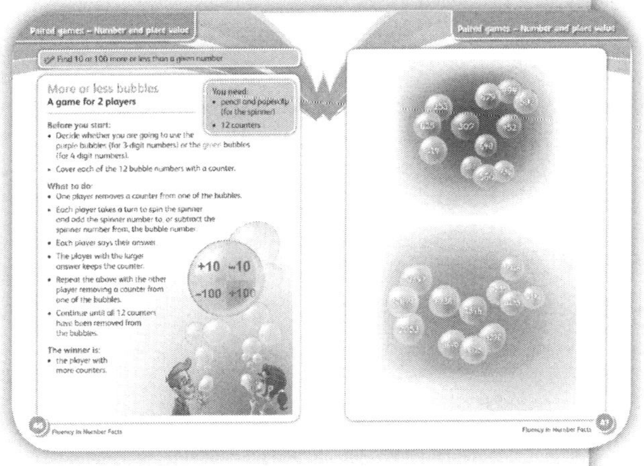

- pencil and paperclip (for the spinner) (per pair)
- 12 counters (per pair)

Notes

- Before the children play the game, ensure that they are familiar with how to use the spinner (see *Facts and Games: Years 3 & 4* book page 80).
- The purple bubbles involve finding 10 or 100 more or less than a 3-digit number, and the green bubbles finding 10 or 100 more or less than a 4-digit number. Instruct children to play the version of the game that is most appropriate to their needs.

Variations

- Children play the game in groups of three.

or

- The player with the smaller answer keeps the counter.

or

Round any number to the nearest 100 or 1000

- The player whose answer is nearest to a multiple of 100 (for the 3-digit purple bubbles) or multiple of 1000 (for the 4-digit green bubbles) keeps the counter.

Paired games and activities

And the winner is...

Objective

- Count in multiples of 2, 3, 4, 5, 10, 50 and 100

Pupil resources

- *Fluency in Number Facts: Facts and Games: Years 3 & 4* book pages 48 and 49 (per pair); PDFs:

Paired games and activities → Paired games from the *Facts and Games: Years 3 & 4* book

- pencil and paperclip (for the spinners) (per pair)
- 10 counters (per pair)

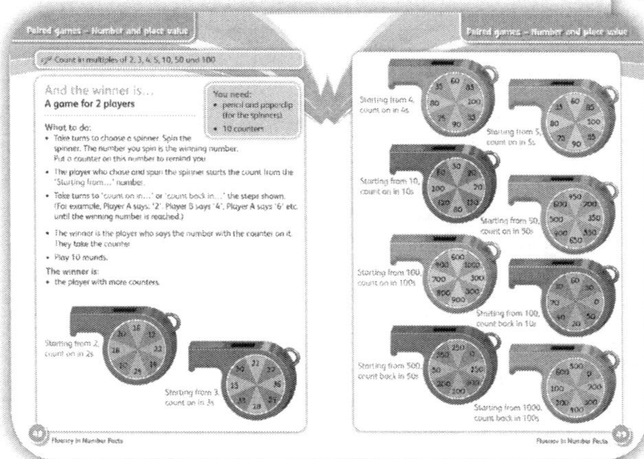

Notes

- This is a paired version of the whole-class game described on page 19.
- You can instruct children to use different whistle spinners to practise and consolidate counting on or back in different multiples. Alternatively, you can instruct them to use just one or two of the spinners to count on and/or back in specific multiples.
- Before the children play the game, ensure that they are familiar with how to use the spinners (see *Facts and Games: Years 3 & 4* book page 80).
- Also ensure that children read each set of whistle instructions carefully, especially as to whether they are to count on or back.

Variations

- Children play the game in groups of three.
- Children play the game individually. If they can reach the winning number within eight counts they keep the counter, otherwise they discard the counter. If necessary suggest the children use their fingers to keep track of the number of counts they make each time. How many of the ten counters can they collect?

Round about flags

Rounding to 10

Rounding to 100

Objective

- Round any number to the nearest 10 or 100

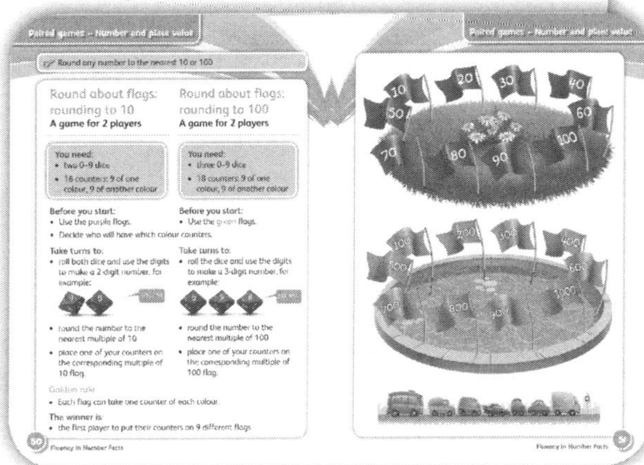

Pupil resources

- *Fluency in Number Facts: Facts and Games: Years 3 & 4* book pages 50 and 51 (per pair); PDFs:

- 2 × 0–9 dice (per pair)
- 18 counters: 9 of one colour, 9 of another colour (per pair)

Notes

- The purple flags involve rounding 2-digit numbers to the nearest multiple of 10, and the green flags rounding 3-digit numbers to the nearest multiple of 100. Instruct children to play the version of the game that is most appropriate to their needs.
- Ensure children realise that the dice can be swapped around to make different 2- or 3-digit numbers, for example:

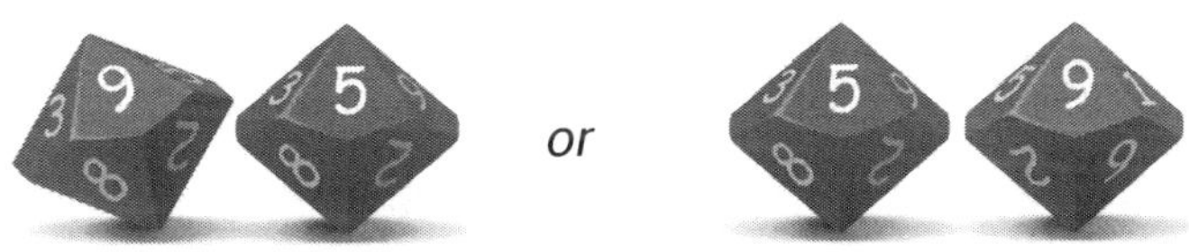

Variations

- Children play the game in groups of three. You need 27 counters: nine each of three different colours.

or

- Begin the game by placing one counter on each of the ten flags, making sure not to cover the number. Children remove a counter from the flag that shows their rounded number. If the counter has already been removed from that flag, they don't collect a counter on that turn. The winner is the first player to collect four counters (if playing in groups of three) or five counters (if playing in pairs).

- Children play the game individually, aiming to put a counter on each of the ten flags.

Decimals in between

Objective

- Compare numbers with the same number of decimal places up to two decimal places

Pupil resources

- *Fluency in Number Facts: Facts and Games: Years 3 & 4* book pages 52 and 53 (per pair); PDFs:

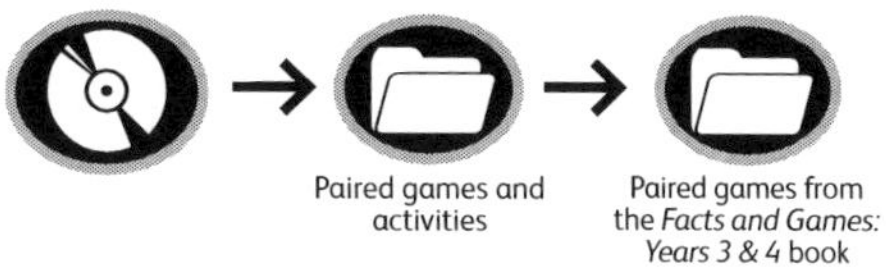

- 2 × 1–6 dice (per pair)
- 30 counters: 15 of one colour, 15 of another colour (per pair)

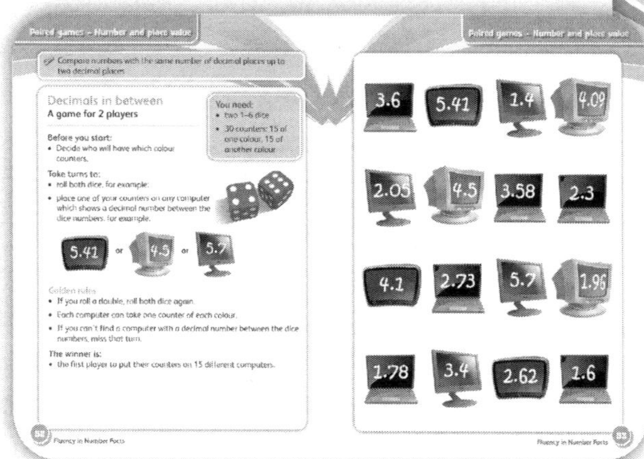
Paired games – Number and place value

Compare numbers with the same number of decimal places up to two decimal places

Decimals in between
A game for 2 players

You need:
- two 1–6 dice
- 30 counters: 15 of one colour, 15 of another colour

Before you start:
- Decide who will have which colour counters.

Take turns to:
- roll both dice, for example:
- place one of your counters on any computer which shows a decimal number between the dice numbers, for example:

5.41 or 4.5 or 5.7

Golden rules
- If you roll a double, roll both dice again.
- Each computer can take one counter of each colour.
- If you can't find a computer with a decimal number between the dice numbers, miss that turn.

The winner is:
- the first player to put their counters on 15 different computers.

Fluency in Number Facts

Paired games – Number and place value

3.6 5.41 1.4 4.09
2.05 4.5 3.58 2.3
4.1 2.73 5.7 1.96
1.78 3.4 2.62 1.6

Fluency in Number Facts

Notes

- Before playing this game ensure children are familiar with decimals with up to two decimal places.

Variations

- Children play the game in groups of three. You need 45 counters: 15 each of 3 different colours.

or

- The winner is the first player to complete a line of four counters.

or

- Begin the game by placing one counter on each of the computers, making sure not to cover the decimals. Children remove a counter from the computer that shows a decimal between their dice numbers. If the counter has already been removed from that computer, they don't collect a counter on that turn. The winner is the first player to collect 6 counters (if playing in groups of 3) or 9 counters (if playing in pairs).

- Children play the game individually. How few turns do they take to complete a line of four counters?

Which is larger?

Objectives

- Read numbers to at least 1000 in numerals
- Order and compare numbers beyond 1000
- Order and compare numbers with up to two decimal places

Pupil resources

→ Whole-class games and activities → Hands-on game boards

- 'Hands-on: 2-digit numbers' game board (per pair)
- 12 counters (per pair)

What to do

- Cover each of the numbers on the whistles with a counter.
- Each child then removes one counter from the whistles.
- The child who removes the counter from the larger number keeps both counters.
- The game continues until all the counters are removed from the whistles.
- The winner is the child with more counters.
- Play three games.

Variations

- Play 'Which is smaller?' The child who removes the counter from the smaller number keeps both counters.
- Use the 'Hands-on: 3-digit numbers' game board (per pair)
- Use the 'Hands-on: 4-digit numbers' game board (per pair)
- Use the 'Hands-on: Tenths' game board (per pair)
- Use the 'Hands-on: Hundredths' game board (per pair)

Whole-class games and activities

Hold it up

Objectives

- Recall and use addition and subtraction facts to 20 fluently, and derive and use related facts up to 100
- Add and subtract numbers mentally, including a 2-digit number and ones, a 2-digit number and tens, two 2-digit numbers, a 3-digit number and ones, a 3-digit number and tens, and a 3-digit number and hundreds

Teacher resources

→ Whole-class games and activities → PowerPoint Slides

- 'Hold it up'

Pupil resources

- set of 0–9 number cards or small individual whiteboard and pen (per child)

What to do

- Using the 'Hold it up: Numbers 1–10' slide, write an addition or subtraction operation in the box at the top of the slide, for example, 28 +.
- Point to one of the coloured 1–10 numbers on the slide.
- Children work out the answer and hold up the appropriate number card(s) / write the answer on their whiteboard.
- Repeat several times.

Variations

- Write different addition or subtraction operations in the box.
- Use the 'Hold it up: Numbers 1–12', 'Hold it up: Numbers 1–20', 'Hold it up: 2-digit numbers' and 'Hold it up: 3-digit numbers' slide.
- Change the numbers on the 'Hold it up' slides.

Gladiators

Objectives

- Recall and use addition and subtraction facts to 20 fluently, and derive and use related facts up to 100
- Add and subtract numbers mentally, including a 2-digit number and ones, a 2-digit number and tens, two 2-digit numbers, a 3-digit number and ones, a 3-digit number and tens, and a 3-digit number and hundreds

Teacher resources

- 'Gladiators'

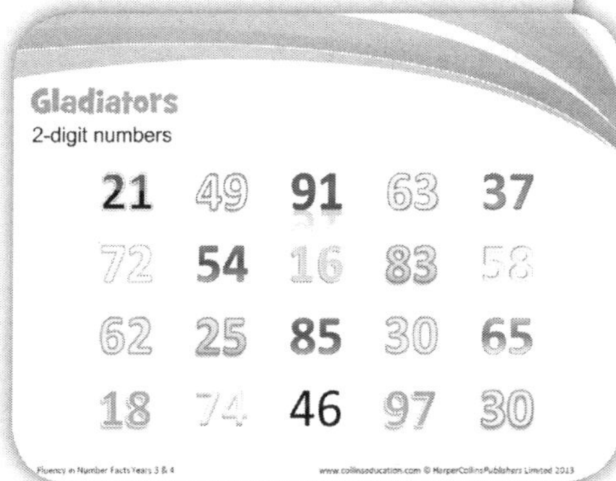

Pupil resources

- 2 × rulers or 'swords'

What to do

- Display the 'Gladiators 2-digit numbers' slide.
- Ask two children to stand either side of the numbers.
- Ask an addition or subtraction calculation where the answer is on the board, for example, *52 add 6 is…*
- The first child to point to the correct answer stays in. The other child sits down.
- Quickly choose another child to come and take the place of the child that just sat down.
- Continue as above.
- Which child can stay in the longest?

Variations

- The children sitting down ask the two children standing by the numbers a question where the answer is on the slide.
- To quicken the game, have two children standing either side of the numbers, one behind the other. When a child loses and has to sit down, there is an immediate replacement.
- Use the 'Gladiators: Numbers 1–10', 'Gladiators: Numbers 1–20', 'Gladiators: 3-digit numbers' and 'Gladiators 2- and 3-digit multiples of 10' slide.

Hands-on

Objectives

- Recall and use addition and subtraction facts to 20 fluently, and derive and use related facts up to 100
- Add and subtract numbers mentally, including a 2-digit number and ones, a 2-digit number and tens, two 2-digit numbers, a 3-digit number and ones, a 3-digit number and tens, and a 3-digit number and hundreds

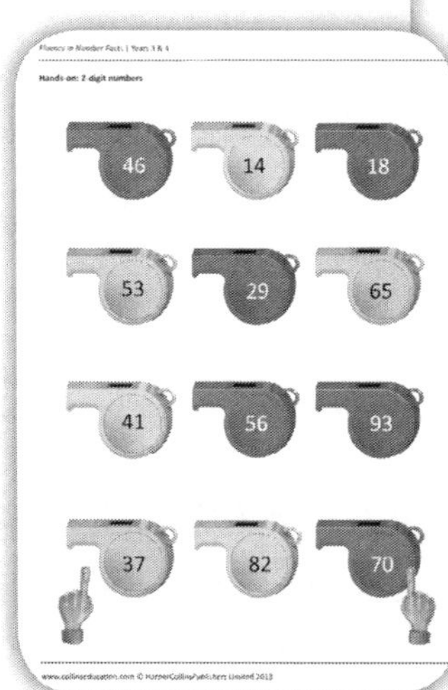

Teacher resources

- none

Pupil resources

- 'Hands-on' game board (per pair)

What to do

- Decide which range of numbers you want the children to use to practise and consolidate the addition and subtraction facts.
- Arrange the children into pairs and provide each pair with a copy of the appropriate 'Hands-on' game board, for example, 'Hands-on: 2-digit numbers' game board.
- Tell the children to put the game board between them and to put their index fingers on a hand at the bottom of the game board.
- Ask an appropriate addition or subtraction calculation that the children are practising, for example, *35 subtract 6*.
- The first child to point to the correct answer wins.
- Children keep count of how many rounds they win.
- Play for as long as is appropriate.
- The winner in each pair is the child who wins more rounds.

Variations

- Provide each pair with a pile of counters. As a child wins a game they take a counter. The winner in each pair is the child who wins more counters.
- Use the 'Hands-on: Numbers 1–10', 'Hands-on: Numbers 1–12', 'Hands-on: Numbers 1–20', 'Hands-on: 3-digit numbers', 'Hands-on: 2- and 3-digit multiples of 10', and 'Hands-on: 4-digit numbers' game boards.

Bingo

Objectives

- Recall and use addition and subtraction facts to 20 fluently, and derive and use related facts up to 100
- Add and subtract numbers mentally, including a 2-digit number and ones, a 2-digit number and tens, two 2-digit numbers, a 3-digit number and ones, a 3-digit number and tens, and a 3-digit number and hundreds

Teacher resources

- 'Bingo'

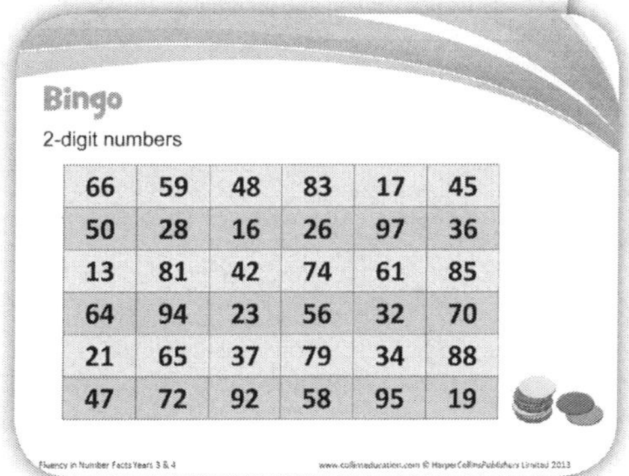

Pupil resources

- pencil and paper or small individual whiteboard and pen (per child)

What to do

- Display the 'Bingo: 2-digit numbers' slide.
- Ask each child to write down any five numbers from the slide.
- Ask questions involving addition and subtraction where the answer is on the slide.
- Children look to find if any of their five numbers is the answer to the question.
- If a child has the answer, they cross out that number.
- The winner is the first child to cross out all five of their numbers and call out 'Bingo!'

(**Note:** Be sure to keep a record of the answers for checking purposes.)

Variations

- Ask the children to write down more or fewer than five numbers from the slide.
- Use the 'Bingo: Numbers 1–20', 'Bingo: 3-digit numbers' and the 'Bingo 2- and 3-digit multiples of 10' slides.

Four in a row

Objectives

- Recall and use addition and subtraction facts to 20 fluently, and derive and use related facts up to 100
- Add and subtract numbers mentally, including a 2-digit number and ones, and a 3-digit number and ones

Teacher resources

→ Whole-class games and activities → PowerPoint slides

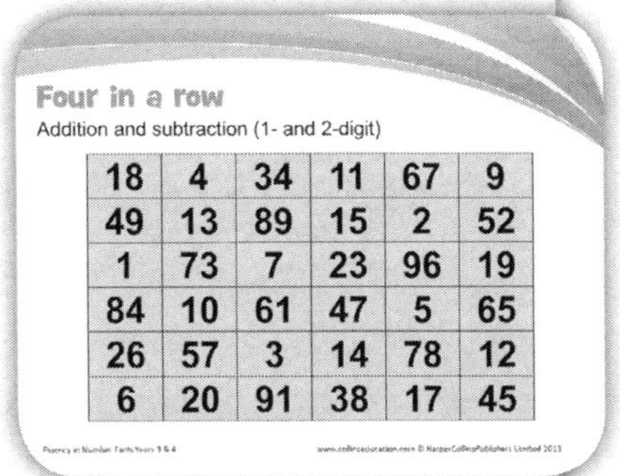
Four in a row
Addition and subtraction (1- and 2-digit)

18	4	34	11	67	9
49	13	89	15	2	52
1	73	7	23	96	19
84	10	61	47	5	65
26	57	3	14	78	12
6	20	91	38	17	45

- 'Four in a row'
- 0–9 dice

Pupil resources

- none

What to do

- Divide the class into two teams – a red team and a blue team.
- Display the 'Four in a row: Addition and subtraction (1- and 2-digit)' slide.
- Explain that the object of the game is for a team to highlight a row of four numbers either side to side, up and down or diagonally.
- To highlight a number, a team must successfully answer an addition or subtraction question.
- Invite a child from the red team to roll the dice and say the number.
- Ask an addition or subtraction question that includes the number rolled and where the answer is on the slide.
- Select a child from the red team to call out the answer.
- If correct, this number is highlighted in red on the slide. If incorrect, ask a child from the blue team to give the answer. If correct, this number is highlighted in blue.
- Next, invite a child from the blue team to roll the dice.
- Repeat the above, at a quick pace, until one team has highlighted a row of four numbers.

Variations

- The team that rolls the dice decides what number to add to, or subtract from, the dice number.
- Display the 'Four in a row: Addition and subtraction (3-digit)' slide and 'Four in a row: 2- and 3-digit multiples of 10' slide.

Tell me the facts

Objectives

- Recall and use addition and subtraction facts to 20 fluently, and derive and use related facts up to 100
- Add and subtract numbers mentally, including a 2-digit number and ones, a 2-digit number and tens, two 2-digit numbers, a 3-digit number and ones, a 3-digit number and tens, and a 3-digit number and hundreds

Teacher resources

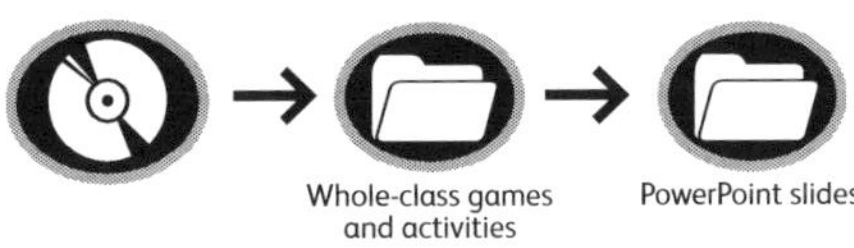

- 'Tell me the facts'

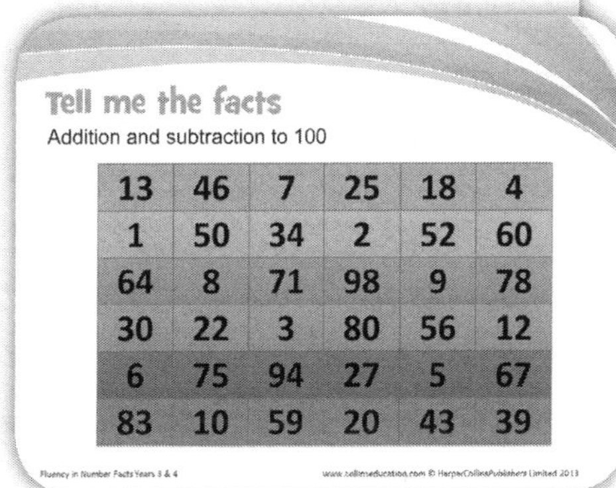

13	46	7	25	18	4
1	50	34	2	52	60
64	8	71	98	9	78
30	22	3	80	56	12
6	75	94	27	5	67
83	10	59	20	43	39

Pupil resources

- none

What to do

- Display the 'Tell me the facts: Addition and subtraction to 100' slide.
- Ask a child to highlight two numbers next to each other either side to side, up and down, or diagonally and say a known addition or subtraction number fact about these two numbers, i.e. *I know that the sum of 52 and 9 is 61.*
- Repeat, asking other children to come and highlight two other numbers, saying a known addition or subtraction number fact about the two numbers.

Variations

- Ask questions such as:
  - *Point to two numbers next to each other that have a total of 28.*
  - *Point to two numbers next to each other that have a difference of 18.*
- Use the 'Tell me the facts: Addition and subtraction to 10', 'Tell me the facts: Addition and subtraction to 20', 'Tell me the facts: Addition and subtraction to 1000' and 'Tell me the facts: 2- and 3-digit multiples of 10' slides.

Tell me your numbers

Objectives

- Recall and use addition and subtraction facts to 20 fluently, and derive and use related facts up to 100
- Add and subtract numbers mentally, including a 2-digit number and ones, a 2-digit number and tens, two 2-digit numbers, and a 3-digit number and ones

Teacher resources

- none

Pupil resources

→ Number cards

- '1–12 number cards' (but only use the 1–9 number cards) or '2-digit number cards' (one card per child)

What to do

- Provide each child with a 1–9 number card, 2-digit number card, or 2- and 3-digit multiples of 10 number cards.
- Quickly call out two children's names.
- Both children stand and say the number on their card.
- Ask these two children an appropriate addition or subtraction question using the two numbers on the cards.
- The two children sit down.
- Repeat for other pairs of children.

Variations

- Provide each child with a 1–9 number card or 3-digit number card. Ensure that when you call out two children's names that one child has a 1–9 number card and the other child a 3-digit number card.
- Provide each child with a 1–9 digit card or 2- and 3-digit multiples of 10 number card. Ensure that when you call out two children's names that one child has a 1–9 number card and the other child a 2- and 3-digit multiples of 10 number card.

Who's left standing?

Objectives

- Recall and use addition and subtraction facts to 20 fluently, and derive and use related facts up to 100
- Add and subtract numbers mentally, including a 2-digit number and ones, a 2-digit number and tens, two 2-digit numbers, a 3-digit number and ones, a 3-digit number and tens, and a 3-digit number and hundreds

Teacher resources

- none

Pupil resources

Number cards

- '1–20 number cards' or '2-digit number cards' or '3-digit number cards' or '2- and 3-digit multiples of 10 number cards' (one card per child)

What to do

Game 1: Recall and use addition facts to 20

- Provide each child with a 1–20 number card.
- Say: *Everyone stand up. Look at the number on your card. Sit down if the number on your card is the answer to:*
  - *5 plus 3* (8)
  - *13 add 7* (20)
  - *2 more than 3* (5)
  - *9 add 7* (16)
  - *1 add 1* (2)
  - *3 plus 4* (7)
  - *8 add 6* (14)
  - *11 add 4* (15)
  - *1 more than 2* (3)
  - *14 plus 5* (19)
  - *3 more than 6* (9)
  - *8 plus 3* (11)
  - *1 add zero* (1)
  - *13 add 4* (17)
  - *8 plus 5* (13)
  - *5 add 7* (12)
  - *2 more than 8* (10)
  - *5 plus 1* (6)
  - *7 add 11* (18)

The winners are the children still standing with 4 on their cards.

(continued)

Who's left standing?

(continued)

Game 2: Recall and use subtraction facts to 20

- Provide each child with a 1–20 number card.
- Say: *Everyone stand up. Look at the number on your card. Sit down if the number on your card is the answer to:*
  - *3 less than 18* (15)
  - *19 subtract 5* (14)
  - *14 minus 12* (2)
  - *18 take away 5* (13)
  - *the difference between 11 and 14* (3)
  - *2 less than 20* (18)
  - *20 take away 11* (9)
  - *17 subtract 5* (12)
  - *13 minus 6* (7)
  - *19 minus 3* (16)
  - *the difference between 10 and 16* (6)
  - *20 subtract zero* (20)
  - *2 less than 19* (17)
  - *12 minus 4* (8)
  - *10 take away 9* (1)
  - *the difference between 20 and 15* (5)
  - *1 less than 20* (19)
  - *16 subtract 12* (4)
  - *the difference between 17 and 7* (10)

The winners are the children still standing with 11 on their cards.

Game 3: Recall and use addition and subtraction facts to 20

- Provide each child with a 1–20 number card.
- Say: *Everyone stand up. Look at the number on your card. Sit down if the number on your card is the answer to:*
  - *8 plus 5* (13)
  - *14 take away 12* (2)
  - *17 minus 10* (7)
  - *9 add 5* (14)
  - *the difference between 17 and 13* (4)
  - *7 plus 8* (15)
  - *16 subtract 13* (3)
  - *14 add 4* (18)
  - *9 subtract 8* (1)
  - *9 add 8* (17)
  - *7 plus 4* (11)
  - *15 minus 6* (9)
  - *12 add 4* (16)
  - *19 minus 9* (10)
  - *14 subtract 6* (8)
  - *14 add 6* (20)
  - *20 take away 14* (6)
  - *16 add 3* (19)
  - *the difference between 14 and 19* (5)

The winners are the children still standing with 12 on their cards.

Who's left standing?

(continued)

Game 4: Add numbers mentally, including a 2-digit number and ones

- Provide each child with a 2-digit number card. (**Note:** Ensure you use the 12 '2-digit number cards' provided on the CD-ROM.)
- Say: *Everyone stand up. Look at the number on your card. Sit down if the number on your card is the answer to:*
  - *18 add 6* (24)
  - *29 plus 8* (37)
  - *46 add 7* (53)
  - *2 more than 73* (75)
  - *19 plus 9* (28)
  - *36 plus 5* (41)
  - *3 more than 56* (59)
  - *78 add 6* (84)
  - *37 plus 9* (46)
  - *52 add 8* (60)
  - *85 plus 7* (92)

The winners are the children still standing with 32 on their cards.

Game 5: Subtract numbers mentally, including a 2-digit number and ones

- Provide each child with a 2-digit number card. (**Note:** Ensure you use the 12 '2-digit number cards' provided on the CD-ROM.)
- Say: *Everyone stand up. Look at the number on your card. Sit down if the number on your card is the answer to:*
  - *38 subtract 6* (32)
  - *92 minus 8* (84)
  - *53 take away 7* (46)
  - *the difference between 84 and 9* (75)
  - *5 less than 33* (28)
  - *28 subtract 4* (24)
  - *the difference between 40 and 3* (37)
  - *61 minus 8* (53)
  - *65 take away 5* (60)
  - *99 subtract 7* (92)
  - *2 less than 61* (59)

The winners are the children still standing with 41 on their cards.

Game 6: Add and subtract numbers mentally, including a 2-digit number and ones

- Provide each child with a 2-digit number card. (**Note:** Ensure you use the 12 '2-digit number cards' provided on the CD-ROM.)
- Say: *Everyone stand up. Look at the number on your card. Sit down if the number on your card is the answer to:*
  - *56 plus 4* (60)
  - *40 minus 8* (32)
  - *78 add 6* (84)
  - *97 take away 5* (92)
  - *34 plus 7* (41)
  - *9 less than 33* (24)
  - *30 add 7* (37)
  - *the difference between 59 and 6* (53)
  - *5 more than 41* (46)
  - *67 plus 8* (75)
  - *2 less than 30* (28)

The winners are the children still standing with 59 on their cards.

(*continued*)

Who's left standing?

(continued)

Game 7: Add numbers mentally, including a 2-digit number and tens

- Provide each child with a 2-digit number card. (**Note:** Ensure you use the 12 '2-digit number cards' provided on the CD-ROM.)
- Say: *Everyone stand up. Look at the number on your card. Sit down if the number on your card is the answer to:*
  - *19 add 40* (59)
  - *27 plus 10* (37)
  - *23 plus 30* (53)
  - *21 add 20* (41)
  - *10 more than 18* (28)
  - *25 plus 50* (75)
  - *30 add 54* (84)
  - *60 more than 32* (92)
  - *16 plus 30* (46)
  - *20 add 40* (60)
  - *12 plus 20* (32)

The winners are the children still standing with 24 on their cards.

Game 8: Subtract numbers mentally, including a 2-digit number and tens

- Provide each child with a 2-digit number card. (**Note:** Ensure you use the 12 '2-digit number cards' provided on the CD-ROM.)
- Say: *Everyone stand up. Look at the number on your card. Sit down if the number on your card is the answer to:*
  - *20 less than 95* (75)
  - *94 subtract 70* (24)
  - *83 minus 30* (53)
  - *66 take away 20* (46)
  - *10 less than 94* (84)
  - *77 minus 40* (37)
  - *89 subtract 30* (59)
  - *81 minus 40* (41)
  - *78 subtract 50* (28)
  - *92 minus 60* (32)
  - *20 less than 80* (60)

The winners are the children still standing with 92 on their cards.

Game 9: Add and subtract numbers mentally, including a 2-digit number and tens

- Provide each child with a 2-digit number card. (**Note:** Ensure you use the 12 '2-digit number cards' provided on the CD-ROM.)
- Say: *Everyone stand up. Look at the number on your card. Sit down if the number on your card is the answer to:*
  - *77 subtract 40* (37)
  - *92 minus 60* (32)
  - *29 plus 30* (59)
  - *10 more than 31* (41)
  - *98 minus 70* (28)
  - *25 plus 50* (75)
  - *74 subtract 50* (24)
  - *42 plus 50* (92)
  - *24 plus 60* (84)
  - *the difference between 76 and 30* (46)
  - *30 add 30* (60)

The winners are the children still standing with 53 on their cards.

Who's left standing?

(continued)

Game 10: Add numbers mentally, including two 2-digit numbers

- Provide each child with a 2-digit number card. (**Note:** Ensure you use the 12 '2-digit number cards' provided on the CD-ROM.)
- Say: *Everyone stand up. Look at the number on your card. Sit down if the number on your card is the answer to:*
  - *28 add 25* (53)
  - *37 plus 55* (92)
  - *the sum of 25 and 12* (37)
  - *31 add 28* (59)
  - *29 plus 17* (46)
  - *47 plus 28* (75)
  - *12 add 12* (24)
  - *27 plus 14* (41)
  - *the total of 32 and 28* (60)
  - *11 more than 17* (28)
  - *14 add 18* (32)

The winners are the children still standing with 84 on their cards.

Game 11: Subtract numbers mentally, including two 2-digit numbers

- Provide each child with a 2-digit number card. (**Note:** Ensure you use the 12 '2-digit number cards' provided on the CD-ROM.)
- Say: *Everyone stand up. Look at the number on your card. Sit down if the number on your card is the answer to:*
  - *92 minus 17* (75)
  - *71 subtract 47* (24)
  - *60 take away 19* (41)
  - *99 minus 15* (84)
  - *the difference between 32 and 60* (28)
  - *16 less than 48* (32)
  - *92 minus 55* (37)
  - *91 subtract 32* (59)
  - *85 take away 39* (46)
  - *81 minus 28* (53)
  - *12 less than 72* (60)

The winners are the children still standing with 92 on their cards.

Game 12: Add and subtract numbers mentally, including two 2-digit numbers

- Provide each child with a 2-digit number card. (**Note:** Ensure you use the 12 '2-digit number cards' provided on the CD-ROM.)
- Say: *Everyone stand up. Look at the number on your card. Sit down if the number on your card is the answer to:*
  - *37 plus 38* (75)
  - *74 minus 42* (32)
  - *25 add 28* (53)
  - *97 minus 38* (59)
  - *16 plus 44* (60)
  - *75 take away 34* (41)
  - *82 subtract 45* (37)
  - *the difference between 80 and 56* (24)
  - *the sum of 38 and 46* (84)
  - *63 subtract 17* (46)
  - *46 add 46* (92)

The winners are the children still standing with 28 on their cards.

(continued)

Who's left standing?

(continued)

Game 13: Add numbers mentally, including a 3-digit number and ones

- Provide each child with a 3-digit number card. (**Note:** Ensure you use the 12 '3-digit number cards' provided on the CD-ROM.)
- Say: *Everyone stand up. Look at the number on your card. Sit down if the number on your card is the answer to:*
  - *505 plus 7* (512)
  - *9 more than 715* (724)
  - *262 plus 6* (268)
  - *2 more than 678* (680)
  - *771 add 5* (776)
  - *4 more than 337* (341)
  - *688 add 5* (693)
  - *128 add 7* (135)
  - *348 plus 9* (357)
  - *854 plus 8* (862)
  - *929 add 8* (937)

The winners are the children still standing with 409 on their cards.

Game 14: Subtract numbers mentally, including a 3-digit number and ones

- Provide each child with a 3-digit number card. (**Note:** Ensure you use the 12 '3-digit number cards' provided on the CD-ROM.)
- Say: *Everyone stand up. Look at the number on your card. Sit down if the number on your card is the answer to:*
  - *142 subtract 7* (135)
  - *362 minus 5* (357)
  - *784 take away 8* (776)
  - *4 less than 272* (268)
  - *411 minus 2* (409)
  - *699 subtract 6* (693)
  - *870 minus 8* (862)
  - *9 less than 350* (341)
  - *519 take away 7* (512)
  - *728 subtract 4* (724)
  - *943 minus 6* (937)

The winners are the children still standing with 680 on their cards.

Game 15: Add and subtract numbers mentally, including a 3-digit number and ones

- Provide each child with a 3-digit number card. (**Note:** Ensure you use the 12 '3-digit number cards' provided on the CD-ROM.)
- Say: *Everyone stand up. Look at the number on your card. Sit down if the number on your card is the answer to:*
  - *338 add 3* (341)
  - *732 subtract 8* (724)
  - *687 plus 6* (693)
  - *853 add 9* (862)
  - *142 take away 7* (135)
  - *363 minus 6* (357)
  - *4 less than 272* (268)
  - *414 subtract 5* (409)
  - *675 add 5* (680)
  - *768 plus 8* (776)
  - *946 minus 9* (937)

The winners are the children still standing with 512 on their cards.

Who's left standing?

(continued)

Game 16: Add numbers mentally, including a 3-digit number and tens

- Provide each child with a 3-digit number card. (**Note:** Ensure you use the 12 '3-digit number cards' provided on the CD-ROM.)
- Say: *Everyone stand up. Look at the number on your card. Sit down if the number on your card is the answer to:*
  - *620 add 60* (680)
  - *726 plus 50* (776)
  - *684 add 40* (724)
  - *623 plus 70* (693)
  - *782 plus 80* (862)
  - *267 plus 90* (357)
  - *10 more than 927* (937)
  - *281 add 60* (341)
  - *492 add 20* (512)
  - *178 plus 90* (268)
  - *379 plus 30* (409)

The winners are the children still standing with 135 on their cards.

Game 17: Subtract numbers mentally, including a 3-digit number and tens

- Provide each child with a 3-digit number card. (**Note:** Ensure you use the 12 '3-digit number cards' provided on the CD-ROM.)
- Say: *Everyone stand up. Look at the number on your card. Sit down if the number on your card is the answer to:*
  - *391 subtract 50* (341)
  - *427 take away 70* (357)
  - *814 minus 90* (724)
  - *328 subtract 60* (268)
  - *562 minus 50* (512)
  - *733 minus 40* (693)
  - *922 subtract 60* (862)
  - *499 take away 90* (409)
  - *710 minus 30* (680)
  - *846 subtract 70* (776)
  - *215 minus 80* (135)

The winners are the children still standing with 937 on their cards.

Game 18: Add and subtract numbers mentally, including a 3-digit number and tens

- Provide each child with a 3-digit number card. (**Note:** Ensure you use the 12 '3-digit number cards' provided on the CD-ROM.)
- Say: *Everyone stand up. Look at the number on your card. Sit down if the number on your card is the answer to:*
  - *185 take away 50* (135)
  - *932 minus 70* (862)
  - *261 add 80* (341)
  - *723 subtract 30* (693)
  - *349 add 60* (409)
  - *654 add 70* (724)
  - *397 minus 40* (357)
  - *422 plus 90* (512)
  - *760 take away 80* (680)
  - *726 plus 50* (776)
  - *897 plus 40* (937)

The winners are the children still standing with 268 on their cards.

(*continued*)

Who's left standing?

(continued)

Game 19: Add numbers mentally, including a 3-digit number and hundreds

- Provide each child with a 3-digit number card. (**Note:** Ensure you use the 12 '3-digit number cards' provided on the CD-ROM.)
- Say: *Everyone stand up. Look at the number on your card. Sit down if the number on your card is the answer to:*
  - *662 add 200* (862)
  - *224 plus 500* (724)
  - *109 plus 300* (409)
  - *237 plus 700* (937)
  - *241 add 100* (341)
  - *176 add 600* (776)
  - *168 plus 100* (268)
  - *380 add 300* (680)
  - *157 plus 200* (357)
  - *193 plus 500* (693)
  - *100 more than 412* (512)

The winners are the children still standing with 135 on their cards.

Game 20: Subtract numbers mentally, including a 3-digit number and hundreds

- Provide each child with a 3-digit number card. (**Note:** Ensure you use the 12 '3-digit number cards' provided on the CD-ROM.)
- Say: *Everyone stand up. Look at the number on your card. Sit down if the number on your card is the answer to:*
  - *924 subtract 200* (724)
  - *835 minus 700* (135)
  - *993 subtract 300* (693)
  - *668 minus 400* (268)
  - *709 take away 300* (409)
  - *957 subtract 600* (357)
  - *100 less than 962* (862)
  - *741 minus 400* (341)
  - *880 take away 200* (680)
  - *812 minus 300* (512)
  - *876 subtract 100* (776)

The winners are the children still standing with 937 on their cards.

Game 21: Add and subtract numbers mentally, including a 3-digit number and hundreds

- Provide each child with a 3-digit number card. (**Note:** Ensure you use the 12 '3-digit number cards' provided on the CD-ROM.)
- Say: *Everyone stand up. Look at the number on your card. Sit down if the number on your card is the answer to:*
  - *200 more than 480* (680)
  - *324 add 400* (724)
  - *912 minus 400* (512)
  - *609 subtract 200* (409)
  - *476 plus 300* (776)
  - *768 take away 500* (268)
  - *362 plus 500* (862)
  - *541 subtract 200* (341)
  - *935 minus 800* (135)
  - *493 plus 200* (693)
  - *137 add 800* (937)

The winners are the children still standing with 357 on their cards.

Who's left standing?

(continued)

Game 22: Add numbers mentally, including pairs of 2- and 3-digit multiples of 10

- Provide each child with a 2- or 3-digit multiple of 10 number card. (**Note:** Ensure you use the 12 '2- and 3-digit multiples of 10 number cards' provided on the CD-ROM.)
- Say: *Everyone stand up. Look at the number on your card. Sit down if the number on your card is the answer to:*
  - *10 more than 20* (30)
  - *40 add 80* (120)
  - *820 plus 50* (870)
  - *570 add 70* (640)
  - *20 add 20* (40)
  - *130 plus 30* (160)
  - *410 add 80* (490)
  - *690 plus 60* (750)
  - *30 add 40* (70)
  - *190 plus 90* (280)
  - *50 more than 480* (530)

The winners are the children still standing with 310 on their cards.

Game 23: Subtract numbers mentally, including pairs of 2- and 3-digit multiples of 10

- Provide each child with a 2- or 3-digit multiple of 10 number card. (**Note:** Ensure you use the 12 '2- and 3-digit multiples of 10 number cards' provided on the CD-ROM.)
- Say: *Everyone stand up. Look at the number on your card. Sit down if the number on your card is the answer to:*
  - *540 subtract 50* (490)
  - *160 minus 40* (120)
  - *830 take away 80 (750)*
  - *100 subtract 70* (30)
  - *590 minus 60* (530)
  - *10 less than 50* (40)
  - *370 minus 60* (310)
  - *250 subtract 90* (160)
  - *30 less than 900* (870)
  - *310 minus 30* (280)
  - *150 subtract 80* (70)

The winners are the children still standing with 640 on their cards.

Game 24: Add and subtract numbers mentally, including pairs of 2- and 3-digit multiples of 10

- Provide each child with a 2- or 3-digit multiple of 10 number card. (**Note:** Ensure you use the 12 '2- and 3-digit multiples of 10 number cards' provided on the CD-ROM.)
- Say: *Everyone stand up. Look at the number on your card. Sit down if the number on your card is the answer to:*
  - *590 add 50* (640)
  - *550 subtract 60* (490)
  - *320 take away 40* (280)
  - *120 minus 80* (40)
  - *70 add 50* (120)
  - *250 plus 60* (310)
  - *20 less than 50* (30)
  - *80 add 80* (160)
  - *460 plus 70* (530)
  - *940 minus 70* (870)
  - *160 take away 90* (70)

The winners are the children still standing with 750 on their cards.

Stand up

Objectives

- Recall and use addition and subtraction facts to 20 fluently, and derive and use related facts up to 100
- Add and subtract numbers mentally, including a 2-digit number and ones, a 2-digit number and tens, two 2-digit numbers, a 3-digit number and ones, a 3-digit number and tens, and a 3-digit number and hundreds

Teacher resources

- none

Pupil resources

Number cards

- '1–12 number cards' or '2-digit number cards' or '3-digit number cards' or '2- and 3-digit multiples of 10 number cards' (one card per child)

What to do

Game 1: Recall and use addition facts to 20 fluently

- Provide each child with a '1–12 number card'.
- Say: *Look at the number on your card. Add 3 to the number on your card. If the total is 11, stand up.*
- Ask: *Who can tell me what number is on Tom's and Gaynor's cards?* (8)
- Ask the children standing to show their cards.
- The children standing then sit down.
- Repeat for the following:
  - *Add 6 to the number on your card. If the total is 16, stand up.* (10)
  - *Add 8 to the number on your card. If the sum is 13, stand up.* (5)
  - *Add 13 to the number on your card. If the total is 17, stand up.* (4)
  - *Add 7 to the number on your card. If the sum is 19, stand up.* (12)
  - *Add 5 to the number on your card. If the total is 6, stand up.* (1)
  - *Add 4 to the number on your card. If the total is 10, stand up.* (6)
  - *Add 11 to the number on your card. If the total is 14, stand up.* (3)
  - *Add 4 to the number on your card. If the total is 15, stand up.* (11)
  - *Add 10 to the number on your card. If the answer is 12, stand up.* (2)
  - *Add 9 to the number on your card. If the answer is 18, stand up.* (9)
  - *Add 13 to the number on your card. If the sum is 20, stand up.* (7)

Stand up

(continued)

Game 2: Recall and use subtraction facts to 20

- Provide each child with a '1–12 number card'.
- Say: *Look at the number on your card. Stand up if your card shows the answer to 17 subtract 7.*
- Ask: *Who can tell me what number is on William's and Leona's cards?* (10)
- Ask the children standing to show their cards.
- The children standing then sit down.
- Repeat for the following:
  - *Stand up if your card shows the answer to 19 subtract 11.* (8)
  - *Stand up if your card shows the answer to 17 subtract 14.* (3)
  - *Stand up if your card shows the answer to 13 minus 7.* (6)
  - *Stand up if your card shows the answer to 20 subtract 8.* (12)
  - *Stand up if your card shows the answer to 15 take away 10.* (5)
  - *Stand up if your card shows the answer to 12 minus 5.* (7)
  - *Stand up if your card shows the answer to 14 subtract 13.* (1)
  - *Stand up if your card shows the answer to 18 take away 9.* (9)
  - *Stand up if your card shows the answer to 9 subtract 5.* (4)
  - *Stand up if your card shows the answer to 19 subtract 8.* (11)
  - *Stand up if your card shows the answer to 16 subtract 14.* (2)

Game 3: Recall and use addition and subtraction facts to 20

- Provide each child with a '1–12 number card'.
- Say: *Look at the number on your card. Stand up if your card shows the answer to 12 subtract 9.*
- Ask: *Who can tell me what number is on Peter's and Juan's cards?* (3)
- Ask the children standing to show their cards.
- The children standing then sit down.
- Repeat for the following:
  - *Add 5 to the number on your card. If the total is 7, stand up.* (2)
  - *Stand up if your card shows the answer to 13 subtract 5.* (8)
  - *Add 11 to the number on your card. If the answer is 18, stand up.* (7)
  - *Stand up if your card shows the answer to 20 subtract 9.* (11)
  - *Stand up if your card shows the answer to 13 take away 7.* (6)
  - *Add 13 to the number on your card. If the sum is 17, stand up.* (4)
  - *Stand up if your card shows the answer to 15 take away 14.* (1)
  - *Add 6 to the number on your card. If the sum is 16, stand up.* (10)
  - *Add 7 to the number on your card. If the answer is 19, stand up.* (12)
  - *Stand up if your card shows the answer to 17 minus 8.* (9)
  - *Add 8 to the number on your card. If the answer is 13, stand up.* (5)

(continued)

Stand up

(continued)

Game 4: Add numbers mentally, including a 2-digit number and ones

- Provide each child with a '2-digit number card'. (**Note:** Ensure you use the 12 '2-digit number cards' provided on the CD-ROM.)
- Say: *Look at the number on your card. Add 6 to the number on your card. If the total is 30, stand up.*
- Ask: *Who can tell me what number is on Harry's and Paul's cards?* (24)
- Ask the children standing to show their cards.
- The children standing then sit down.
- Repeat for the following:
  - *Add 7 to the number on your card. If the total is 35, stand up.* (28)
  - *Add 5 to the number on your card. If the total is 37, stand up.* (32)
  - *Add 9 to the number on your card. If the sum is 62, stand up.* (53)
  - *Add 4 to the number on your card. If the answer is 63, stand up.* (59)
  - *Add 6 to the number on your card. If the total is 66, stand up.* (60)
  - *Add 3 to the number on your card. If the total is 40, stand up.* (37)
  - *Add 8 to the number on your card. If the answer is 49, stand up.* (41)
  - *Add 5 to the number on your card. If the total is 51, stand up.* (46)
  - *Add 7 to the number on your card. If the total is 82, stand up.* (75)
  - *Add 4 to the number on your card. If the total is 88, stand up.* (84)
  - *Add 5 to the number on your card. If the answer is 97, stand up.* (92)

Game 5: Subtract numbers mentally, including a 2-digit number and ones

- Provide each child with a '2-digit number card'. (**Note:** Ensure you use the 12 '2-digit number cards' provided on the CD-ROM.)
- Say: *Look at the number on your card. Stand up if your card shows the answer to 61 subtract 8.*
- Ask: *Who can tell me what number is on Helen's and Oliver's cards?* (53)
- Ask the children standing to show their cards.
- The children standing then sit down.
- Repeat for the following:
  - *Stand up if your card shows the answer to 63 take away 4.* (59)
  - *Stand up if your card shows the answer to 66 minus 6.* (60)
  - *Stand up if your card shows the answer to 46 subtract 9.* (37)
  - *Stand up if your card shows the answer to 53 take away 7.* (46)
  - *Stand up if your card shows the answer to 45 subtract 4.* (41)
  - *Stand up if your card shows the answer to 30 minus 2.* (28)
  - *Stand up if your card shows the answer to 83 minus 8.* (75)
  - *Stand up if your card shows the answer to 99 take away 7.* (92)
  - *Stand up if your card shows the answer to 88 minus 4.* (84)
  - *Stand up if your card shows the answer to 30 subtract 6.* (24)
  - *Stand up if your card shows the answer to 37 take away 5.* (32)

Stand up

(continued)

Game 6: Add and subtract numbers mentally, including a 2-digit number and ones

- Provide each child with a '2-digit number card'. (**Note:** Ensure you use the 12 '2-digit number cards' provided on the CD-ROM.)
- Say: *Look at the number on your card. Stand up if your card shows the answer to 83 subtract 8.*
- Ask: *Who can tell me what number is on Martin's and Arshin's cards?* (75)
- Ask the children standing to show their cards.
- The children standing then sit down.
- Repeat for the following:
  - *Add 9 to the number on your card. If the total is 62, stand up.* (53)
  - *Stand up if your card shows the answer to 44 minus 7.* (37)
  - *Add 6 to the number on your card. If the total is 30, stand up.* (24)
  - *Stand up if the number on your card is 2 less than 61.* (59)
  - *Add 7 to the number on your card. If the answer is 91, stand up.* (84)
  - *Add 8 to the number on your card. If the total is 49, stand up.* (41)
  - *Add 5 to the number on your card. If the sum is 33, stand up.* (28)
  - *Stand up if your card shows the answer to 40 take away 8.* (32)
  - *Stand up if your card shows the answer to 52 subtract 6.* (46)
  - *Add 4 to the number on your card. If the total is 64, stand up.* (60)
  - *Stand up if your card shows the answer to 97 subtract 5.* (92)

Game 7: Add numbers mentally, including a 2-digit number and tens

- Provide each child with a '2-digit number card'. (**Note:** Ensure you use the 12 '2-digit number cards' provided on the CD-ROM.)
- Say: *Look at the number on your card. Add 30 to the number on your card. If the total is 76, stand up.*
- Ask: *Who can tell me what number is on Mile's and Tom's cards?* (46)
- Ask the children standing to show their cards.
- The children standing then sit down.
- Repeat for the following:
  - *Add 20 to the number on your card. If the sum is 61, stand up.* (41)
  - *Add 10 to the number on your card. If the answer is 94, stand up.* (84)
  - *Add 40 to the number on your card. If the total is 77, stand up.* (37)
  - *Add 60 to the number on your card. If the total is 92, stand up.* (32)
  - *Add 50 to the number on your card. If the sum is 74, stand up.* (24)
  - *Add 20 to the number on your card. If the total is 48, stand up.* (28)
  - *Add 30 to the number on your card. If the answer is 90, stand up.* (60)
  - *Add 40 to the number on your card. If the total is 93, stand up.* (53)
  - *Add 20 to the number on your card. If the answer is 79, stand up.* (59)
  - *Add 10 to the number on your card. If the total is 102, stand up.* (92)
  - *Add 20 to the number on your card. If the total is 95, stand up.* (75)

(continued)

Stand up

(continued)

Game 8: Subtract numbers mentally, including a 2-digit number and tens

- Provide each child with a '2-digit number card'. (**Note:** Ensure you use the 12 '2-digit number cards' provided on the CD-ROM.)
- Say: *Look at the number on your card. Stand up if your card shows the answer to 83 subtract 30.*
- Ask: *Who can tell me what number is on Brian's and Gillian's cards?* (53)
- Ask the children standing to show their cards.
- The children standing then sit down.
- Repeat for the following:
  - *Stand up if your card shows the answer to 77 subtract 40.* (37)
  - *Stand up if your card shows the answer to 95 take away 20.* (75)
  - *Stand up if your card shows the answer to 84 minus 60.* (24)
  - *Stand up if your card shows the answer to 70 subtract 10.* (60)
  - *Stand up if your card shows the answer to 86 take away 40.* (46)
  - *Stand up if your card shows the answer to 92 minus 60.* (32)
  - *Stand up if your card shows the answer to 102 take away 10.* (92)
  - *Stand up if your card shows the answer to 98 minus 70.* (28)
  - *Stand up if your card shows the answer to 94 subtract 10.* (84)
  - *Stand up if your card shows the answer to 71 minus 30.* (41)
  - *Stand up if your card shows the answer to 79 take away 20.* (59)

Game 9: Add and subtract numbers mentally, including a 2-digit number and tens

- Provide each child with a '2-digit number card'. (**Note:** Ensure you use the 12 '2-digit number cards' provided on the CD-ROM.)
- Say: *Look at the number on your card. Stand up if your card shows the answer to 90 take away 30.*
- Ask: *Who can tell me what number is on Allison's and Michael's cards?* (60)
- Ask the children standing to show their cards.
- The children standing then sit down.
- Repeat for the following:
  - *Add 40 to the number on your card. If the answer is 99, stand up.* (59)
  - *Add 10 to the number on your card. If the total is 94, stand up.* (84)
  - *Stand up if your card shows the answer to 102 minus 10.* (92)
  - *Add 20 to the number on your card. If the total is 95, stand up.* (75)
  - *Stand up if your card shows the answer to 83 subtract 30.* (53)
  - *Add 30 to the number on your card. If the total is 67, stand up.* (37)
  - *Stand up if your card shows the answer to 61 minus 20.* (41)
  - *Add 40 to the number on your card. If the total is 68, stand up.* (28)
  - *Add 50 to the number on your card. If the answer is 74, stand up.* (24)
  - *Stand up if your card shows the answer to 92 minus 60.* (32)
  - *Stand up if your card shows the answer to 86 subtract 40.* (46)

Stand up

(continued)

Game 10: Add numbers mentally, including two 2-digit numbers

- Provide each child with a '2-digit number card'. (**Note:** Ensure you use the 12 '2-digit number cards' provided on the CD-ROM.)
- Say: *Look at the number on your card. Add 34 to the number on your card. If the answer is 75, stand up.*
- Ask: *Who can tell me what number is on Paula's and Robyn's cards?* (41)
- Ask the children standing to show their cards.
- The children standing then sit down.
- Repeat for the following:
  - *Add 26 to the number on your card. If the total is 54, stand up.* (28)
  - *Add 35 to the number on your card. If the total is 94, stand up.* (59)
  - *Add 16 to the number on your card. If the answer is 100, stand up.* (84)
  - *Add 54 to the number on your card. If the sum is 86, stand up.* (32)
  - *Add 28 to the number on your card. If the total is 88, stand up.* (60)
  - *Add 37 to the number on your card. If the sum is 83, stand up.* (46)
  - *Add 21 to the number on your card. If the total is 96, stand up.* (75)
  - *Add 45 to the number on your card. If the total is 82, stand up.* (37)
  - *Add 59 to the number on your card. If the answer is 83, stand up.* (24)
  - *Add 36 to the number on your card. If the total is 89, stand up.* (53)
  - *Add 11 to the number on your card. If the total is 103, stand up.* (92)

Game 11: Subtract numbers mentally, including two 2-digit numbers

- Provide each child with a '2-digit number card'. (**Note:** Ensure you use the 12 '2-digit number cards' provided on the CD-ROM.)
- Say: *Look at the number on your card. Stand up if your card shows the answer to 85 minus 32.*
- Ask: *Who can tell me what number is on Deirdre's and Johannes's cards?* (53)
- Ask the children standing to show their cards.
- The children standing then sit down.
- Repeat for the following:
  - *Stand up if your card shows the answer to 91 subtract 32.* (59)
  - *Stand up if your card shows the answer to 85 take away 25.* (60)
  - *Stand up if your card shows the answer to 93 subtract 18.* (75)
  - *Stand up if your card shows the answer to 64 minus 23.* (41)
  - *Stand up if your card shows the answer to 95 minus 11.* (84)
  - *Stand up if your card shows the answer to 102 take away 10.* (92)
  - *Stand up if your card shows the answer to 62 subtract 25.* (37)
  - *Stand up if your card shows the answer to 81 minus 49.* (32)
  - *Stand up if your card shows the answer to 74 subtract 28.* (46)
  - *Stand up if your card shows the answer to 81 take away 57.* (24)
  - *Stand up if your card shows the answer to 64 take away 36.* (28)

(continued)

Stand up

(continued)

Game 12: Add and subtract numbers mentally, including two 2-digit numbers

- Provide each child with a '2-digit number card'. (**Note:** Ensure you use the 12 '2-digit number cards' provided on the CD-ROM.)
- Say: *Look at the number on your card. Stand up if your card shows the answer to 65 subtract 37.*
- Ask: *Who can tell me what number is on Fiona's and Keith's cards?* (28)
- Ask the children standing to show their cards.
- The children standing then sit down.
- Repeat for the following:
  - *Add 42 to the number on your card. If the total is 83, stand up.* (41)
  - *Stand up if your card shows the answer to 99 take away 15.* (84)
  - *Add 27 to the number on your card. If the sum is 86, stand up.* (59)
  - *Stand up if your card shows the answer to 81 subtract 49.* (32)
  - *Add 39 to the number on your card. If the total is 85, stand up.* (46)
  - *Stand up if your card shows the answer to 74 minus 14.* (60)
  - *Add 8 to the number on your card. If the answer is 100, stand up.* (92)
  - *Add 36 to the number on your card. If the answer is 73, stand up.* (37)
  - *Stand up if your card shows the answer to 81 take away 28.* (53)
  - *Add 58 to the number on your card. If the total is 82, stand up.* (24)
  - *Stand up if your card shows the answer to 94 subtract 19.* (75)

Game 13: Add numbers mentally, including a 3-digit number and ones

- Provide each child with a '3-digit number card'. (**Note:** Ensure you use the 12 '3-digit number cards' provided on the CD-ROM.)
- Say: *Look at the number on your card. Add 7 to the number on your card. If the total is 142, stand up.* Ask: *Who can tell me what number is on Gaby's and Tom's cards?* (135)
- Ask the children standing to show their cards.
- The children standing then sit down.
- Repeat for the following:
  - *Add 6 to the number on your card. If the total is 274, stand up.* (268)
  - *Add 8 to the number on your card. If the sum is 365, stand up.* (357)
  - *Add 7 to the number on your card. If the answer is 416, stand up.* (409)
  - *Add 4 to the number on your card. If the total is 684, stand up.* (680)
  - *Add 9 to the number on your card. If the answer is 702, stand up.* (693)
  - *Add 2 to the number on your card. If the sum is 778, stand up.* (776)
  - *Add 5 to the number on your card. If the total is 867, stand up.* (862)
  - *Add 3 to the number on your card. If the sum is 344, stand up.* (341)
  - *Add 6 to the number on your card. If the answer is 730, stand up.* (724)
  - *Add 7 to the number on your card. If the sum is 519, stand up.* (512)
  - *Add 9 to the number on your card. If the total is 946, stand up.* (937)

Stand up

(continued)

Game 14: Subtract numbers mentally, including a 3-digit number and ones

- Provide each child with a '3-digit number card'. (**Note:** Ensure you use the 12 '3-digit number cards' provided on the CD-ROM.)
- Say: *Look at the number on your card. Stand up if your card has the answer to 731 minus 7.*
- Ask: *Who can tell me what number is on Toby's and Delroy's cards?* (724)
- Ask the children standing to show their cards.
- The children standing then sit down.
- Repeat for the following:
  - *Stand up if your card has the answer to 521 subtract 9.* (512)
  - *Stand up if your card has the answer to 347 minus 6.* (341)
  - *Stand up if your card has the answer to 942 take away 5.* (937)
  - *Stand up if your card has the answer to 413 subtract 4.* (409)
  - *Stand up if your card has the answer to 275 minus 7.* (268)
  - *Stand up if your card has the answer to 701 take away 8.* (693)
  - *Stand up if your card has the answer to 865 subtract 3.* (862)
  - *Stand up if your card has the answer to 144 minus 9.* (135)
  - *Stand up if your card has the answer to 362 take away 5.* (357)
  - *Stand up if your card has the answer to 784 subtract 8.* (776)
  - *Stand up if your card has the answer to 682 minus 2.* (680)

Game 15: Add and subtract numbers mentally, including a 3-digit number and ones

- Provide each child with a '3-digit number card'. (**Note:** Ensure you use the 12 '3-digit number cards' provided on the CD-ROM.)
- Say: *Look at the number on your card. Stand up if your card has the answer to 732 subtract 8.*
- Ask: *Who can tell me what number is on Gregory's and Natalie's cards?* (724)
- Ask the children standing to show their cards.
- The children standing then sit down.
- Repeat for the following:
  - *Add 8 to the number on your card. If the total is 701, stand up.* (693)
  - *Stand up if your card shows the answer to 871 take away 9.* (862)
  - *Add 7 to the number on your card. If the sum is 687, stand up.* (680)
  - *Stand up if your card shows the answer to 415 subtract 6.* (409)
  - *Add 9 to the number on your card. If the total is 277, stand up.* (268)
  - *Stand up if your card shows the answer to 781 minus 5.* (776)
  - *Add 8 to the number on your card. If the answer is 945, stand up.* (937)
  - *Add 6 to the number on your card. If the answer is 363, stand up.* (357)
  - *Stand up if your card shows the answer to 345 take away 4.* (341)
  - *Add 7 to the number on your card. If the total is 519, stand up.* (512)
  - *Stand up if your card shows the answer to 142 subtract 7.* (135)

(continued)

Stand up

(continued)

Game 16: Add numbers mentally, including a 3-digit number and tens

- Provide each child with a '3-digit number card'. (**Note:** Ensure you use the 12 '3-digit number cards' provided on the CD-ROM.)
- Say: *Look at the number on your card. Add 60 to the number on your card. If the sum is 740, stand up*
- Ask: *Who can tell me what number is on Rachel's and Oliver's cards?* (680)
- Ask the children standing to show their cards.
- The children standing then sit down.
- Repeat for the following:
  - *Add 20 to the number on your card. If the sum is 361, stand up.* (341)
  - *Add 80 to the number on your card. If the answer is 804, stand up.* (724)
  - *Add 30 to the number on your card. If the total is 298, stand up.* (268)
  - *Add 50 to the number on your card. If the total is 185, stand up.* (135)
  - *Add 40 to the number on your card. If the answer is 733, stand up.* (693)
  - *Add 90 to the number on your card. If the sum is 866, stand up.* (776)
  - *Add 70 to the number on your card. If the sum is 427, stand up.* (357)
  - *Add 60 to the number on your card. If the sum is 572, stand up.* (512)
  - *Add 10 to the number on your card. If the total is 947, stand up.* (937)
  - *Add 80 to the number on your card. If the answer is 489, stand up.* (409)
  - *Add 50 to the number on your card. If the total is 912, stand up.* (862)

Game 17: Subtract numbers mentally, including a 3-digit number and tens

- Provide each child with a '3-digit number card'. (**Note:** Ensure you use the 12 '3-digit number cards' provided on the CD-ROM.)
- Say: *Look at the number on your card. Stand up if your card has the answer to 499 minus 90.*
- Ask: *Who can tell me what number is on Earl's and Hannah's cards?* (409)
- Ask the children standing to show their cards.
- The children standing then sit down.
- Repeat for the following:
  - *Stand up if your card has the answer to 328 minus 60.* (268)
  - *Stand up if your card has the answer to 814 subtract 90.* (724)
  - *Stand up if your card has the answer to 175 minus 40.* (135)
  - *Stand up if your card has the answer to 427 take away 70.* (357)
  - *Stand up if your card has the answer to 592 subtract 80.* (512)
  - *Stand up if your card has the answer to 723 take away 30.* (693)
  - *Stand up if your card has the answer to 391 minus 50.* (341)
  - *Stand up if your card has the answer to 997 take away 60.* (937)
  - *Stand up if your card has the answer to 892 subtract 30.* (862)
  - *Stand up if your card has the answer to 846 subtract 70.* (776)
  - *Stand up if your card has the answer to 770 minus 90.* (680)

Stand up

(continued)

Game 18: Add and subtract numbers mentally, including a 3-digit number and tens

- Provide each child with a '3-digit number card'. (**Note:** Ensure you use the 12 '3-digit number cards' provided on the CD-ROM.)
- Say: *Look at the number on your card. Stand up if your card has the answer to 836 subtract 60.*
- Ask: *Who can tell me what number is on Eric's and Ruby's cards?* (776)
- Ask the children standing to show their cards.
- The children standing then sit down.
- Repeat for the following:
  - *Add 60 to the number on your card. If the total is 417, stand up.* (357)
  - *Stand up if your card shows the answer to 582 take away 70.* (512)
  - *Add 90 to the number on your card. If the sum is 814, stand up.* (724)
  - *Stand up if your card shows the answer to 723 subtract 30.* (693)
  - *Add 50 to the number on your card. If the total is 730, stand up.* (680)
  - *Stand up if your card shows the answer to 225 minus 90.* (135)
  - *Add 40 to the number on your card. If the answer is 977, stand up.* (937)
  - *Add 70 to the number on your card. If the answer is 932, stand up.* (862)
  - *Stand up if your card shows the answer to 318 take away 50.* (268)
  - *Add 80 to the number on your card. If the total is 489, stand up.* (409)
  - *Stand up if your card shows the answer to 421 subtract 80.* (341)

Game 19: Add numbers mentally, including a 3-digit number and hundreds

- Provide each child with a '3-digit number card'. (**Note:** Ensure you use the 12 '3-digit number cards' provided on the CD-ROM.)
- Say: *Look at the number on your card. Add 400 to the number on your card. If the sum is 741, stand up.*
- Ask: *Who can tell me what number is on Mark's and Karen's cards?* (341)
- Ask the children standing to show their cards.
- The children standing then sit down.
- Repeat for the following:
  - *Add 600 to the number on your card. If the sum is 957, stand up.* (357)
  - *Add 200 to the number on your card. If the sum is 712, stand up.* (512)
  - *Add 200 to the number on your card. If the sum is 976, stand up.* (776)
  - *Add 100 to the number on your card. If the answer is 824, stand up.* (724)
  - *Add 700 to the number on your card. If the total is 968, stand up.* (268)
  - *Add 800 to the number on your card. If the sum is 935, stand up.* (135)
  - *Add 300 to the number on your card. If the answer is 709, stand up.* (409)
  - *Add 200 to the number on your card. If the total is 880, stand up.* (680)
  - *Add 100 to the number on your card. If the total is 962, stand up.* (862)
  - *Add 100 to the number on your card. If the total is 1037, stand up.* (937)
  - *Add 200 to the number on your card. If the answer is 893, stand up.* (693)

(continued)

Stand up

(continued)

Game 20: Subtract numbers mentally, including a 3-digit number and hundreds

- Provide each child with a '3-digit number card'. (**Note:** Ensure you use the 12 '3-digit number cards' provided on the CD-ROM.)
- Say: *Look at the number on your card. Stand up if your card has the answer to 880 minus 200.*
- Ask: *Who can tell me what number is on Leo's and Penny's cards?* (680)
- Ask the children standing to show their cards.
- The children standing then sit down.
- Repeat for the following:
  - *Stand up if your card has the answer to 709 minus 300.* (409)
  - *Stand up if your card has the answer to 912 subtract 400.* (512)
  - *Stand up if your card has the answer to 541 minus 200.* (341)
  - *Stand up if your card has the answer to 993 take away 300.* (693)
  - *Stand up if your card has the answer to 962 subtract 100.* (862)
  - *Stand up if your card has the answer to 868 minus 600.* (268)
  - *Stand up if your card has the answer to 976 subtract 200.* (776)
  - *Stand up if your card has the answer to 735 minus 600.* (135)
  - *Stand up if your card has the answer to 857 take away 500.* (357)
  - *Stand up if your card has the answer to 924 subtract 200.* (724)
  - *Stand up if your card has the answer to 1037 take away 100.* (937)

Game 21: Add and subtract numbers mentally, including a 3-digit number and hundreds

- Provide each child with a '3-digit number card'. (**Note:** Ensure you use the 12 '3-digit number cards' provided on the CD-ROM.)
- Say: *Look at the number on your card. Stand up if your card has the answer to 935 subtract 800.*
- Ask: *Who can tell me what number is on Yolanda's and Ursula's cards?* (135)
- Ask the children standing to show their cards.
- The children standing then sit down.
- Repeat for the following:
  - *Stand up if your card shows the answer to 857 minus 500.* (357)
  - *Add 200 to the number on your card. If the answer is 880, stand up.* (680)
  - *Add 100 to the number on your card. If the answer is 876, stand up.* (776)
  - *Stand up if your card shows the answer to 741 take away 400.* (341)
  - *Add 200 to the number on your card. If the total is 924, stand up.* (724)
  - *Stand up if your card shows the answer to 912 subtract 400.* (512)
  - *Add 100 to the number on your card. If the total is 1037, stand up.* (937)
  - *Stand up if your card shows the answer to 868 take away 600.* (268)
  - *Add 400 to the number on your card. If the sum is 809, stand up.* (409)
  - *Stand up if your card shows the answer to 893 subtract 200.* (693)
  - *Add 100 to the number on your card. If the total is 962, stand up.* (862)

Stand up

(continued)

Game 22: Add numbers mentally, including pairs of 2- and 3-digit multiples of 10

- Provide each child with a '2- or 3-digit multiple of 10 number card'. (**Note:** Ensure you use the 12 '2- and 3-digit multiples of 10 number cards' provided on the CD-ROM.)
- Say: *Look at the number on your card. Add 70 to the number on your card. If the total is 230, stand up.*
- Ask: *Who can tell me what number is on Ellie's and Amy's cards?* (160)
- Ask the children standing to show their cards.
- The children standing then sit down.
- Repeat for the following:
  - *Add 80 to the number on your card. If the sum is 120, stand up.* (40)
  - *Add 60 to the number on your card. If the sum is 550, stand up.* (490)
  - *Add 20 to the number on your card. If the sum is 770, stand up.* (750)
  - *Add 90 to the number on your card. If the answer is 400, stand up.* (310)
  - *Add 70 to the number on your card. If the total is 710, stand up.* (640)
  - *Add 80 to the number on your card. If the sum is 200, stand up.* (120)
  - *Add 30 to the number on your card. If the answer is 60, stand up.* (30)
  - *Add 20 to the number on your card. If the total is 890, stand up.* (870)
  - *Add 40 to the number on your card. If the total is 320, stand up.* (280)
  - *Add 10 to the number on your card. If the total is 80, stand up.* (70)
  - *Add 80 to the number on your card. If the answer is 610, stand up.* (530)

Game 23: Subtract numbers mentally, including pairs of 2- and 3-digit multiples of 10

- Provide each child with a '2- or 3-digit multiple of 10 number card'. (**Note:** Ensure you use the 12 '2- and 3-digit multiples of 10 number cards' provided on the CD-ROM.)
- Say: *Look at the number on your card. Stand up if your card has the answer to 380 subtract 70.*
- Ask: *Who can tell me what number is on Trevor's and Matt's cards?* (310)
- Ask the children standing to show their cards.
- The children standing then sit down.
- Repeat for the following:
  - *Stand up if your card has the answer to 150 minus 30.* (120)
  - *Stand up if your card has the answer to 680 subtract 40.* (640)
  - *Stand up if your card has the answer to 50 minus 20.* (30)
  - *Stand up if your card has the answer to 520 take away 30.* (490)
  - *Stand up if your card has the answer to 830 subtract 80.* (750)
  - *Stand up if your card has the answer to 110 minus 70.* (40)
  - *Stand up if your card has the answer to 250 subtract 90.* (160)
  - *Stand up if your card has the answer to 930 minus 60.* (870)
  - *Stand up if your card has the answer to 120 take away 50.* (70)
  - *Stand up if your card has the answer to 610 subtract 80.* (530)
  - *Stand up if your card has the answer to 320 take away 40.* (280)

(continued)

Stand up

(continued)

Game 24: Add and subtract numbers mentally, including pairs of 2- and 3-digit multiples of 10

- Provide each child with a '2- or 3-digit multiple of 10 number card'. (**Note:** Ensure you use the 12 '2- and 3-digit multiples of 10 number cards' provided on the CD-ROM.)
- Say: *Look at the number on your card. Stand up if your card shows the answer to 620 minus 90.*
- Ask: *Who can tell me what number is on Sheila's and John's cards?* (530)
- Ask the children standing to show their cards.
- The children standing then sit down.
- Repeat for the following:
  - *Stand up if your card shows the answer to 830 minus 80.* (750)
  - *Add 30 to the number on your card. If the answer is 340, stand up.* (310)
  - *Add 80 to the number on your card. If the answer is 720, stand up.* (640)
  - *Stand up if your card shows the answer to 530 take away 40.* (490)
  - *Add 70 to the number on your card. If the total is 940, stand up.* (870)
  - *Stand up if your card shows the answer to 120 subtract 90.* (30)
  - *Add 50 to the number on your card. If the total is 210, stand up.* (160)
  - *Stand up if your card shows the answer to 130 take away 60.* (70)
  - *Add 60 to the number on your card. If the sum is 340, stand up.* (280)
  - *Stand up if your card shows the answer to 120 subtract 80.* (40)
  - *Add 90 to the number on your card. If the total is 210, stand up.* (120)

Whole-class, paired or individual activities

Using the Maths Facts in the *Facts and Games* book

Objectives

- Recall and use addition and subtraction facts to 20 fluently, and derive and use related facts up to 100
- Add and subtract numbers mentally, including a 2-digit number and ones, two 2-digit multiples of 10 and a 2-digit multiple of 10 and a 3-digit multiple of 10

Teacher resources

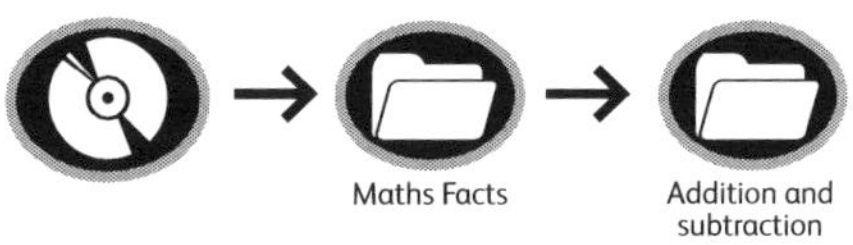

Pupil resources

- *Fluency in Number Facts: Facts and Games: Years 3 & 4* book pages 4–17 (per child or pair)

Introduction

The Maths Facts on pages 4–17 of the *Fluency in Number Facts: Facts and Games: Years 3 & 4* book cover the key addition and subtraction number facts that children need to be able to recall instantly by the end of Lower Key Stage 2.

These pages aim to develop children's fluency by:

- securing a thorough conceptual understanding of the addition and subtraction number facts
- identifying patterns and the relationship between addition and subtraction
- developing strategic approaches to recalling and deriving the answers to addition and subtraction number facts.

To assist in achieving these aims, the addition and subtraction number facts contained in the *Facts and Games: Years 3 & 4* book are presented in the following ways:

- Addition and subtraction numbers facts to 20 (pages 4–6)
- Addition and subtraction trios to 20 (pages 7–13)
- Addition number facts to 10 and 20 tables (page 14)
- Addition of 1-digit and 2-digit numbers to 20 tables (page 15)
- Multiples of 10 addition and subtraction table (pages 16 and 17)

The following pages include a brief description of each of these presentations, along with suggestions of how to focus on these Maths Facts either with the whole class, or with children working in pairs or individually.

(*continued*)

Whole-class, paired or individual activities

Using the Maths Facts in the *Facts and Games* book

(continued)

Addition and subtraction numbers facts to 20 (pages 4–6)

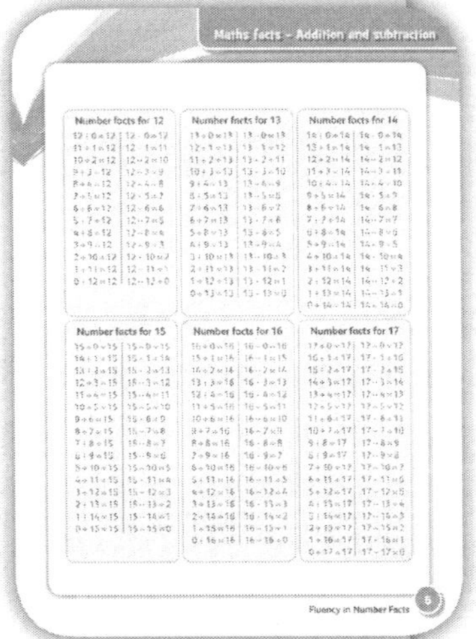

The facts are organised into 'number fact families', for example, Number facts for 12, which are presented in two columns – an addition column and a subtraction column. This presentation shows the number pattern in each addition and subtraction 'family' as well as the relationship between the addition and the subtraction number facts.

At this stage, children should be able to recall all the addition and subtraction facts to 20 fluently, and use these facts to derive related facts up to 100.

How to use the Maths Facts

Whole class

- Focus on just one 'number fact family' at a time, for example, Number facts for 12. However, the eventual aim is to have the class focus on several 'number fact families' simultaneously.
- Display the appropriate PDF file, (CD-ROM / Maths Facts / Addition and Subtraction) and provide each child or pair with a copy of the *Facts and Games: Years 3 & 4* book and direct their attention to the relevant 'number fact family' on pages 4–6.
- Begin by asking the children to identify different patterns in both lists of calculations and discuss these with the class.
- Can the children see any relationships between the two columns of calculations?
- Discuss with the children how knowing the addition and subtraction number facts to 20 can help them derive answers to related number facts to 100, for example, 7 + 5 = 12, therefore 70 + 50 = 120; 12 – 5 = 7, therefore 120 – 50 = 70.
- Repeat for other addition and subtraction number facts and the related facts up to 100.
- Conclude by hiding the PDF file, asking the children to close their copy of the *Facts and Games: Years 3 & 4* book and ask the class questions similar to the following:
  - *What is 6 add 6?*
  - *How many more do you need to add to 4 to make 12?*
  - *9 and what other number total 12?*
  - *If 5 add 7 is 12, then what is 50 add 70?*
  - *30 and what other number make 120?*
  - *What is 12 subtract / minus / take away 8?*
  - *What is the difference between 12 and 5?*
  - *What is 5 less than 12?*
  - *What is 120 subtract 70?*

Whole-class, paired or individual activities

Using the Maths Facts in the *Facts and Games* book

(continued)

Pairs

- Begin by telling the children to focus on just one 'number fact family', for example, Number facts for 12. However, the eventual aim is to have the children focus on several 'number fact families' simultaneously.
- Provide each pair with a copy of the *Facts and Games: Years 3 & 4* book and direct their attention to the relevant 'number fact family' on pages 4–6. Alternatively, ask the children to choose a 'family' that they know they need to develop greater fluency of.
- Children spend just two or three minutes individually looking at the addition and subtraction facts with the aim of developing greater fluency of the facts.
- Children then take turns to take charge of the book and ask each other questions similar to those on page 76, including the related facts up to 100.

Individual

- Begin by telling the child to focus on just one 'number fact family', for example, Number facts for 12. However, the eventual aim is to have the child focus on several 'number fact families' simultaneously.
- Provide the child with a copy of the *Facts and Games: Years 3 & 4* book and direct their attention to the relevant 'number fact family' on pages 4–6. Alternatively, ask the child to choose a 'family' that they know they need to develop greater fluency of.
- It is recommended that the child spends just five or ten minutes each time, focussing their attention on developing greater fluency of the facts.
- To provide some personal challenge, suggest the child:
  - covers the number facts with their hand and recites the facts to themselves
  - recalls the related facts up to 100, for example, 12 + 0 = 12 and 120 + 0 = 120; 11 + 1 = 12 and 110 + 10 = 120… 4 + 8 = 12 and 40 + 80 = 120…

(*continued*)

Whole-class, paired or individual activities

Using the Maths Facts in the *Facts and Games* book

(continued)

Addition and subtraction trios to 20 (pages 7–13)

'Trios' show the relationship between the three numbers that make up an addition fact and the related subtraction fact. They also show that addition of two numbers can be done in any order (commutative) and how this law does *not* apply to subtraction.

At this stage, children should be able to recall all the addition and subtraction facts to 20 fluently, and use these facts to derive related facts up to 100.

How to use the Maths Facts

Whole class

- Focus on just one set of addition and subtraction 'trios' at a time, for example, 'Addition and subtraction trios for 12'.
- Display the appropriate PDF file (CD-ROM / Maths Facts / Addition and subtraction) and provide each child or pair with a copy of the *Facts and Games: Years 3 & 4* book and direct their attention to the relevant trios on pages 7–13.
- Begin by asking the children to identify different patterns between the four calculations in the first trio.
- Ensure the children realise that each trio consists of only three numbers, i.e. 4, 8 and 12, and that these three numbers produce four calculations: two addition calculations (8 + 4 = 12 and 4 + 8 = 12), and two subtraction calculations (12 – 4 = 8 and 12 – 8 = 4).
- Referring to the two addition calculations, discuss with the children how addition of two numbers can be done in any order (commutative law).
- Then, referring to the two subtraction calculations, discuss with the children how the commutative law does *not* apply to subtraction.
- Move on to discussing the inverse relationship between addition and subtraction.
- Repeat the above for the remaining trios in the set.
- Discuss with the children how knowing the addition and subtraction number facts to 20 can help them derive answers to related number facts to 100, for example, 8 + 4 = 12, therefore 80 + 40 = 120; 12 – 4 = 8, therefore 120 – 40 = 80.
- Repeat for other addition and subtraction number facts and the related facts up to 100.
- Conclude by hiding the PDF file, asking the children to close their copy of the *Facts and Games: Years 3 & 4* book, and ask the class questions similar to the following:
  - *Tell me an addition calculation you can make using only the numbers 4, 8 and 12.*
  - *Can you tell me another addition calculation that only uses the same three numbers?*
  - *Tell me a subtraction calculation that only uses the numbers 4, 8 and 12.*
  - *Is there another subtraction calculation that only uses these numbers?*
  - *What four calculations can you make using the numbers 40, 80 and 120?*

Whole-class, paired or individual activities

Using the Maths Facts in the *Facts and Games* book

(continued)

Pairs

- Provide each pair with a copy of the *Facts and Games: Years 3 & 4* book and direct their attention to the relevant set of addition and subtraction trios on pages 7–13. Alternatively, ask the children to choose a set of trios that they know they need to develop greater fluency of.
- Children take turns to choose one of the trios and place their hand/fingers over the list of four calculations.
- Referring to the three numbers on the triangle, the other child the other child has to say the two addition and two subtraction number facts.
- Once they have done this, the child covering the facts removes their hand/finger to reveal the four calculations.
- Occasionally, vary the activity by asking children to say the related facts up to 100.

Individual

- Provide each child with a copy of the *Facts and Games: Years 3 & 4* book and direct their attention to the relevant set of addition and subtraction trios on pages 7–13. Alternatively, ask the child to choose a set of trios that they know they need to develop greater fluency of.
- It is recommended that the child spend just five or ten minutes each time, focussing their attention on one set of addition and subtraction trios with the aim of developing greater fluency of the facts.
- To provide some personal challenge, as for the paired activity above, suggest the child:
  - places their hand/fingers over the list of four calculations and recites the facts to themselves
  - recalls the related facts up to 100, for example, 80 + 40 = 120, 40 + 80 = 120, 120 – 80 = 40 and 120 – 40 = 80

(*continued*)

Whole-class, paired or individual activities

Using the Maths Facts in the *Facts and Games* book

(continued)

Addition number facts to 10 and 20 tables (page 14)

Addition of 1-digit and 2-digit numbers to 20 table (page 15)

Multiples of 10 addition and subtraction table (pages 16 and 17)

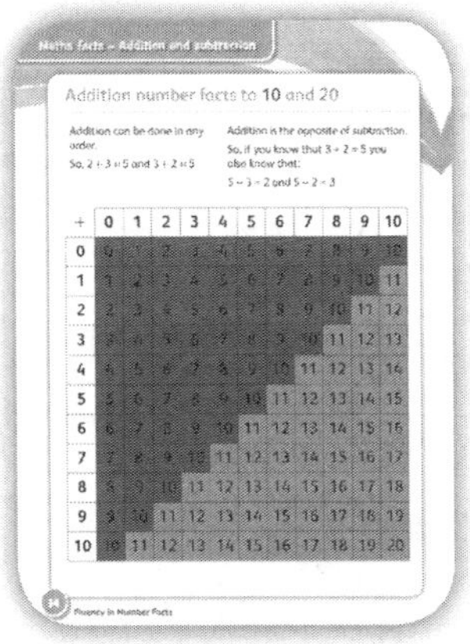

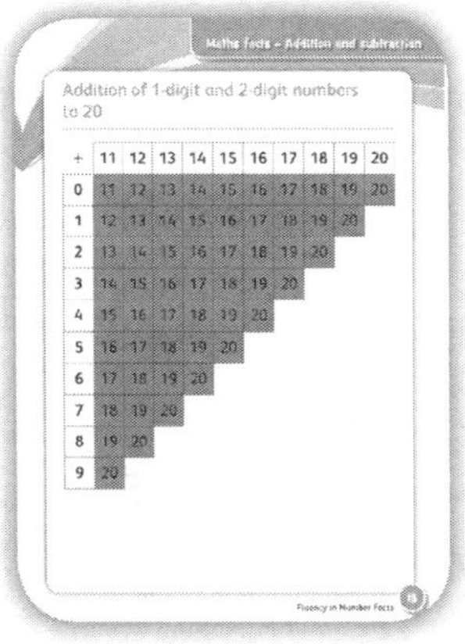

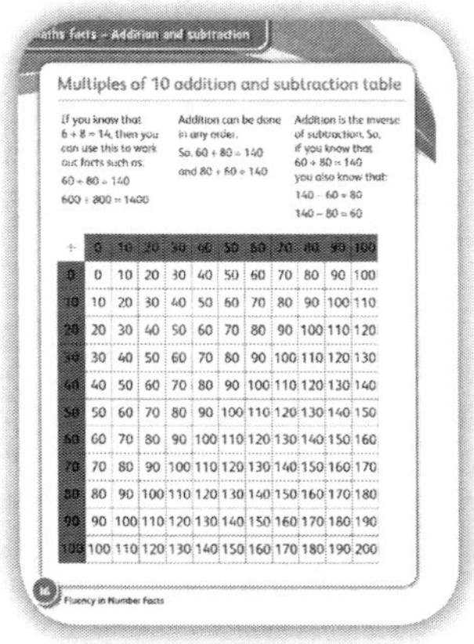

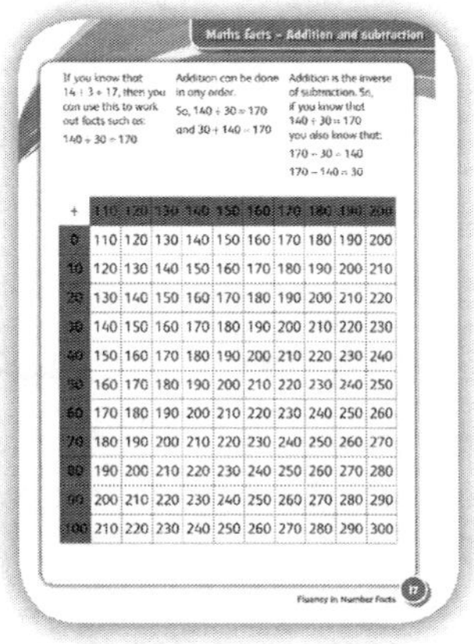

The table on page 14 shows all the addition number facts to 20 involving the numbers 0 to 10. The answers in blue are all the number facts to 10, and the answers in green are all the number facts from 11 to 20. The table therefore, shows children the progressive nature of the number facts from 0 to 20.

The table on page 15 shows all the addition number facts to 20 involving the 1 to 9 digits and the 'teen' numbers.

The two tables on pages 16 and 17 show all the addition number facts for the multiples of 10 from 10 to 200. These tables mirror the 'Addition number facts to 10 and 20' table and the 'Addition of 1-digit and 2-digit numbers to 20' tables on pages 14 and 15.

At this stage, children should be able to recall all the addition and subtraction facts to 20 fluently, and use these facts to derive related facts up to 100.

The tables also show that addition of two numbers can be done in any order (commutative) and that addition is the opposite (inverse) of subtraction.

How to use the Maths Facts

Whole class

- Display the appropriate PDF file (CD-ROM Maths Facts / Addition and subtraction) and provide each child or pair with a copy of the *Facts and Games: Years 3 & 4* book and direct their attention to the two tables on pages 14 and 15.
- Begin by discussing the 'Addition number facts to 10 and 20' table on page 14 with the children. Ask the children to identify different patterns in the table and discuss these with the class. Draw their attention to the patterns of numbers in each row, column and diagonal. In particular, highlight the row of numbers at the top of the table and the column of numbers down the left-hand side of the table.

Whole-class, paired or individual activities

Using the Maths Facts in the *Facts and Games* book

(continued)

- If necessary, remind the children how to use the table. Put one finger on 5 in the column of numbers down the left-hand side of the table and another finger on 7 in the row of numbers at the top of the table, and then move both fingers across and down the table until they meet at the answer, i.e. 12.
- Discuss with the children how 5 + 7 is the same as 7 + 5 (commutative).
- Repeat several times.
- Once the children are secure with reading the table for addition, remind them how the table can also be used for subtraction. Put one finger on 5 in the column of numbers down the left-hand side of the table, and then move another finger across the row until you land on 12. Once your finger is on 12, move up the column until you land on 7 in the row of numbers at the top of the table.
- Discuss with the children that if they know that 5 + 7 = 12 then they also know that 12 – 5 = 7 and 12 – 7 = 5.
- Repeat several times.
- Repeat the above for the 'Addition of 1-digit and 2-digit numbers to 20' table on page 15.
- Next, draw children's attention to the two 'Multiples of 10 addition and subtraction' tables on pages 16 and 17. Discuss with the children the similarities between the tables on pages 14 and 16, and the tables on pages 15 and 17 (although the table on page 17 extends to answers from 200 to 300).
- Highlight the following to the children:
  - the tables on pages 16 and 17 show all of the addition number facts for the multiples of 10 from 10 to 200
  - if you know that 14 + 3 = 17 (as shown on the table on page 15), then you also know that 140 + 30 = 170 (as shown on the table on page 17)
  - addition can be done in any order, so 140 + 30 = 170 and 30 + 140 = 170
  - addition is the inverse of subtraction, so if you know that 140 + 30 = 170 you also know that 170 – 30 = 140 and 170 – 140 = 30.
- Referring to the relevant PDF file on display, conclude by asking the class questions similar to the following:
  - *Toby, will you come out and show us how to get the answer to 5 add 9?*
  - *So, if we know that 5 add 9 is 14, what is the answer to 9 add 5? How can we check this on the table?*
  - *If we know that 5 plus 9 is 14, and 9 add 5 is 14, what is the answer to 14 subtract 5? How does the table help us check? What about 14 minus 9?*
  - *If we know that 5 plus 9 is 14, what is the answer to 50 add 90? What about 90 plus 50? What about 140 subtract 50? What is the answer to 140 minus 90?*

(continued)

Whole-class, paired or individual activities

Using the Maths Facts in the *Facts and Games* book

(continued)

Pairs

- Provide each pair with a copy of the *Facts and Games: Years 3 & 4* book and direct their attention to either the two tables on pages 14 and 15 or the two tables on pages 16 and 17.
- Children spend just two or three minutes individually looking at the table(s) with the aim of developing greater fluency on the facts.
- Children then take turns to ask each other questions similar to the following:
  - *Show me how to find the answer to 8 add 7.*
  - *What is 4 plus 7?*
  - *What is 9 subtract 5?*
  - *Show me the answer to 60 add 50.*
  - *What is the answer to 210 subtract 30?*

Individual

- Provide each child with a copy of the *Facts and Games: Years 3 & 4* book and direct their attention to either the two tables on pages 14 and 15 or the two tables on pages 16 and 17.
- It is recommended that the child spend just five or ten minutes each time, focussing their attention on developing greater fluency of the facts.
- To provide some personal challenge, suggest the child covers the answers on the table leaving only the numbers in the top row and left-hand column visible. The child tests themselves on the addition (and subtraction) number facts to 20 and the addition (and subtraction) of 1-digit and 2-digit numbers to 20 (pages 14 and 15) or the addition (and subtraction) of multiples of 10 from 10 to 200 (pages 16 and 17).

Button up

Objective

- Add and subtract mentally two 2-digit multiples of 10

Pupil resources

- *Fluency in Number Facts: Facts and Games: Years 3 & 4* book pages 54 and 55 (per pair); PDFs:

→ Paired games and activities → Paired games from the *Facts and Games: Years 3 & 4* book

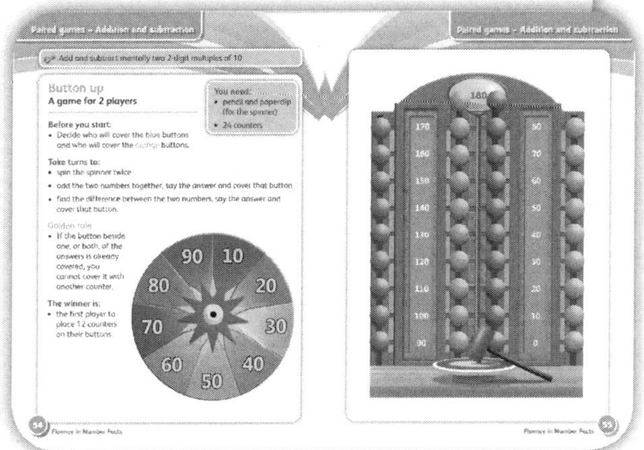

- pencil and paperclip (for the spinner) (per pair)
- 24 counters (per pair)

Notes

- Before the children play the game, ensure that they are familiar with how to use the spinner (see *Facts and Games: Years 3 & 4* book page 80).

Variations

- Play the game in groups of three. Each player takes eight counters which they can place on both blue and orange buttons. The winner is the first player to place all eight of their counters on buttons.
- Children play the game individually using the blue buttons. The orange buttons are used to keep track of the number of turns taken, covering one orange button with a counter each turn. Can the child cover 12 blue buttons before 12 orange buttons are covered?

Star catcher

Addition
Subtraction

Objective

- Add and subtract mentally a 2-digit number and ones

Pupil resources

- *Fluency in Number Facts: Facts and Games: Years 3 & 4* book pages 56 and 57 (per pair); PDFs:

- 0–9 dice (per pair)
- 20 counters (per pair)

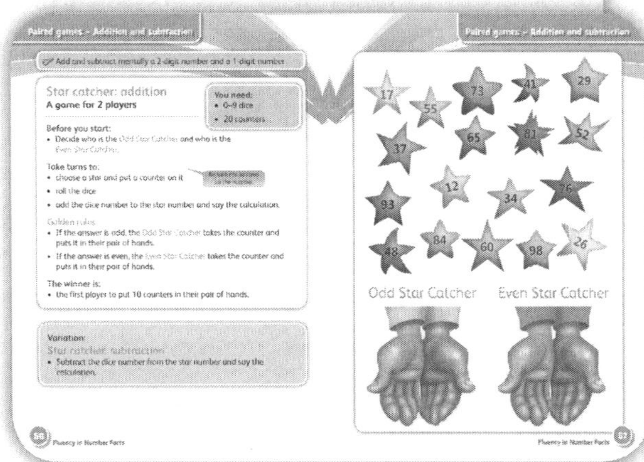
Paired games – Addition and subtraction
Add and subtract mentally a 2-digit number and a 1-digit number
Star catcher: addition
A game for 2 players
You need:
- 0–9 dice
- 20 counters

Before you start:
- Decide who is the Odd Star Catcher and who is the Even Star Catcher.

Take turns to:
- choose a star and put a counter on it
- roll the dice
- add the dice number to the star number and say the calculation.

Golden rules:
- If the answer is odd, the Odd Star Catcher takes the counter and puts it in their pair of hands.
- If the answer is even, the Even Star Catcher takes the counter and puts it in their pair of hands.

The winner is:
- the first player to put 10 counters in their pair of hands.

Variation:
Star catcher: subtraction
- Subtract the dice number from the star number and say the calculation.

56 Fluency in Number Facts

Paired games – Addition and subtraction
17 55 73 41 29 37 65 81 52 12 34 76 93 84 60 98 26 48
Odd Star Catcher
Even Star Catcher
Fluency in Number Facts 57

Variations

Add mentally a 2-digit number and ones

Before you start:

- Decide who is the Odd Star Catcher and who is the Even Star Catcher.
- Each player places five counters in their pair of hands.

Take turns to:

- pick a star, saying out loud the number on it
- roll the dice
- add the dice number to the star number and say the number sentence.

Golden rules:

- If the player is the Odd Star Catcher, they can cover that star with one of their counters if the total is odd. If the total is even, they miss that turn.
- If the player is the Even Star Catcher, they can cover that star with one of their counters if the total is even. If the total is odd, they miss that turn.
- Only one counter can be placed on each star.

The winner is:

- the first player to put all five of their counters on stars.

Subtract mentally a 2-digit number and ones

- Children play the variation above for subtraction, subtracting the dice number from the star number.
- Children play the game individually, deciding whether they want to catch even numbers or odd numbers. Can they put ten counters in their chosen pair of hands before there are ten counters in the other pair of hands?

The coin decides

Addition
Subtraction

Objective

- Add and subtract mentally two 2-digit numbers

Pupil resources

- *Fluency in Number Facts: Facts and Games: Years 3 & 4* book pages 58 and 59 (per pair); PDFs:

→ Paired games and activities → Paired games from the *Facts and Games: Years 3 & 4* book

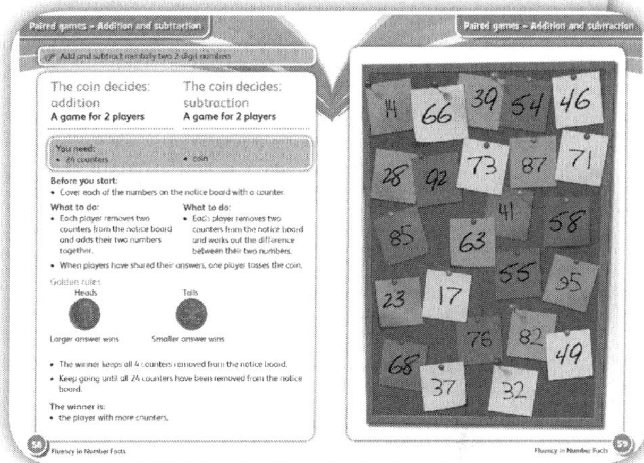

- 24 counters (per pair)
- coin (per pair)

Note

- More able children may complete this game quite quickly so you may want to suggest that they play the best of three games.

Variations

or

- Change the Golden rule to 'Heads': even answer wins; 'Tails': odd answer wins. Each child with a winning answer keeps one counter, i.e. each turn both players may have a winning answer, only one player may have a winning answer or neither players have a winning answer.

  This variation can be used for 'The coin decides: Addition' and 'The coin decides: Subtraction'.

- Children play the variation above individually, seeing how many counters they can collect by the end of the game.

Paired games and activities

The Ferris wheel

Addition
Subtraction

Objective

- Add and subtract mentally a 3-digit number and ones

Pupil resources

- *Fluency in Number Facts: Facts and Games: Years 3 & 4* book pages 60 and 61 (per pair); PDFs:

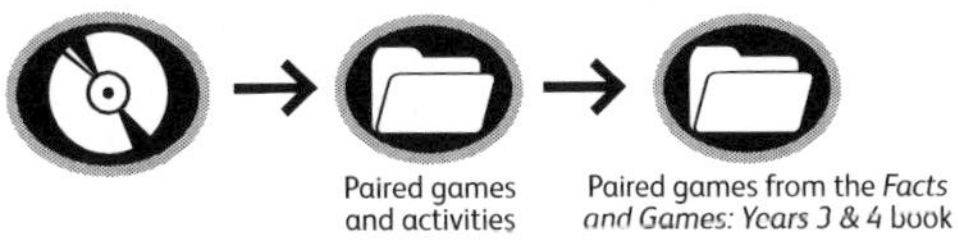

- button (per pair)
- two 0–9 dice: one for each player (per pair)
- 20 counters (per pair)

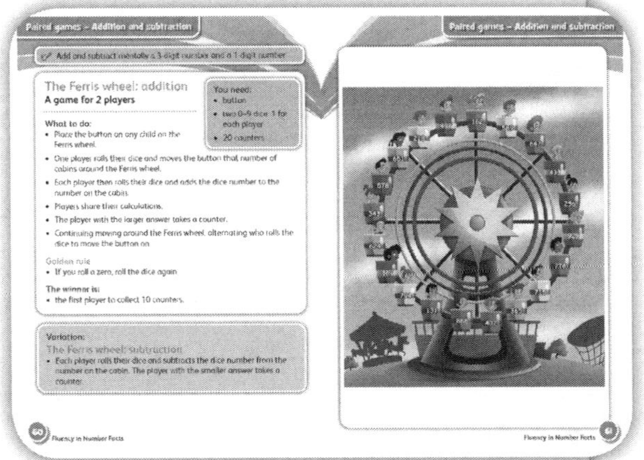
Paired games – Addition and subtraction
Add and subtract mentally a 3-digit number and a 1-digit number

The Ferris wheel: addition
A game for 2 players

You need:
- button
- two 0–9 dice: 1 for each player
- 20 counters

What to do:
- Place the button on any child on the Ferris wheel.
- One player rolls their dice and moves the button that number of cabins around the Ferris wheel.
- Each player then rolls their dice and adds the dice number to the number on the cabin.
- Players share their calculations.
- The player with the larger answer takes a counter.
- Continuing moving around the Ferris wheel, alternating who rolls the dice to move the button on.

Golden rule
- If you roll a zero, roll the dice again

The winner is:
- the first player to collect 10 counters.

Variation:
The Ferris wheel: subtraction
- Each player rolls their dice and subtracts the dice number from the number on the cabin. The player with the smaller answer takes a counter.

60 Fluency in Number Facts

Paired games – Addition and subtraction

Fluency in Number Facts 61

Variations

- Children play the game in groups of three. You need three 0–9 dice, one for each player. The winner is the player with most counters once all the counters have been used.

or

- Using a pencil and paperclip, children use the Ferris wheel as a spinner, taking turns to spin the spinner to choose the 3-digit number.

or

- Rather than the larger (or the smaller) answer winning, even answers win. Each child with a winning answer keeps one counter, i.e. each turn both players may have a winning answer, only one player may have a winning answer or neither players have a winning answer.

  This variation can be used for 'The Ferris wheel: Addition' and 'The Ferris wheel: Subtraction'.

Six cars win

Objective

- Add and subtract mentally a 3-digit number and tens

Pupil resources

- *Fluency in Number Facts: Facts and Games: Years 3 & 4* book pages 62 and 63 (per pair); PDFs:

Paired games and activities — Paired games from the *Facts and Games: Years 3 & 4* book

- 12 counters: 6 for each player (per pair)
- button (per pair)
- pencil and paperclip (for the spinner) (per pair)

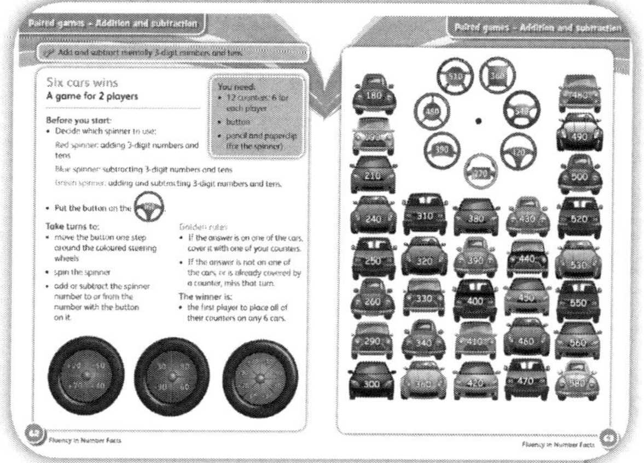

Notes

- Before the children play the game, ensure that they are familiar with how to use the spinners (see *Facts and Games: Years 3 & 4* book page 80).
- The red spinner involves adding 3-digit numbers and tens, the blue spinner subtracting 3-digit numbers and tens, and the green spinner adding and subtracting 3-digit numbers and tens. Instruct children to play the version of the game that is most appropriate to their needs.

Variations

- Children play the game in groups of three. You need 18 counters: six for each player.

or

(**Note:** This activity is suitable for more able children, as it requires them to carry out four or eight calculations each turn.)

Provide the children with 20 counters.

(Decide which wheel from page 62 is most appropriate.) Children take turns to use the circle of steering wheels at the top of page 63 as a spinner and perform the operations of the red wheel, blue wheel or green wheel at the bottom of page 62 to the 3-digit number spun. For example, if the number 480 is spun and children are using the red wheel, they can decide whether to add 20, 40, 50 or 70 to the number spun.

Children put a counter on the car that has that answer.

The winner is the first player to complete a line of four counters. A line can go sideways, up and down or diagonally.

Paired games and activities

Hit the target

Objective

- Add and subtract mentally a 3-digit number and hundreds

Pupil resources

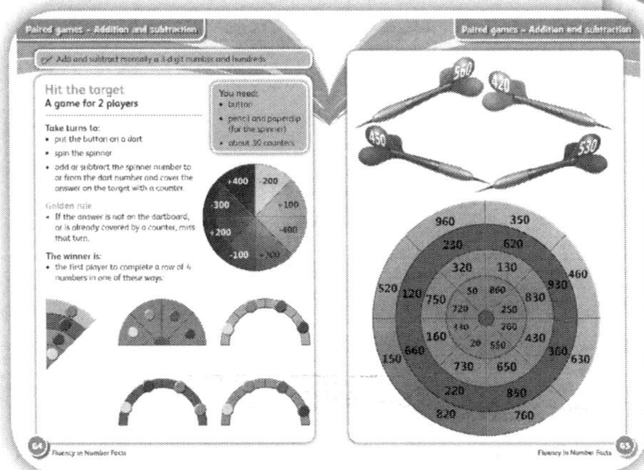

- *Fluency in Number Facts: Facts and Games: Years 3 & 4* book pages 64 and 65 (per pair); PDFs:

→ Paired games and activities → Paired games from the *Facts and Games: Years 3 & 4* book

- button (per pair)
- pencil and paperclip (for the spinner) (per pair)
- about 30 counters (per pair)

Notes

- Before the children play the game, ensure that they are familiar with how to use the spinner (see *Facts and Games: Years 3 & 4* book page 80).

Variation

or

(**Note:** This activity is suitable for more able children, as it requires them to carry out four calculations each turn.)

- Use the dartboard on page 65 as a spinner as well as the operation spinner on page 64.
- Provide each child with four counters.

Take turns to:

- spin both spinners
- carry out the operation spun by the operation spinner on the four numbers spun by the dartboard spinner.

Golden rules:

- If any of the four answers matches a number on a dart, put a counter on that dart, but not covering the number. A dart can have more than one counter on it.

The winner is:

- the first player to place all four of their counters on darts.

Paired games and activities

Adding the dice

Objective

- Recall and use addition facts to 20 fluently

Pupil resources

- 'Hands-on: Numbers 1–12' game board (per pair)
- two 1–6 dice (per pair)
- 20 counters: 10 of one colour, 10 of another colour (per pair)

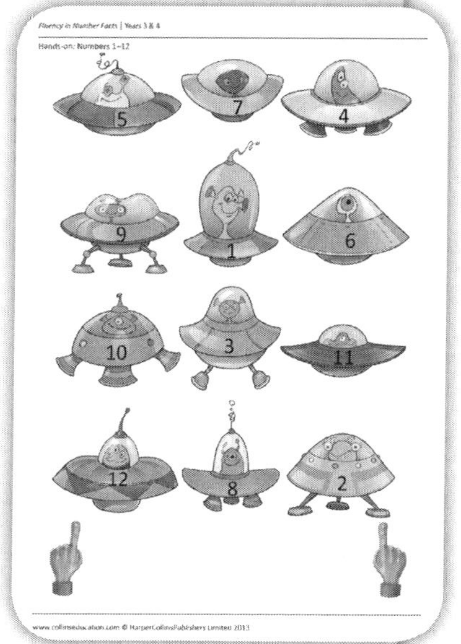

What to do

- Before you start decide who will have which colour counters.
- Take turns to:
  - roll both dice, for example, 6 and 3
  - add the two numbers together, i.e. 9
  - cover the answer, i.e. 9, using one of your counters.
- If the number is already covered, miss that turn.
- The winner is the player with more counters on the game board once all the numbers, except for number 1, have a counter on them.

Variations

- Use the 'Hands-on: Numbers 1–20 game board' (per pair), two 0–9 dice and 24 counters: 12 of one colour, 12 of another colour (per pair)
- The winner is the player with more counters on the game board once all the numbers, except for numbers 19 and 20, have a counter on them.

Individual activities

Addition and subtraction Flip Facts cards

Objective

- Recall and use addition and subtraction facts to 20 fluently

Resources

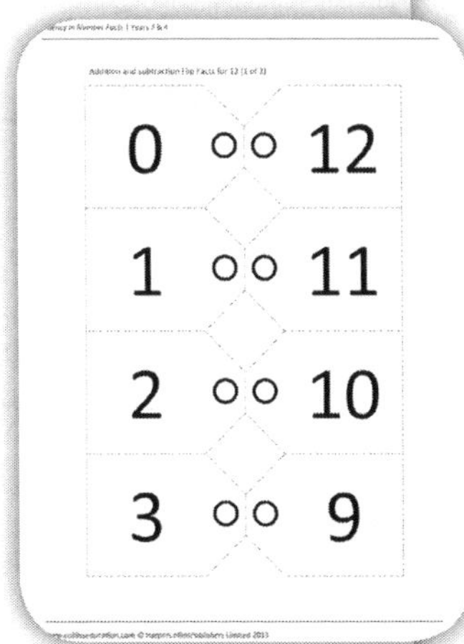

- 'Addition and subtraction Flip Facts cards'
- scissors
- glue
- hole punch
- small piece of string or paper fastener

What to do

- Cut out the cards along the dashed lines.
- Fold each card along the dotted lines to form two-sided cards.
- Glue together the back of each card.
- Punch a hole in the centre of each card.
- Arrange the cards in order with the smallest number on top.
- Fasten the set of cards together with string or a paper fastener.

To practise the addition facts for 12

- Use the 'Addition and subtraction Flip Facts cards for 12'.
- Start with the 0 card on top.
- Ask yourself: *0, how many more to make 12?* (12) Turn over the card to check. *1, how many more to make 12?* (11) Turn over the card to check. *2, how many more to make 12?* (10) Turn over the card to check.
- Continue until you reach the card showing 6 and once again ask: *6, how many more to make 12?* (6).
- Now turn the pack of cards around asking: *6, how many more to make 12?* (6). Turn over the card to check. *7, how many more to make 12?* (5). Turn over the card to check. *8, how many more to make 12?* (4) and so on.
- Repeat several times, quickening the pace as you go.

To practise the subtraction facts for 12

- Use the 'Addition and subtraction Flip Facts cards for 12'.
- Start with the 0 card on top.
- Ask yourself: *12 take away 0 is?* (12). Turn over the card to check. *12 take away 1 is?* (11). Turn over the card to check. 12 *take away 2 is?* (10). Turn over the card to check.
- Continue until you reach the card showing 6 and once again ask: *12 take away 6 is?* (6).
- Now turn the pack of cards around, asking: *12 take away 6 is?* (6). Turn over the card to check. *12 take away 7 is?* (5) and so on.
- Repeat several times, quickening the pace as you go.
- Children spend just five or ten minutes each time, focussing their attention on learning the addition and subtraction facts off by heart.

Individual activities

To practise the subtraction facts for 12

- Use the 'Addition and subtraction Flip Facts cards for 12'.
- Start with the 0 card on top.
- Ask yourself: *12 take away 0 is?* (12). Turn over the card to check. *12 take away 1 is?* (11). Turn over the card to check. *12 take away 2 is?* (10). Turn over the card to check.
- Continue until you reach the card showing 6 and once again ask: *12 take away 6 is?* (6).
- Now turn the pack of cards around asking: *12 take away 6 is?* (6). Turn over the card to check. *12 take away 7 is?* (5). Turn over the card to check. *12 take away 8 is?* (4) and so on.
- Repeat several times, quickening the pace as you go.
- Children spend just five or ten minutes each time, focussing their attention on learning the addition and subtraction facts off by heart.

Variation

- Use other sets of Flip Facts cards to practise the addition and subtraction facts for 1–11, 13–20.

Whole-class games and activities

Hold it up

Objective

- Recall multiplication and division facts for multiplication tables up to 12 × 12

Teacher resources

→ Whole-class games and activities → PowerPoint slides

- 'Hold it up'

Pupil resources

- set of 0–9 number cards or small individual whiteboard and pen (per child)

What to do

- Using either the 'Hold it up: Numbers 1–10' slide or 'Hold it up: Numbers 1–12' slide, write the multiplication symbol and multiplication table you want the children to practise and consolidate in the box at the top of the slide, for example, × 4.
- Point to one of the coloured 1–10 or 1–12 numbers on the slide.
- Children work out the answer and hold up the appropriate number card(s), for example, 4 × 3 = 12, so the children should hold up a 1 and a 2 number card to show '12': then children can write the answer on their whiteboard.
- Repeat several times.

Variations

- Use the eleven 'Hold it up' times tables slides to practise the division facts for multiplication tables up to 12 × 12.

Around the clock

Objective

- Recall multiplication and division facts for multiplication tables up to 12 × 12

Teacher resources

→ Whole-class games and activities → PowerPoint slides

- 'Around the clock'

Pupil resources

→ Number cards

- set of 'Multiples of…number cards' or small individual whiteboard and pen (per child)

What to do

- Using the 'Around the clock' slide, write the multiplication table you want the children to practise and consolidate on the circle in the centre of the clock, for example, × 4.
- Provide each child with the corresponding set of 'Multiples of...number cards' or an individual whiteboard and pen.
- Point to one of the 1–12 numbers on the clock face.
- Children work out the answer and hold up the appropriate multiples card or write the answer on their whiteboard.
- Repeat several times.

Variations

- Provide pairs of children with a set of multiples cards, and ask them to work together.
- *Don't* write the multiplication table on the circle in the centre of the clock and *don't* provide the children with the multiples number cards. Point to one of the 1–12 numbers on the clock face, say: *times 2, times 3…* or *times 12*. Children work out the answer and put up their hand or write the answer on their whiteboard.

Gladiators

Objective

- Recall multiplication and division facts for multiplication tables up to 12 × 12

Teacher resources

- 'Gladiators'

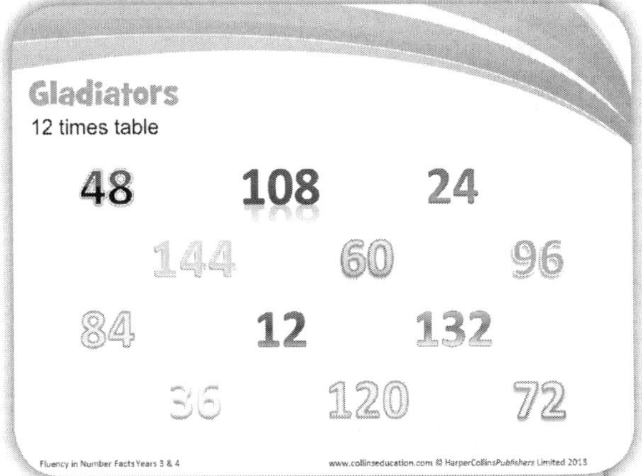

Pupil resources

- '2 × rulers or 'swords'

What to do

- Decide which multiplication table you want the children to practise and consolidate, and display the appropriate 'Gladiators' times-table slide.
- Ask two children to stand either side of the numbers.
- Ask a multiplication fact for the corresponding multiplication table, for example: *6 multiplied by 4 is…*
- The first child to point to the correct answer stays in. The other child sits down.
- Quickly choose another child to come and take the place of the child that just sat down.
- Continue as above.
- Which child can stay in the longest?

Variations

- The children sitting down ask the two children standing by the numbers a question where the answer is on the slide.
- To quicken the game, have two children standing either side of the numbers, one behind the other. When a child loses and has to sit down, there is an immediate replacement.
- Use the other 'Gladiators: Times tables' slides and the 'Gladiators: Division facts' slide.

Hands-on

Objective

- Recall multiplication and division facts for multiplication tables up to 12 × 12

Teacher resources

- none

Pupil resources

- 'Hands-on: Multiples of...' game board or 'Hands-on: Numbers 1–12' game board (per pair)

What to do

- Decide which multiplication table you want the children to practise and consolidate. If practising the multiplication facts for one of the multiplication tables up to 12 × 12, use the corresponding 'Hands-on: Multiples of…' game board. If practising the division facts for one of the multiplication tables up to 12 × 12 use the 'Hands-on: Numbers 1– 12' game board.
- Arrange the children into pairs and provide each pair with a copy of the appropriate 'Hands-on' game board.
- Tell the children to put the game board between them and to put their index fingers on a hand at the bottom of the game board.
- Ask an appropriate multiplication or division fact for the multiplication table the children are practising, for example: *9 times 4* (if practising the multiplication facts for the 4 multiplication table) or *32 divided by 4* (if practising the division facts for the 4 multiplication table).
- The first child to point to the correct answer wins.
- Children keep count of how many games they win.
- Play for as long as is appropriate.
- The winner in each pair is the child who wins more rounds.

Variation

- Provide each pair with a pile of counters. As a child wins a game they take a counter. The winner in each pair is the child who wins more counters.

Bingo

Objectives

- Recall multiplication and division facts for the 2, 3, 4, 5, 8 and 10 multiplication tables
- Recall multiplication and division facts for multiplication tables up to 12 × 12

Teacher resources

→ Whole-class games and activities → PowerPoint slides

- 'Bingo'

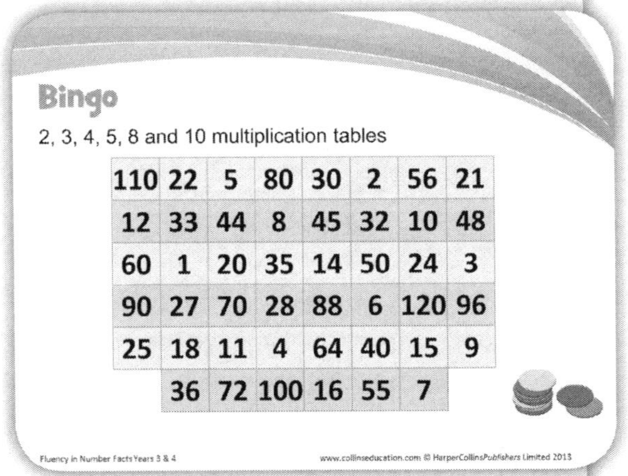

Pupil resources

- pencil and paper or small individual whiteboard and pen (per child)

What to do

- Display the 'Bingo: 2, 3, 4, 5, 8 and 10 multiplication tables' slide.
- Ask each child to write down any five numbers from the slide.
- Ask questions involving the multiplication and division facts for the 2, 3, 4, 5, 8 and 10 multiplication tables.
- Children look to find if any of their five numbers is the answer to the question.
- If a child has the answer, they cross out that number.
- The winner is the first child to cross out all five of their numbers and call out 'Bingo!'

(**Note:** Be sure to keep a record of the answers for checking purposes.)

Variations

- Ask the children to write down more or fewer than five numbers from the slide.
- Use the 'Bingo: 12 × 12 multiplication tables' slide. Ask the children questions involving the multiplication and division facts for multiplication tables up to 12 × 12.

Four in a row

Objectives

- Recall multiplication and division facts for the 2, 3, 4, 5, 8 and 10 multiplication tables
- Recall multiplication and division facts for multiplication tables up to 12 × 12

Teacher resources

- 'Four in a row'
- 1–12 dice

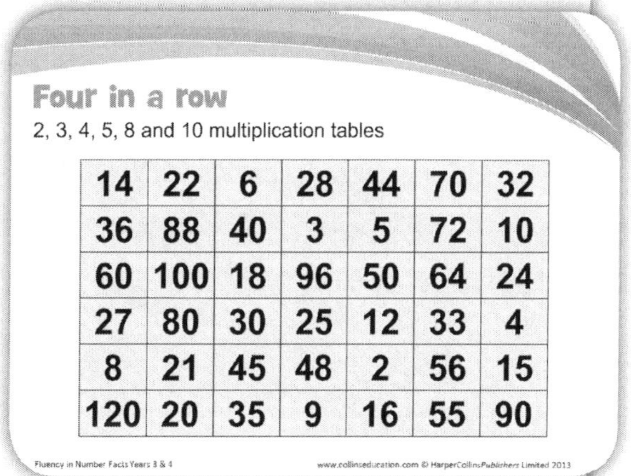

14	22	6	28	44	70	32
36	88	40	3	5	72	10
60	100	18	96	50	64	24
27	80	30	25	12	33	4
8	21	45	48	2	56	15
120	20	35	9	16	55	90

Pupil resources

- none

What to do

- Divide the class into two teams – a red team and a blue team.
- Display the 'Four in a row: 2, 3, 4, 5, 8 and 10 multiplication tables' slide.
- Explain that the object of the game is for a team to highlight a row of four numbers either side to side, up and down or diagonally.
- To highlight a number, a team must successfully answer a 2, 3, 4, 5, 8 or 10 times table question.
- Invite a child from the red team to roll the dice and say the number, for example, 6.
- Decide whether to multiply the dice number by 2, 3, 4, 5, 8 or 10 and say the corresponding calculation, for example: *6 times 8*. (**Note:** 110, the answer to 10 × 11, is not on the slide.)
- Select a child from the red team to call out the answer.
- If correct, this number is highlighted in red on the slide. If incorrect, ask a child from the blue team to give the answer. If correct, this number is highlighted in blue.
- Next, invite a child from the blue team to roll the dice.
- Repeat the above, at a quick pace, until one team has highlighted a row of four numbers.

Variations

- The team that rolls the dice decides whether to multiply the dice number by 2, 3, 4, 5, 8 or 10.
- Use the 'Four in a row: 12 × 12 multiplication tables' slide.

Tell me the facts

Objective

- Recall multiplication and division facts for multiplication tables up to 12 × 12

Teacher resources

→ Whole-class games and activities → PowerPoint slides

- 'Tell me the facts'

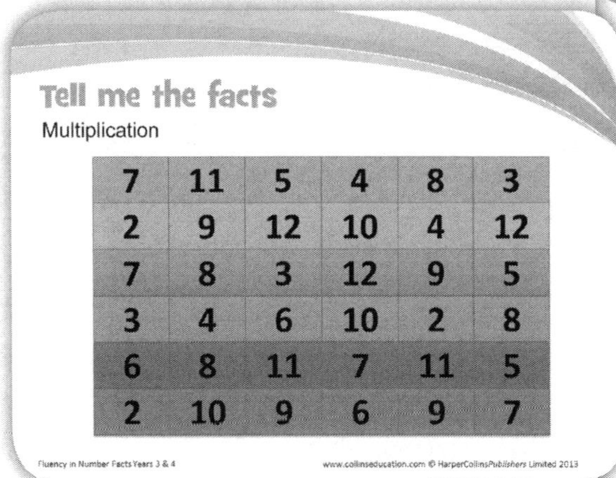

7	11	5	4	8	3
2	9	12	10	4	12
7	8	3	12	9	5
3	4	6	10	2	8
6	8	11	7	11	5
2	10	9	6	9	7

Pupil resources

- none

What to do

- Display the 'Tell me the facts: Multiplication' slide.
- Ask a child to highlight two numbers next to each other either side to side, up and down, or diagonally and say a known multiplication number fact about these two numbers, i.e. *I know that 6 multiplied by 8 equals 48.*
- Repeat, asking other children to come and highlight two other numbers, saying a known multiplication fact about the two numbers.

Variations

- Ask questions such as:
  - *Point to two numbers next to each other that have a product of 48.*
- Use the 'Tell me the facts: 2, 5, 10 division' slide, 'Tell me the facts: 3, 4, 8 division' slide, 'Tell me the facts: 6, 7, 9, 11 and 12 division' slide or 'Tell me the facts: 12 × 12 division' slide, asking questions such as:
  - *Point to two numbers next to each other that give an answer of 8 when the larger number is divided by the smaller number.*

Who's left standing?

Objective

- Recall multiplication and division facts for multiplication tables up to 12 × 12

Teacher resources

- none

Pupil resources

Number cards

- 'Multiples of…number cards' or '1–12 number cards' (one card per child)

What to do

- Decide which multiplication table you want the children to practise and consolidate. If practising the multiplication facts for one of the multiplication tables up to 12 × 12, use the corresponding 'Multiples of…number cards'. If practising the division facts for one of the multiplication tables up to 12 × 12 use the '1–12 number cards'.

Game 1: Recall and use multiplication facts for the 2 multiplication table

- Provide each child with a 'Multiples of 2 number card'.
- Say: *Everyone stand up. Look at the number on your card. Sit down if the number on your card is the answer to:*
  - *6 sets of 2* (12)
  - *9 lots of 2* (18)
  - *10 times 2* (20)
  - *2 times 2* (4)
  - *3 groups of 2* (6)
  - *5 times 2* (10)
  - *4 times 2* (8)
  - *11 multiplied by 2* (22)
  - *7 multiplied by 2* (14)
  - *12 times 2* (24)
  - *1 times 2* (2)

The winners are the children still standing with 16 on their cards.

Game 2: Recall and use multiplication facts for the 3 multiplication table

- Provide each child with a 'Multiples of 3 number card'.
- Say: *Everyone stand up. Look at the number on your card. Sit down if the number on your card is the answer to:*
  - *3 times 3* (9)
  - *6 times 3* (18)
  - *11 lots of 3* (33)
  - *7 times 3* (21)
  - *1 set of 3* (3)
  - *9 multiplied by 3* (27)
  - *12 multiplied by 3* (36)
  - *4 multiplied by 3* (12)
  - *10 groups of 3* (30)
  - *8 times 3* (24)
  - *2 times 3* (6)

The winners are the children still standing with 15 on their cards.

Game 3: Recall and use multiplication facts for the 4 multiplication table

- Provide each child with a 'Multiples of 4 number card'.
- Say: *Everyone stand up. Look at the number on your card. Sit down if the number on your card is the answer to:*
  - *5 times 4* (20)
  - *2 times 4* (8)
  - *4 lots of 4* (16)
  - *7 times 4* (28)
  - *9 sets of 4* (36)
  - *10 multiplied by 4* (40)
  - *1 multiplied by 4* (4)
  - *12 multiplied by 4* (48)
  - *3 groups of 4* (12)
  - *11 times 4* (44)
  - *8 times 4* (32)

The winners are the children still standing with 24 on their cards.

Who's left standing?

(continued)

Game 4: Recall and use multiplication facts for the 5 multiplication table

- Provide each child with a 'Multiples of 5 number card'.
- Say: *Everyone stand up. Look at the number on your card. Sit down if the number on your card is the answer to:*
  - *12 times 5* (60)
  - *4 times 5* (20)
  - *11 multiplied by 5* (55)
  - *1 times 5* (5)
  - *5 times 5* (25)
  - *7 sets of 5* (35)
  - *2 multiplied by 5* (10)
  - *10 times 5* (50)
  - *3 lots of 5* (15)
  - *9 multiplied by 5* (45)
  - *8 groups of 5* (40)

The winners are the children still standing with 30 on their cards.

Game 5: Recall and use multiplication facts for the 6 multiplication table

- Provide each child with a 'Multiples of 6 number card'.
- Say: *Everyone stand up. Look at the number on your card. Sit down if the number on your card is the answer to:*
  - *3 times 6* (18)
  - *10 times 6* (60)
  - *5 multiplied by 6* (30)
  - *11 times 6* (66)
  - *6 times 6* (36)
  - *12 sets of 6* (72)
  - *1 multiplied by 6* (6)
  - *7 times 6* (42)
  - *9 lots of 6* (54)
  - *4 multiplied by 6* (24)
  - *8 groups of 6* (48)

The winners are the children still standing with 12 on their cards.

Game 6: Recall and use multiplication facts for the 7 multiplication table

- Provide each child with a 'Multiples of 7 number card'.
- Say: *Everyone stand up. Look at the number on your card. Sit down if the number on your card is the answer to:*
  - *6 times 7* (42)
  - *10 times 7* (70)
  - *4 multiplied by 7* (28)
  - *1 times 7* (7)
  - *3 times 7* (21)
  - *5 sets of 7* (35)
  - *8 multiplied by 7* (56)
  - *9 times 7* (63)
  - *7 lots of 7* (49)
  - *12 multiplied by 7* (84)
  - *2 groups of 7* (14)

The winners are the children still standing with 77 on their cards.

Game 7: Recall and use multiplication facts for the 8 multiplication table

- Provide each child with a 'Multiples of 8 number card'.
- Say: *Everyone stand up. Look at the number on your card. Sit down if the number on your card is the answer to:*
  - *1 times 8* (8)
  - *6 times 8* (48)
  - *11 multiplied by 8* (88)
  - *9 times 8* (72)
  - *8 times 8* (64)
  - *4 sets of 8* (32)
  - *2 multiplied by 8* (16)
  - *7 times 8* (56)
  - *3 lots of 8* (24)
  - *12 multiplied by 8* (96)
  - *10 groups of 8* (80)

The winners are the children still standing with 40 on their cards.

Who's left standing?

(continued)

Game 8: Recall and use multiplication facts for the 9 multiplication table

- Provide each child with a 'Multiples of 9 number card'.
- Say: *Everyone stand up. Look at the number on your card. Sit down if the number on your card is the answer to:*
  - *3 times 9* (27)
  - *9 times 9* (81)
  - *8 multiplied by 9* (72)
  - *4 times 9* (36)
  - *1 times 9* (9)
  - *12 sets of 9* (108)
  - *7 multiplied by 9* (63)
  - *2 times 9* (18)
  - *5 lots of 9* (45)
  - *10 multiplied by 9* (90)
  - *6 groups of 9* (54)

The winners are the children still standing with 99 on their cards.

Game 9: Recall and use multiplication facts for the 10 multiplication table

- Provide each child with a 'Multiples of 10 number card'.
- Say: *Everyone stand up. Look at the number on your card. Sit down if the number on your card is the answer to:*
  - *9 multiplied by 10* (90)
  - *11 multiplied by 10* (110)
  - *5 sets of 10* (50)
  - *7 times 10* (70)
  - *10 groups of 10* (100)
  - *3 times 10* (30)
  - *8 lots of 10* (80)
  - *12 times 10* (120)
  - *6 times 10* (60)
  - *1 multiplied by 10* (10)
  - *4 times 10* (40)

The winners are the children still standing with 20 on their cards.

Game 10: Recall and use multiplication facts for the 11 multiplication table

- Provide each child with a 'Multiples of 11 number card'.
- Say: *Everyone stand up. Look at the number on your card. Sit down if the number on your card is the answer to:*
  - *6 times 11* (66)
  - *2 times 11* (22)
  - *9 multiplied by 11* (99)
  - *8 times 11* (88)
  - *1 times 11* (11)
  - *3 sets of 11* (33)
  - *12 multiplied by 11* (132)
  - *7 times 11* (77)
  - *10 lots of 11* (110)
  - *11 multiplied by 11* (121)
  - *5 groups of 11* (55)

The winners are the children still standing with 44 on their cards.

Game 11: Recall and use multiplication facts for the 12 multiplication table

- Provide each child with a 'Multiples of 12 number card'.
- Say: *Everyone stand up. Look at the number on your card. Sit down if the number on your card is the answer to:*
  - *5 times 12* (60)
  - *4 times 12* (48)
  - *11 multiplied by 12* (132)
  - *1 times 12* (12)
  - *12 times 12* (144)
  - *7 sets of 12* (84)
  - *2 multiplied by 12* (24)
  - *10 times 12* (120)
  - *3 lots of 12* (36)
  - *9 multiplied by 12* (108)
  - *8 groups of 12* (96)

The winners are the children still standing with 72 on their cards.

Who's left standing?

(continued)

Game 12: Recall and use division facts for the 2 multiplication table

- Provide each child with a '1–12 number card'.
- Say: *Everyone stand up. Look at the number on your card. Sit down if the number on your card is the answer to:*
  - *12 shared between 2* (6)
  - *22 divided by 2* (11)
  - *24 divided by 2* (12)
  - *18 shared between 2* (9)
  - *8 divided by 2* (4)
  - *20 divided by 2* (10)
  - *10 divided by 2* (5)
  - *4 shared between 2* (2)
  - *2 divided by 2* (1)
  - *14 shared between 2* (7)
  - *16 divided by 2* (8)

The winners are the children still standing with 3 on their cards.

Game 13: Recall and use division facts for the 3 multiplication table

- Provide each child with a '1–12 number card'.
- Say: *Everyone stand up. Look at the number on your card. Sit down if the number on your card is the answer to:*
  - *36 divided by 3* (12)
  - *27 shared between 3* (9)
  - *15 divided by 3* (5)
  - *6 shared between 3* (2)
  - *12 divided by 3* (4)
  - *21 shared between 3* (7)
  - *24 divided by 3* (8)
  - *3 divided by 3* (1)
  - *30 divided by 3* (10)
  - *18 shared between 3* (6)
  - *9 divided by 3* (3)

The winners are the children still standing with 11 on their cards.

Game 14: Recall and use division facts for the 4 multiplication table

- Provide each child with a '1–12 number card'.
- Say: *Everyone stand up. Look at the number on your card. Sit down if the number on your card is the answer to:*
  - *24 shared between 4* (6)
  - *32 divided by 4* (8)
  - *48 divided by 4* (12)
  - *36 shared between 4* (9)
  - *16 divided by 4* (4)
  - *40 divided by 4* (10)
  - *12 divided by 4* (3)
  - *8 shared between 4* (2)
  - *4 divided by 4* (1)
  - *44 divided by 4* (11)
  - *28 shared between 4* (7)

The winners are the children still standing with 5 on their cards.

Game 15: Recall and use division facts for the 5 multiplication table

- Provide each child with a '1–12 number card'.
- Say: *Everyone stand up. Look at the number on your card. Sit down if the number on your card is the answer to:*
  - *55 divided by 5* (11)
  - *50 divided by 5* (10)
  - *30 divided by 5* (6)
  - *25 shared between 5* (5)
  - *15 shared between 5* (3)
  - *40 divided by 5* (8)
  - *10 shared between 5* (2)
  - *20 divided by 5* (4)
  - *45 shared between 5* (9)
  - *5 divided by 5* (1)
  - *60 divided by 5* (12)

The winners are the children still standing with 7 on their cards.

Who's left standing?

(continued)

Game 16: Recall and use division facts for the 6 multiplication table

- Provide each child with a '1–12 number card'.
- Say: *Everyone stand up. Look at the number on your card. Sit down if the number on your card is the answer to:*
  - *66 divided by 6* (11)
  - *42 divided by 6* (7)
  - *60 divided by 6* (10)
  - *72 divided by 6* (12)
  - *36 divided by 6* (6)
  - *18 shared between 6* (3)
  - *30 shared between 6* (5)
  - *54 shared between 6* (9)
  - *6 divided by 6* (1)
  - *48 divided by 6* (8)
  - *12 shared between 6* (2)

The winners are the children still standing with 4 on their cards.

Game 17: Recall and use division facts for the 7 multiplication table

- Provide each child with a '1–12 number card'.
- Say: *Everyone stand up. Look at the number on your card. Sit down if the number on your card is the answer to:*
  - *7 divided by 7* (1)
  - *21 shared between 7* (3)
  - *70 divided by 7* (10)
  - *84 divided by 7* (12)
  - *42 divided by 7* (6)
  - *35 shared between 7* (5)
  - *49 divided by 7* (7)
  - *63 shared between 7* (9)
  - *28 divided by 7* (4)
  - *14 shared between 7* (2)
  - *56 divided by 7* (8)

The winners are the children still standing with 11 on their cards.

Game 18: Recall and use division facts for the 8 multiplication table

- Provide each child with a '1–12 number card'.
- Say: *Everyone stand up. Look at the number on your card. Sit down if the number on your card is the answer to:*
  - *64 divided by 8* (8)
  - *72 shared between 8* (9)
  - *96 divided by 8* (12)
  - *24 shared between 8* (3)
  - *88 divided by 8* (11)
  - *40 shared between 8* (5)
  - *32 divided by 8* (4)
  - *48 divided by 8* (6)
  - *16 shared between 8* (2)
  - *56 divided by 8* (7)
  - *8 divided by 8* (1)

The winners are the children still standing with 10 on their cards.

Game 19: Recall and use division facts for the 9 multiplication table

- Provide each child with a '1–12 number card'.
- Say: *Everyone stand up. Look at the number on your card. Sit down if the number on your card is the answer to:*
  - *54 divided by 9* (6)
  - *108 divided by 9* (12)
  - *18 shared between 9* (2)
  - *27 shared between 9* (3)
  - *63 divided by 9* (7)
  - *90 divided by 9* (10)
  - *45 shared between 9* (5)
  - *81 shared between 9* (9)
  - *9 divided by 9* (1)
  - *99 divided by 9* (11)
  - *36 divided by 9* (4)

The winners are the children still standing with 8 on their cards.

Who's left standing?

(continued)

Game 20: Recall and use division facts for the 10 multiplication table

- Provide each child with a '1–12 number card'.
- Say: *Everyone stand up. Look at the number on your card. Sit down if the number on your card is the answer to:*
  - *80 divided by 10* (8)
  - *20 shared between 10* (2)
  - *100 divided by 10* (10)
  - *120 divided by 10* (12)
  - *110 divided by 10* (11)
  - *70 divided by 10* (7)
  - 40 divided by 10 (4)
  - *90 shared between 10* (9)
  - *10 divided by 10* (1)
  - *30 shared between 10* (3)
  - *50 shared between 10* (5)

The winners are the children still standing with 6 on their cards.

Game 21: Recall and use division facts for the 11 multiplication table

- Provide each child with a '1–12 number card'.
- Say: *Everyone stand up. Look at the number on your card. Sit down if the number on your card is the answer to:*
  - *110 divided by 11* (10)
  - *44 divided by 11* (4)
  - *99 shared between 11* (9)
  - *66 divided by 11* (6)
  - *77 divided by 11* (7)
  - *11 divided by 11* (1)
  - *33 shared between 11* (3)
  - *121 divided by 11* (11)
  - *55 shared between 11* (5)
  - *88 divided by 11* (8)
  - *22 shared between 11* (2)

The winners are the children still standing with 12 on their cards.

Game 22: Recall and use division facts for the 12 multiplication table

- Provide each child with a '1–12 number card'.
- Say: *Everyone stand up. Look at the number on your card. Sit down if the number on your card is the answer to:*
  - *36 shared between 12* (3)
  - *60 shared between 12* (5)
  - *48 divided by 12* (4)
  - *144 divided by 12* (12)
  - *96 divided by 12* (8)
  - *84 divided by 12* (7)
  - *24 shared between 12* (2)
  - *72 shared between 12* (6)
  - *132 divided by 12* (11)
  - *12 divided by 12* (1)
  - *120 divided by 12* (10)

The winners are the children still standing with 9 on their cards.

Forming groups

Objective

- Recall multiplication and division facts for multiplication tables up to 12 × 12

Teacher resources

- none

Pupil resources

Number cards

- 'Multiples of…number cards' or '2-digit number cards' (one card per child)

What to do

- Decide which multiplication table you want the children to practise and consolidate and provide each child with either one of the corresponding 'Multiples of…number cards' or one of the '2-digit number cards'. (**Note:** It is recommended that you use the '2-digit number cards' provided on the CD-ROM).
- If, for example, you are practising the 4 times table, point and say: *Everyone stand up. Look at the number on your card. When I say 'Go!' I want everyone who has a card with a number on it that is a multiple of 4 to move to this side of the room, and everyone who has a card with a number on it that is not a multiple of 4 to move to this side of the room. Ready? Go!*
- Once the two groups have formed, ask the members of each group in turn to call out their number. Say: *Everyone hold up your number card. The multiples of 4 group, starting with Toby, call out your numbers. Now the group that have cards that are not multiples of 4, starting with Ollie, tell us your numbers.*
- If appropriate, ask each group to order themselves smallest to largest.

Variation

- Rather than providing each child with a 'Multiples of…number card' or a '2-digit number card', use two different sets of multiples cards to provide each child with a card, for example, the 'Multiples of 4 number cards' and the 'Multiples of 5 number cards'. Do the children that have the cards that are common multiples, for example, 20, 40 and 60, realise that they belong to both groups?

Stand up

Objective

- Recall multiplication and division facts for multiplication tables up to 12 × 12

Teacher resources

- none

Pupil resources

Number cards

- '1–12 number cards' (one card per child)

What to do

- Decide which multiplication or division facts for the multiplication tables up to 12 × 12 you want the children to practise and consolidate.
- Provide each child with a '1–12 number card'.

To practise the multiplication facts for the 2 multiplication table:

- Say: *Look at the number on your card. Multiply the number on your card by 2. Stand up if the answer is 12.*
- Ask: *Who can tell me what number is on Matt's and Sam's cards?* (6)
- Ask the children standing to show their cards.
- The children standing then sit down.
- Repeat, saying: *Multiply the number on your card by 2. Stand up if the answer is:*

22 (11)	*20* (10)	*14* (7)	*18* (9)	*24* (12)	*2* (1)
4 (2)	*16* (8)	*8* (4)	*6* (3)	*10* (5)	

To practise the division facts for the 2 multiplication table:

- Say: *Divide 16 by 2. Look at the number on your card. If you have the answer on your card, stand up.*
- Ask: *Who can tell me what number is on Luke's and Julia's cards?* (8)
- Ask the children standing to show their cards.
- The children standing then sit down.
- Repeat for the following:

6 (3)	*24* (12)	*10* (5)	*20* (10)	*4* (2)	*22* (11)
2 (1)	*12* (6)	*8* (4)	*14* (7)	*18* (9)	

Stand up

(continued)

Variations

To practise the multiplication facts for the 3 multiplication table:

- Say: *Multiply the number on your card by 3. Stand up if the answer is:*

6 (2)	*21* (7)	*24* (8)	*9* (3)	*36* (12)	*15* (5)
27 (9)	*12* (4)	*3* (1)	*18* (6)	*30* (10)	*33* (11)

To practise the division facts for the 3 multiplication table:

- Say: *Divide 21 by 3. Look at the number on your card. If you have the answer on your card, stand up.* (7). Repeat for the following:

24 (8)	*3* (1)	*6* (2)	*36* (12)	*18* (6)	*12* (4)
30 (10)	*27* (9)	*9* (3)	*15* (5)	*33* (11)	

To practise the multiplication facts for the 4 multiplication table:

- Say: *Multiply the number on your card by 4. Stand up if the answer is:*

24 (6)	*4* (1)	*48* (12)	*32* (8)	*20* (5)	*44* (11)
12 (3)	*40* (10)	*16* (4)	*8* (2)	*36* (9)	*28* (7)

To practise the division facts for the 4 multiplication table:

- Say: *Divide 36 by 4. Look at the number on your card. If you have the answer on your card, stand up.* (9). Repeat for the following:

16 (4)	*24* (6)	*8* (2)	*44* (11)	*12* (3)	*48* (12)
28 (7)	*32* (8)	*4* (1)	*40* (10)	*20* (5)	

To practise the multiplication facts for the 5 multiplication table:

- Say: *Multiply the number on your card by 5. Stand up if the answer is:*

25 (5)	*15* (3)	*55* (11)	*5* (1)	*35* (7)	*20* (4)
10 (2)	*45* (9)	*30* (6)	*40* (8)	*60* (12)	*50* (10)

To practise the division facts for the 5 multiplication table:

- Say: *Divide 25 by 5. Look at the number on your card. If you have the answer on your card, stand up.* (5). Repeat for the following:

55 (11)	*10* (2)	*40* (8)	*60* (12)	*15* (3)	*30* (6)
5 (1)	*50* (10)	*20* (4)	*35* (7)	*45* (9)	

To practise the multiplication facts for the 6 multiplication table:

- Say: *Multiply the number on your card by 6. Stand up if the answer is:*

6 (1)	*48* (8)	*36* (6)	*30* (5)	*66* (11)	*42* (7)
60 (10)	*18* (3)	*12* (2)	*54* (9)	*24* (4)	*72* (12)

To practise the division facts for the 6 multiplication table:

- Say: *Divide 60 by 6. Look at the number on your card. If you have the answer on your card, stand up.* (10). Repeat for the following:

18 (3)	*24* (4)	*6* (1)	*48* (8)	*12* (2)	*54* (9)
72 (12)	*36* (6)	*30* (5)	*66* (11)	*42* (7)	

(continued)

Stand up

(continued)

To practise the multiplication facts for the 7 multiplication table:

- Say: *Multiply the number on your card by 7. Stand up if the answer is:*

63 (9)	*28* (4)	*21* (3)	*14* (2)	*84* (12)	*35* (5)
7 (1)	*70* (10)	*49* (7)	*56* (8)	*42* (6)	*77* (11)

To practise the division facts for the 7 multiplication table:

- Say: *Divide 14 by 7. Look at the number on your card. If you have the answer on your card, stand up.* (2). Repeat for the following:

21 (3)	*7* (1)	*70* (10)	*35* (5)	*63* (9)	*28* (4)
49 (7)	*56* (8)	*42* (6)	*77* (11)	*84* (12)	

To practise the multiplication facts for the 8 multiplication table:

- Say: *Multiply the number on your card by 8. Stand up if the answer is:*

96 (12)	*16* (2)	*72* (9)	*64* (8)	*32* (4)	*80* (10)
24 (3)	*56* (7)	*8* (1)	*40* (5)	*88* (11)	*48* (6)

To practise the division facts for the 8 multiplication table:

- Say: *Divide 96 by 8. Look at the number on your card. If you have the answer on your card, stand up.* (12). Repeat for the following:

8 (1)	*40* (5)	*64* (8)	*32* (4)	*24* (3)	*56* (7)
16 (2)	*72* (9)	*88* (11)	*48* (6)	*80* (10)	

To practise the multiplication facts for the 9 multiplication table:

- Say: *Multiply the number on your card by 9. Stand up if the answer is:*

45 (5)	*27* (3)	*54* (6)	*99* (11)	*9* (1)	*81* (9)
72 (8)	*108* (12)	*18* (2)	*36* (4)	*90* (10)	*63* (7)

To practise the division facts for the 9 multiplication table:

- Say: *Divide 45 by 9. Look at the number on your card. If you have the answer on your card, stand up.* (5). Repeat for the following:

54 (6)	*99* (11)	*9* (1)	*81* (9)	*27* (3)	*72* (8)
18 (2)	*36* (4)	*90* (10)	*63* (7)	*108* (12)	

To practise the multiplication facts for the 10 multiplication table:

- Say: *Multiply the number on your card by 10. Stand up if the answer is:*

30 (3)	*70* (7)	*50* (5)	*10* (1)	*60* (6)	*100* (10)
110 (11)	*20* (2)	*90* (9)	*80* (8)	*120* (12)	*40* (4)

Stand up

(continued)

To practise the division facts for the 10 multiplication table:

- Say: *Divide 20 by 10. Look at the number on your card. If you have the answer on your card, stand up.* (2). Repeat for the following:

70 (7)	*30* (3)	*50* (5)	*60* (6)	*40* (4)	*90* (9)
80 (8)	*10* (1)	*100* (10)	*120* (12)	*110* (11)	

To practise the multiplication facts for the 11 multiplication table:

- Say: *Multiply the number on your card by 11. Stand up if the answer is:*

110 (10)	*33* (3)	*77* (7)	*66* (6)	*22* (2)	*99* (9)
55 (5)	*121* (11)	*44* (4)	*88* (8)	*11* (1)	*132* (12)

To practise the division facts for the 11 multiplication table:

- Say: *Divide 88 by 11. Look at the number on your card. If you have the answer on your card, stand up.* (8). Repeat for the following:

11 (1)	*132* (12)	*22* (2)	*99* (9)	*66* (6)	*110* (10)
33 (3)	*77* (7)	*55* (5)	*44* (4)	*121* (11)	

To practise the multiplication facts for the 12 multiplication table:

- Say: *Multiply the number on your card by 12. Stand up if the answer is:*

36 (3)	*48* (4)	*96* (8)	*60* (5)	*72* (6)	*24* (2)
84 (7)	*108* (9)	*12* (1)	*144* (12)	*120* (10)	*132* (11)

To practise the division facts for the 12 multiplication table:

Say: *Divide 36 by 12. Look at the number on your card. If you have the answer on your card, stand up.* (3). Repeat for the following:

96 (8)	*60* (5)	*24* (2)	*72* (6)	*48* (4)	*84* (7)
120 (10)	*132* (11)	*12* (1)	*144* (12)	*108* (9)	

Whole-class, paired or individual activities

Using the Maths Facts in the *Facts and Games* book

Objective

- Recall multiplication and division facts for multiplication tables up to 12 × 12

Teacher resources

→ Maths Facts → Multiplication and division

Pupil resources

- *Fluency in Number Facts: Facts and Games: Years 3 & 4* book pages 18–41 (per child or pair)

Introduction

The Maths Facts on pages 18–41 of the *Fluency in Number Facts: Facts and Games: Years 3 & 4* book cover the key multiplication and division number facts that children need to be able to recall instantly by the end of Lower Key Stage 2.

These pages aim to develop children's fluency by:

- securing a thorough conceptual understanding of the multiplication and division number facts
- identifying patterns and the relationship between multiplication and division
- developing strategic approaches to recalling and deriving the answers to multiplication and division number facts.

To assist in achieving these aims, the multiplication and division number facts contained in the *Facts and Games: Years 3 & 4* book are presented in the following ways:

- Multiplication tables to 12 × 12 (pages 18–21)
- Division facts relating to the multiplication tables to 12 × 12 (pages 22–25)
- Multiples up to 12 × 12 (pages 26–28)
- Multiplication square to 12 × 12 (pages 29 and 30)
- Trios for the multiplication tables to 12 × 12 (pages 31–41)

The following pages include a brief description of each of these presentations, along with suggestions of how to focus on these Maths Facts either with the whole class, or with children working in pairs or individually.

Whole-class, paired or individual activities

Using the Maths Facts in the *Facts and Games Book*

(continued)

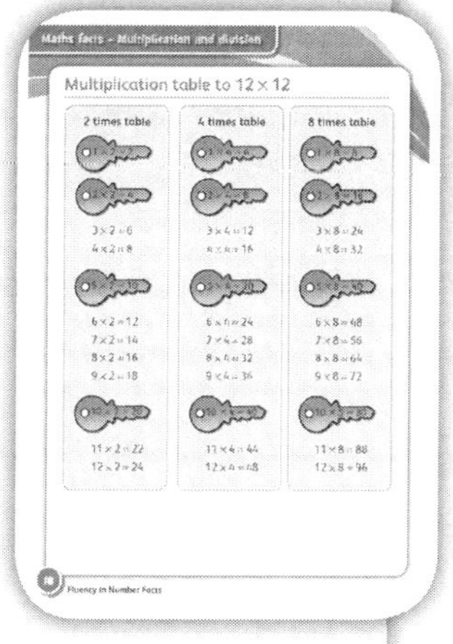

Multiplication tables to 12 × 12 (pages 18–21)

These pages show the times tables facts for the multiplication tables to 12 × 12.

The 2, 4, and 8 times tables are in red, the 3, 6, and 12 times tables in green, and the 5 and 10 times tables in blue. This corresponds with the colours used on pages 22–41. The use of colour has been used to highlight the relationship between different multiplication tables.

These pages also show the four 'key facts', i.e. 1 × , 2 × , 5 × and 10 ×, for each of the multiplication tables to 12 × 12. These 'key facts' once secure, can be used to help derive the answers to unknown related facts.

How to use the Maths Facts

Whole class

- Focus on the multiplication facts for one of the multiplication tables. However, the eventual aim is to have the class focussing on several tables at a time. It is also recommended that you begin by simultaneously working on both the multiplication and division facts for the same multiplication table so that children gain a deeper understanding of the relationship between multiplication and division.
- Display the appropriate PDF file (CD-ROM / Maths Facts / Multiplication and division) and provide each child or pair with a copy of the *Facts and Games: Years 3 & 4* book and direct their attention to the relevant multiplication facts on pages 18–21.
- Begin by asking the children to identify different patterns in the list of calculations and discuss these with the class. What do they notice about the first, the second and in particular the third number in each calculation? Can the children see any relationships between these numbers?

(*continued*)

Whole-class, paired or individual activities

Using the Maths Facts in the *Facts and Games Book*

(continued)

- Next, draw children's attention to the four 'key facts', i.e. 1 ×, 2 ×, 5 ×, 10 ×. Discuss with the children how it is important that they learn and remember these 'key facts' first as, once secure, they can use them to help derive the answers to unknown related facts.
- Ask individual children to chant the facts, for example: *Rochelle, please read out the 8 times table facts.* After the child has said approximately half of the facts say: *David, please continue the 8 times table facts.*
- Ask specific groups of children to chant the facts, for example:
  - *1 times 8 is 8* (boys); *2 times 8 is 16* (girls); *3 times 8 is 24* (boys); *4 times 8 is 32* (girls)…
  - *1 times 8 is 8* (Group A); *2 times 8 is 16* (Group B); *3 times 8 is 24* (Group C); *4 times 8 is 32* (Group A)…
- Ask the whole class to chant the facts.
- Tell the children to spend just two or three minutes looking at the multiplication facts with the aim of focussing their attention on learning these facts off by heart.
- Conclude by hiding the PDF file, asking the children to close their copy of the *Facts and Games: Years 3 & 4* book and ask the class questions similar to the following:
  - *What is 7 times 8?*
  - *What is 5 multiplied by 8?*
  - *What is 8 lots of 2?*
  - *What is the product of 8 and 10?*
- After several sessions, draw children's attention to the use of colour, i.e. the 2, 4, and 8 times tables are in red, the 3, 6, and 12 times tables in green, and the 5 and 10 times tables in blue. Discuss with the children the relationship between different multiplication tables:
  - the answers to the 4 times table are double the answers to the 2 times table, for example, 3 × 2 = 6 and 3 × 4 = 12
  - the answers to the 8 times table are double the answers to the 4 times table, for example, 3 × 4 = 12 and 3 × 8 = 24
  - the answers to the 6 times table are double the answers to the 3 times table, for example, 7 × 3 = 21 and 7 × 6 = 42
  - the answers to the 12 times table are double the answers to the 6 times table, for example, 7 × 6 = 42 and 7 × 12 = 84.
- Ensure the children realise that, just like the 'key facts', knowing the relationship between different multiplication tables can help them derive the answers to unknown facts.

Whole-class, paired or individual activities

Using the Maths Facts in the *Facts and Games* Book

(continued)

Pairs

- Begin by asking the children to focus on one of the multiplication tables up to 12 × 12. However, the eventual aim is to have the children focus on several multiplication tables simultaneously.
- Provide each pair with a copy of the *Facts and Games: Years 3 & 4* book and direct their attention to the relevant multiplication facts on pages 18–21. Alternatively, ask the children to choose a multiplication table that they know they need to develop greater fluency of.
- Children spend just two or three minutes individually looking at the multiplication facts with the aim of learning these facts off by heart.
- Children then take turns to take charge of the book and ask each other questions similar to those on page 112.

Individual

- Begin by asking the child to focus on one of the multiplication tables up to 12 × 12. However, the eventual aim is to have the child focus on several multiplication tables simultaneously.
- Provide the child with a copy of the *Facts and Games: Years 3 & 4* book and direct their attention to the relevant multiplication facts on pages 18–21. Alternatively, ask the child to choose a multiplication table that they know they need to develop greater fluency of.
- It is recommended that the child spends just five or ten minutes each time, focussing their attention on learning the multiplication facts off by heart.
- To provide some personal challenge, suggest the child covers the multiplication facts and recites the facts to themselves.

(*continued*)

Whole-class, paired or individual activities

Using the Maths Facts in the *Facts and Games Book*

(continued)

Division facts relating to the multiplication tables to 12 × 12 (pages 22–25)

These pages show the division facts for the multiplication tables to 12 × 12.

The division facts for the 2, 4 and 8 multiplication tables are in red, the division facts for the 3, 6 and 12 multiplication tables in green, and the division facts for the 5 and 10 multiplication tables in blue. This corresponds with the colours used on pages 18–21 and 26–41. The use of colour has been used to highlight the relationship between different multiplication tables.

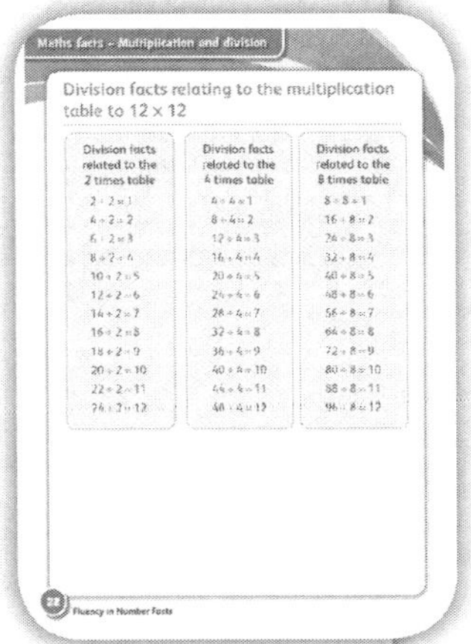
Maths facts – Multiplication and division

Division facts relating to the multiplication table to 12 × 12

Division facts related to the 2 times table	Division facts related to the 4 times table	Division facts related to the 8 times table
2 ÷ 2 = 1	4 ÷ 4 = 1	8 ÷ 8 = 1
4 ÷ 2 = 2	8 ÷ 4 = 2	16 ÷ 8 = 2
6 ÷ 2 = 3	12 ÷ 4 = 3	24 ÷ 8 = 3
8 ÷ 2 = 4	16 ÷ 4 = 4	32 ÷ 8 = 4
10 ÷ 2 = 5	20 ÷ 4 = 5	40 ÷ 8 = 5
12 ÷ 2 = 6	24 ÷ 4 = 6	48 ÷ 8 = 6
14 ÷ 2 = 7	28 ÷ 4 = 7	56 ÷ 8 = 7
16 ÷ 2 = 8	32 ÷ 4 = 8	64 ÷ 8 = 8
18 ÷ 2 = 9	36 ÷ 4 = 9	72 ÷ 8 = 9
20 ÷ 2 = 10	40 ÷ 4 = 10	80 ÷ 8 = 10
22 ÷ 2 = 11	44 ÷ 4 = 11	88 ÷ 8 = 11
24 ÷ 2 = 12	48 ÷ 4 = 12	96 ÷ 8 = 12

22 Fluency in Number Facts

How to use the Maths Facts

Whole class

- Focus on the division facts for one of the multiplication tables. However, the eventual aim is to have the class focussing on the division facts for several multiplication tables at a time. It is also recommended that you begin by simultaneously working on both the multiplication and division facts for the same multiplication table so that children gain a deeper understanding of the relationship between multiplication and division.
- Display the appropriate PDF file (CD-ROM / Maths Facts / Multiplication and division) and provide each child or pair with a copy of the *Facts and Games: Years 3 & 4* book and direct their attention to the relevant division facts on pages 22–25.
- Begin by asking the children to identify different patterns in the list of calculations and discuss these with the class. What do they notice about the first, the second and the third number in each calculation? Can the children see any relationships between these numbers?
- Next, draw children's attention to the corresponding multiplication facts on the appropriate PDF file (CD-ROM / Maths Facts / Multiplication and division) and pages 18–21 of the *Facts and Games: Years 3 & 4* book. In particular, ensure they are made aware of how the same colour has been used to link the related multiplication and division facts.
- Discuss with the children the inverse relationship between multiplication and division and how they can use a known multiplication fact to help them derive the answer to an unknown division fact (and vice versa), for example, 9 × 8 = 72 and 72 ÷ 8 = 9.
- Ask individual children to chant the facts, for example: *Sam, please read out the division facts for the 8 times table*. After the child has said approximately half of the facts, say: *Toni, please continue to say the facts.*

Whole-class, paired or individual activities

Using the Maths Facts in the *Facts and Games* Book

(continued)

- Ask specific groups of children to chant the facts, for example:
  - *8 divided by 8 is 1* (boys); *16 divided by 8 is 2* (girls); *24 divided by 8 is 3* (boys); *32 divided by 8 is 4* (girls)…
  - *8 divided by 8 is 1* (Group A); *16 divided by 8 is 2* (Group B); *24 divided by 8 is 3* (Group C); *32 divided by 8 is 4* (Group A)…
- Ask the whole class to chant the facts.
- Tell the children to spend just two or three minutes looking at the division facts with the aim of focussing their attention on learning these facts off by heart.
- Conclude by hiding the PDF file and asking the children to close their copy of the *Facts and Games: Years 3 & 4* book, and ask the class questions similar to the following:
  - *What is 56 divided by 8?*
  - *What is 88 shared between 8?*
  - *How many eights are there in 16?*
  - *Share 24 between 8. How many is this each?*

Pairs

- Begin by asking the children to focus on the division facts for one of the multiplication tables up to 12 × 12. However, the eventual aim is to have the children focus on several multiplication tables simultaneously.
- Provide each pair with a copy of the *Facts and Games: Years 3 & 4* book and direct their attention to the relevant division facts on pages 22–25. Alternatively, ask them to choose the division facts that they know they need to develop greater fluency of.
- Children spend just two or three minutes individually looking at the division facts with the aim of learning these facts off by heart.
- Children then take turns to take charge of the book and ask each other questions similar to those above.

Individual

- Begin by asking the child to focus on the division facts for one of the multiplication tables up to 12 × 12. However, the eventual aim is to have the child focus on several multiplication tables simultaneously.
- Provide the child with a copy of the *Facts and Games: Years 3 & 4* book and direct their attention to the relevant division facts on pages 22–25. Alternatively, ask the child to choose the division facts that they know they need to develop greater fluency of.
- It is recommended that the child spends just five or ten minutes each time, focussing their attention on learning the division facts off by heart.
- To provide some personal challenge, suggest the child covers the division facts and recites the facts to themselves.

(continued)

Whole-class, paired or individual activities

Using the Maths Facts in the *Facts and Games Book*

(continued)

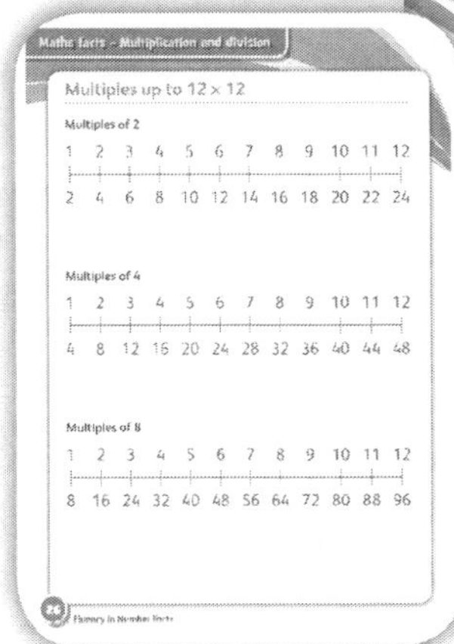
Maths facts – Multiplication and division

Multiples up to 12 × 12

Multiples of 2

1 2 3 4 5 6 7 8 9 10 11 12

2 4 6 8 10 12 14 16 18 20 22 24

Multiples of 4

1 2 3 4 5 6 7 8 9 10 11 12

4 8 12 16 20 24 28 32 36 40 44 48

Multiples of 8

1 2 3 4 5 6 7 8 9 10 11 12

8 16 24 32 40 48 56 64 72 80 88 96

Multiples up to 12 × 12 (pages 26–28)

These pages show the multiplication and related division facts for 2, 3, 4, 5, 6, 7, 8, 9, 10, 11 and 12 up to the 12th multiple, for example: 24 (× 2), 48 (× 4) and 96 (× 8).

The multiples of 2, 4 and 8 are in red, the multiples of 3, 6 and 12 in green, and the multiples of 5 and 10 in blue. This corresponds with the colours used on pages 18–25 and 29–41. The use of colour has been used to highlight the relationship between different multiplication tables.

These number lines are a simple way of showing the relationship between the increasing steps and the corresponding products. They also highlight the link between multiplication and division.

How to use the Maths Facts

Whole class

- Focus on the multiplication and division facts for one of the multiplication tables. However, the eventual aim is to have the class focussing on the multiplication and division facts for several multiplication tables at a time.
- Display the appropriate PDF file (CD-ROM / Maths Facts / Multiplication and division) and provide each child or pair with a copy of the *Facts and Games: Years 3 & 4* book and direct their attention to the relevant number line on pages 26–28.
- Begin by discussing with the children how the line is simply a number line but instead of having one set of numbers along the line, there are two sets of numbers – one set above the line (the numbers 1 to 12) and another set below the line (the corresponding multiples).
- Ask the children to identify any patterns or relationships between the numbers on the number line.
- Then, pointing in turn to each of the numbers 1 to 12 above the number line, and then the corresponding multiples below the line, say the multiplication facts to the children, for example:
  - *1 times 8 is 8*
  - *2 times 8 is 16*
  - *3 times 8 is 24*
  - *4 times 8 is 32…*
- Once the class is secure in using the number line to identify the multiplication facts, ask individual children to repeat the above, chanting the multiplication facts.

Whole-class, paired or individual activities

Using the Maths Facts in the *Facts and Games* Book

(continued)

Next, pointing in turn to each of the multiples below the number line, and then the corresponding number 1–12 above the line, say the division facts to the children, for example:

- *8 divided by 8 is 1*
- *16 divided by 8 is 2*
- *24 divided by 8 is 3*
- *32 divided by 8 is 4…*

- Once the class is secure in using the number line to identify the division facts, ask individual children to repeat the above, chanting the division facts.
- Ask the children to spend just two or three minutes looking at the number line with the aim of focussing their attention on learning the multiplication and division facts for the multiplication table off by heart.
- Conclude by hiding the PDF file, asking the children to close their copy of the *Facts and Games: Years 3 & 4* book, and ask the class questions similar to the following:
  - *What is 8 times / multiplied by / lots of / groups of 9?*
  - *What is 56 divided by / shared between 8?*
  - *How many eights are there in 24?*
  - *Share 80 between 8. How many is this each?*
- After several sessions, draw children's attention to the use of colour: i.e. the multiples of 2, 4 and 8 are in red, the multiples of 3, 6 and 12 in green, and the multiples of 5 and 10 in blue. Discuss with the children the relationship between different multiplication tables:
  - the answers to the 4 times table are double the answers to the 2 times table, for example, 3 × 2 = 6 and 3 × 4 = 12
  - the answers to the 8 times table are double the answers to the 4 times table, for example, 3 × 4 = 12 and 3 × 8 = 24
  - the answers to the 6 times table are double the answers to the 3 times table, for example, 7 × 3 = 21 and 7 × 6 = 42
  - the answers to the 12 times table are double the answers to the 6 times table, for example, 7 × 6 = 42 and 7 × 12 = 84.
- Ensure the children realise that knowing the relationship between different multiplication tables can help them derive the answers to unknown facts.

(*continued*)

Whole-class, paired or individual activities

Using the Maths Facts in the *Facts and Games Book*

(continued)

Pairs

- Begin by telling the children to focus on the multiplication and division facts for one of the multiplication tables up to 12 × 12. However, the eventual aim is to have the children focus on several multiplication tables simultaneously.
- Provide each pair with a copy of the *Facts and Games: Years 3 & 4* book and direct their attention to the relevant number line on pages 26–28. Alternatively, ask the children to choose the multiplication and division facts that they know they need to develop greater fluency of.
- Children spend just two or three minutes individually using the number line to assist them in learning the multiplication and division facts off by heart.
- Children then take turns to take charge of the book and ask each other questions similar to those on page 117.

Individual

- Begin by asking the child to focus on the multiplication and division facts for one of the multiplication tables up to 12 × 12. However, the eventual aim is to have the child focus on several multiplication tables simultaneously.
- Provide the child with a copy of the *Facts and Games: Years 3 & 4* book and direct their attention to the relevant number line on pages 26–28. Alternatively, ask the child to choose the multiplication and division facts that they know they need to develop greater fluency of.
- It is recommended that the child spends just five or ten minutes each time, focussing their attention on learning multiplication and division facts off by heart.
- To provide some personal challenge, suggest the child covers the numbers (multiples) below the number line and recites the multiplication facts to themselves and/or cover the numbers 1 – 12 above the number line and recite the division facts to themselves.

Whole-class, paired or individual activities

Using the Maths Facts in the *Facts and Games Book*

(continued)

Multiplication square to 12 × 12 (pages 29 and 30)

The square on page 29 shows the calculations (without the answers) that make up the multiplication facts up to 12 × 12. The square on page 30 shows the answers (multiples) corresponding to the multiplication calculations. These squares can be used to show that multiplication of two numbers can be done in any order (commutative). The square on page 30 can also be used to show the relationship between multiplication and division.

The multiplication calculations and corresponding multiples for 2, 4 and 8 are in red, the calculations and multiples for 3, 6 and 12 in green, and the calculations and multiples for 5 and 10 in blue. This corresponds with the colours used on pages 18–28 and 31–41. The use of colour has been used to highlight the relationship between different multiplication tables.

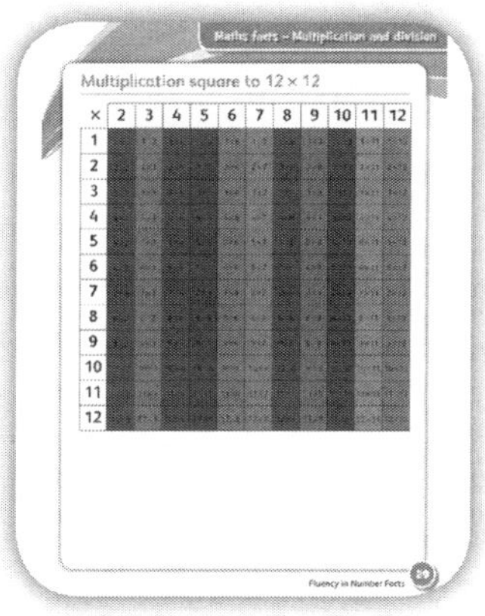

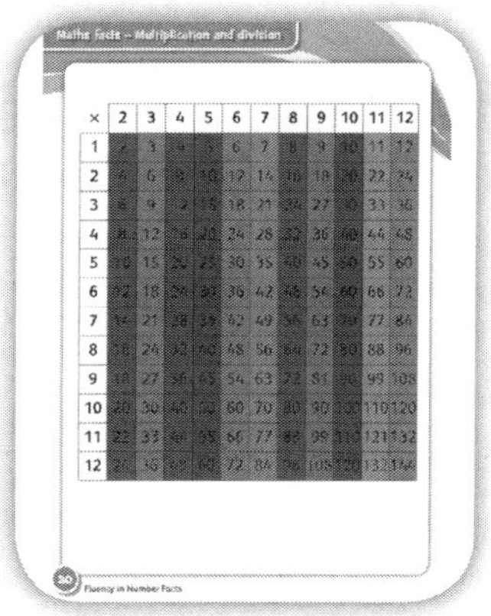

How to use the Maths Facts

Whole class

- Display the appropriate PDF file (CD-ROM / Maths Facts / Multiplication and division) and provide each child or pair with a copy of the *Facts and Games: Years 3 & 4* book and direct their attention to the two squares on pages 29 and 30.
- Begin by discussing the 'Multiplication square to 12 × 12' on page 29 with the children. Ask them to identify different patterns in the square and discuss these. Draw attention to the row of 12 numbers at the top of the square and the column of 12 numbers down the left-hand side of the square.
- Next, move on to showing the children how to use the square. Put one finger on 6 in the column of numbers down the left-hand side of the square and another finger on 8 in the row of numbers at the top of the square, and then move both fingers across and down the square until they meet at the calculation, i.e. 6 × 8.
- Next, display page 30 to the children, which shows the answers (multiples) to the calculations on page 29.
- As with page 29, demonstrate to the children how to find the answer to 6 × 8.
- Repeat the above several times for other calculations, moving between pages 29 and 30 as you go.

(continued)

Whole-class, paired or individual activities

Using the Maths Facts in the *Facts and Games Book*

(continued)

- Once the children are secure with using the squares, identifying a calculation and finding the corresponding answer (multiple), use the squares to demonstrate to the children how, for example, 8 × 6 is the same as 6 × 8 (commutative).
- Repeat several times.
- Next, ask the children to spend just four or five minutes becoming familiar with the squares.
- Referring to the square on page 29, conclude by asking the class questions similar to the following:
  - *What is 7 times 9?*
  - *What is 4 multiplied by 12?*
  - *What is 9 lots of 6?*
  - *What is 8 groups of 8?*
- After each question, display the square on page 30 to check the answer.
- Once the children are confident in using the squares, draw their attention to the use of colour: i.e. the calculations and multiples of 2, 4 and 8 are in red, the calculations and multiples of 3, 6 and 12 in green, and the calculations and multiples of 5 and 10 in blue. Referring to the square on page 30, discuss with the children the relationship between different multiplication tables:
  - the answers to the 4 times table are double the answers to the 2 times table, for example, 3 × 2 = 6 and 3 × 4 = 12
  - the answers to the 8 times table are double the answers to the 4 times table, for example, 3 × 4 = 12 and 3 × 8 = 24
  - the answers to the 6 times table are double the answers to the 3 times table, for example, 7 × 3 = 21 and 7 × 6 = 42
  - the answers to the 12 times table are double the answers to the 6 times table, for example, 7 × 6 = 42 and 7 × 12 = 84.
- Ensure the children realise that knowing the relationship between different multiplication tables can help them derive the answers to unknown multiplication facts.
- The multiplication square on page 30 can also be used to show the relationship between multiplication and division. Once the children are confident in using the square to recall the answers to the multiplication facts, demonstrate how to use the square to help them recall the answers to division facts and their inverse relationship to multiplication.

Pairs

- Begin by asking the children to focus on the multiplication facts for one of the multiplication tables up to 12 × 12. However, the eventual aim is to have the children focus on several multiplication tables simultaneously.
- Provide each pair with a copy of the *Facts and Games: Years 3 & 4* book and direct their attention to one of the columns on the multiplication square on page 29. Alternatively, ask the children to choose the multiplication facts that they know they need to develop greater fluency of.

Whole-class, paired or individual activities

Using the Maths Facts in the *Facts and Games Book*

(continued)

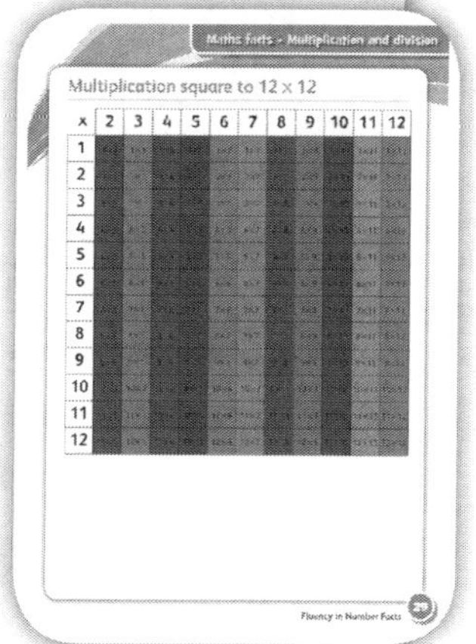

- Children stand the book up so that one child is looking at page 29, while the other child is looking at page 30.
- The child looking at page 30 identifies a multiplication calculation using the row of numbers at the top of the square and the column of numbers down the left-hand side of the square and says the calculation to their partner, for example: *7 times 8*.
- The child looking at page 29 finds that calculation on the square and says the answer to their partner.
- The child looking at page 30 then says whether this answer is correct or not.
- After about five minutes, children swap roles and repeat.
- To use the square to practise and consolidate division facts, children refer to the multiplication square on page 30. They cover the numbers in the left-hand column (or top row) and take turns to ask each other division questions. They check the answer each time by removing the cover on the left-hand column (or top row).

Individual

- Begin by asking the child to focus on the multiplication facts for one of the multiplication tables up to 12 × 12. However, the eventual aim is to have the child focus on several multiplication tables simultaneously.
- Provide the child with a copy of the *Facts and Games: Years 3 & 4* book and direct their attention to one of the columns on the multiplication square on page 29. Alternatively, ask the child to choose the multiplication facts that they know they need to develop greater fluency of.
- Beginning on page 29, the child points to one of the calculations and recalls the answer.

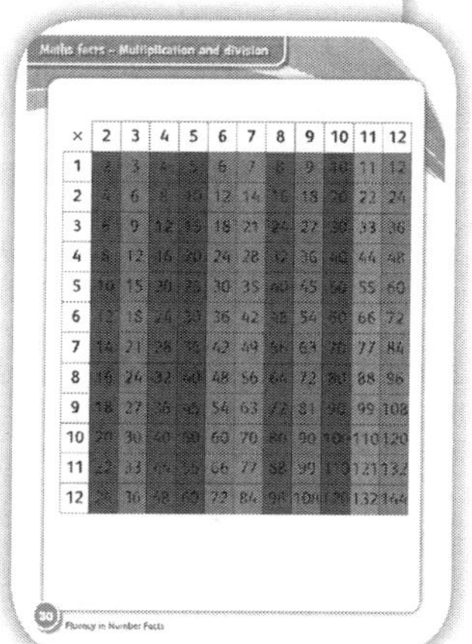

- They then turn over to page 30 to check whether this answer is correct or not.
- It is recommended that the child spends just five or ten minutes each time, focussing their attention on learning the multiplication facts off by heart.
- To use the square to practise and consolidate division facts, the child uses the multiplication square on page 30. They cover the numbers in the left-hand column (or top row) and ask themselves a division question. They check the answer each time by removing the cover on the left-hand column (or top row).

(continued)

Whole-class, paired or individual activities

Using the Maths Facts in the *Facts and Games* Book

(continued)

Trios for the multiplication tables to 12 × 12 (pages 31–41)

'Trios' show the relationship between the three numbers that make up a multiplication fact and the related division fact. They can be used to show that multiplication of two numbers can be done in any order (commutative) and how this law does *not* apply to division.

The trios for 2, 4 and 8 are in red, the trios for 3, 6 and 9 in green, and the trios for 5 and 10 in blue. This corresponds with the colours used on pages 18–30. The use of colour has been used to highlight the relationship between different multiplication tables.

How to use the Maths Facts

Whole class

- Focus on the multiplication and division facts for one of the multiplication tables.
- Display the appropriate PDF file (CD-ROM / Maths Facts / Multiplication and division) and provide each child or pair with a copy of the *Facts and Games: Years 3 & 4* book and direct their attention to the relevant times tables and related division facts on pages 31–41.
- There are 12 sets of trios for each multiplication table, so begin by referring to each set of trios in turn, asking the children to identify different patterns between the four calculations in the trio.
- Ensure the children realise that each trio consists of only three numbers, for example, 3, 8 and 24, and that these three numbers produce four calculations: two multiplication calculations (3 × 8 = 24 and 8 × 3 = 24), and two division calculations (24 ÷ 8 = 3 and 24 ÷ 3 = 8).

Whole-class, paired or individual activities

Using the Maths Facts in the *Facts and Games* Book

(continued)

- Referring to the two multiplication calculations, discuss with the children how multiplication of two numbers can be done in any order (commutative law).
- Then, referring to the two division calculations, discuss with the children how the commutative law does *not* apply to division.
- Move on to discussing the inverse relationship between multiplication and division.
- Next, ask the children to spend just two or three minutes looking at the set of four multiplication and division facts for each trio with the aim of learning the facts off by heart.
- Conclude by hiding the PDF file, asking the children the children to close their copy of the *Facts and Games: Years 3 & 4* book, and ask the class questions similar to the following:
  – *Tell me a multiplication calculation you can make using only the numbers 7, 8 and 56.*
  – *Can you tell me another multiplication calculation that only uses the same three numbers?*
  – *Tell me a division calculation that uses only the numbers 7, 8 and 56.*
  – *Is there another division calculation that uses only these numbers?*
- Repeat the above for the remaining eleven sets of trios as and when appropriate.

Pairs

- Provide each pair with a copy of the *Facts and Games: Years 3 & 4* book and direct their attention to the relevant times tables and related division facts on pages 31–41. Alternatively, ask the children to choose the multiplication table that they know they need to develop greater fluency of.
- Children take turns to choose one of the trios and place their hand/fingers over the list of four calculations.
- Referring to the three numbers on the triangle, the the other child says the two multiplication and two division number facts.
- Once they have done this, the child covering the facts removes their hand/finger to reveal the four calculations.

Individual

- Provide the child with a copy of the *Facts and Games: Years 3 & 4* book and direct their attention to the relevant times tables and related division facts on pages 31–41. Alternatively, ask the child to choose the multiplication table that they know they need to develop greater fluency of.
- It is recommended that the child spends just five or ten minutes each time, focussing their attention on learning the multiplication and division facts off by heart.
- To provide some personal challenge, as for the paired activity above, suggest the child places their hand/fingers over the list of four calculations and recites the facts to themselves.

Team lines

Objective

- Recall multiplication facts for the 2, 5 and 10 multiplication tables

Pupil resources

- *Fluency in Number Facts: Facts and Games: Years 3 & 4* book pages 66 and 67 (per pair); PDFs:

→ Paired games and activities → Paired games from the *Facts and Games: Years 3 & 4* book

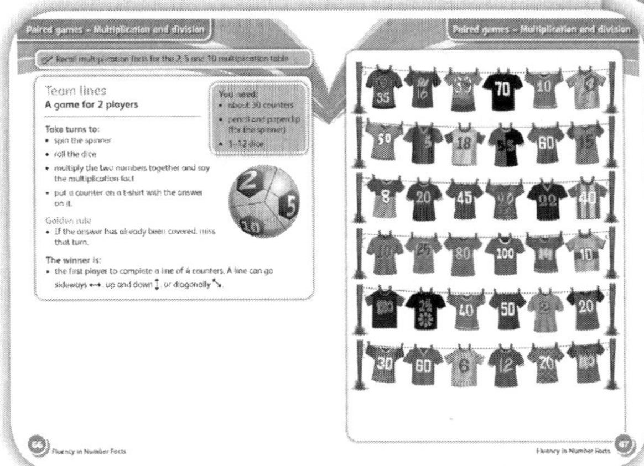

- about 30 counters (per pair)
- pencil and paperclip (for the spinner) (per pair)
- 1–12 dice (per pair)

Notes

- Before the children play the game, ensure that they are familiar with how to use the spinner (see *Facts and Games: Years 3 & 4* book page 80).

Variations

- Children play the game in groups of three.

or

- The winner is the first player to complete a square of four counters.

Recall division facts for the 2, 5 and 10 multiplication tables

or

- Children do not require the 1–12 dice for this variation.

Take turns to:

- spin the spinner, find a t-shirt with a number that can be divided by the spinner number
- say the number sentence and cover that t-shirt with a counter.

The winner is:

- the first player to complete a line of five counters. A line can go sideways, up and down or diagonally.

- Children play the game individually using only nine counters.

You win the game if:

- you can complete a line of three counters. A line can go sideways, up and down or diagonally.

3, 4 and 8 cube

Objective

- Recall multiplication facts for the 3, 4 and 8 multiplication tables

Pupil resources

- *Fluency in Number Facts: Facts and Games: Years 3 & 4* book pages 68 and 69 (per pair); PDFs:

→ Paired games and activities → Paired games from the *Facts and Games: Years 3 & 4* book

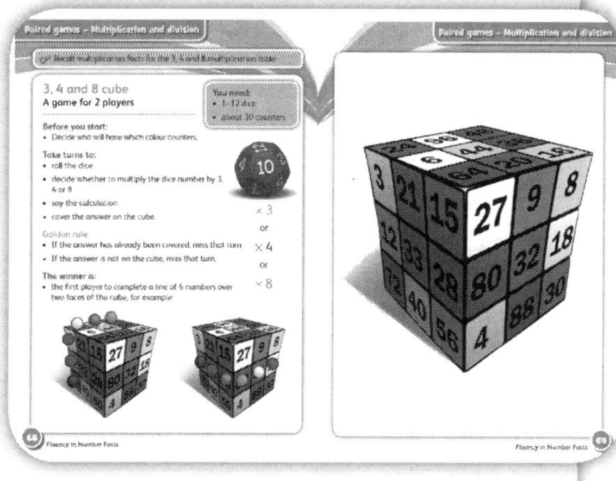
Paired games – Multiplication and division

Recall multiplication facts for the 3, 4 and 8 multiplication tables

3, 4 and 8 cube
A game for 2 players

You need:
- 1–12 dice
- about 30 counters

Before you start:
- Decide who will have which colour counters.

Take turns to:
- roll the dice
- decide whether to multiply the dice number by 3, 4 or 8
- say the calculation
- cover the answer on the cube.

Golden rule
- If the answer has already been covered, miss that turn.
- If the answer is not on the cube, miss that turn.

The winner is:
- the first player to complete a line of 6 numbers over two faces of the cube, for example

×3 or ×4 or ×8

68 Fluency in Number Facts

- 1–12 dice (per pair)
- about 30 counters (per pair)

Variations

- Children play the game in groups of three.

or Recall division facts for the 2, 5 and 10 multiplication tables

- Children do not require the 1–12 dice for this variation. They do however need 27 counters.
- Children cover each of the numbers on the cube with a counter. They take turns to remove a counter from the cube to reveal a number, for example, 64. Each child decides whether to divide the number revealed by 3, 4 or 8. The first child to say a correct number sentence, for example, *64 divided by 8 is 8,* keeps that counter. The winner is the first child to collect six counters.

- Children play the game individually using only nine counters.

You win the game if:

- you can complete a line of three counters.

Paired games and activities

Win the world

Objective

- Recall multiplication facts for the 6, 7, 9, 11 and 12 multiplication tables

Pupil resources

- *Fluency in Number Facts: Facts and Games: Years 3 & 4* book pages 70 and 71 (per pair); PDFs:

→ Paired games and activities → Paired games from the *Facts and Games: Years 3 & 4* book

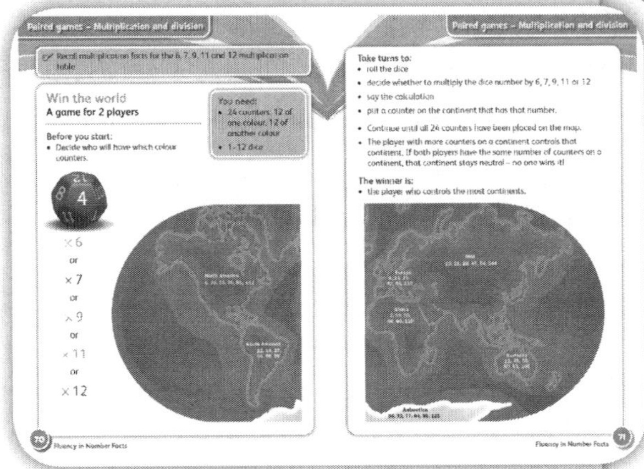

- 24 counters: 12 of one colour, 12 of another colour (per pair)
- 1–12 dice (per pair)

Variations

- Children play the game in groups of three. You need 36 counters: 12 each of three different colours.

- Children play the game individually using only ten counters.

You win the game if:

- you can put a counter on each continent.

Honeycomb

Multiplication
Division

Objective

- Recall multiplication and division facts for multiplication tables up to 12 × 12

Pupil resources

- *Fluency in Number Facts: Facts and Games: Years 3 & 4* book pages 72 and 73 (per pair); PDFs:

Paired games and activities → Paired games from the *Facts and Games: Years 3 & 4* book

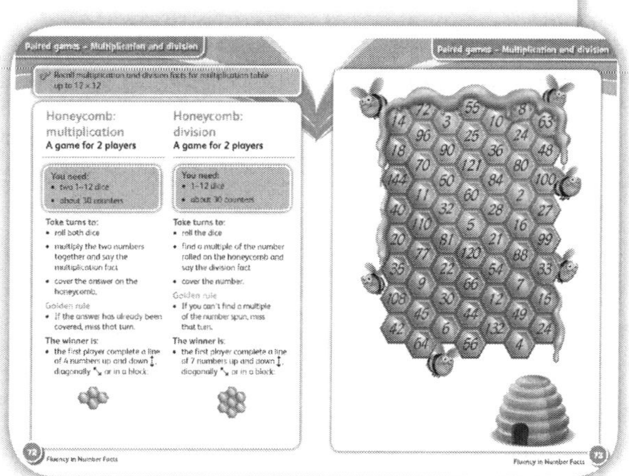
Paired games – Multiplication and division

Recall multiplication and division facts for multiplication tables up to 12 × 12

Honeycomb: multiplication
A game for 2 players

You need:
- two 1–12 dice
- about 30 counters

Take turns to:
- roll both dice
- multiply the two numbers together and say the multiplication fact
- cover the answer on the honeycomb.

Golden rule
- If the answer has already been covered, miss that turn.

The winner is:
- the first player complete a line of 4 numbers up and down, diagonally or in a block.

Honeycomb: division
A game for 2 players

You need:
- 1–12 dice
- about 30 counters

Take turns to:
- roll the dice
- find a multiple of the number rolled on the honeycomb and say the division fact
- cover the number.

Golden rule
- If you can't find a multiple of the number spun, miss that turn.

The winner is:
- the first player complete a line of 7 numbers up and down, diagonally or in a block.

72 Fluency in Number Facts

Fluency in Number Facts 73

- 2 × 1–12 dice: for Honeycomb: Multiplication (per pair)
- 1–12 dice: for Honeycomb: Division (per pair)
- about 30 counters (per pair)

Variations

- Children play the game in groups of three.

Honeycomb: Multiplication

- Children play the game individually using only 14 counters.

You win the game if:

- you can cover four numbers up and down, diagonally or in a block.

Honeycomb: Division

- Children play the game individually using only 14 counters.

You win the game if:

- you can cover seven numbers up and down, diagonally or in a block.

River times

Objective

- Recall multiplication and division facts for multiplication tables up to 12 × 12

Pupil resources

- *Fluency in Number Facts: Facts and Games: Years 3 & 4* book pages 74 and 75 (per pair); PDFs:

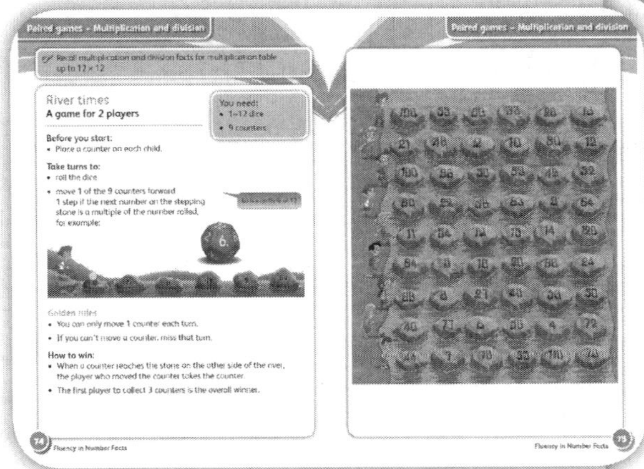

→ Paired games and activities → Paired games from the *Facts and Games: Years 3 & 4* book

- 1–12 dice (per pair)
- 9 counters (per pair)

Variations

- Children play the game in groups of three.

or

- Begin the game by placing a counter to the right of the last stepping stone in each row. Move *one* of the nine counters backwards one step if the next number on the stepping stone is a multiple of the number rolled. When a counter reaches the number on the stone immediately in front of the child, the player who moved the counter takes the counter. The first player to collect three counters is the overall winner.

or *You need:*

- 1–12 dice
- 21 counters all the same colour (per player; each player needs different coloured counters)

Before you start:

- Choose three different paths of stepping stones and place one of your counters on the child at the end of that path. This path now 'belongs' to you.

Take turns to:

- roll the dice, for example, 6
- find a stepping stone on any one of the three paths that belongs to you that has a number that is a multiple of the number rolled, for example, 42.

The winner is:

- the first player to cover all the numbers on one of their paths across the river.

Paired games and activities

Mechanical multiplication

Objective

- Multiply a 2-digit number by a 1-digit number

Pupil resources

- *Fluency in Number Facts: Facts and Games: Years 3 & 4* book pages 76 and 77 (per pair); PDFs:

Paired games and activities → Paired games from the *Facts and Games: Years 3 & 4* book

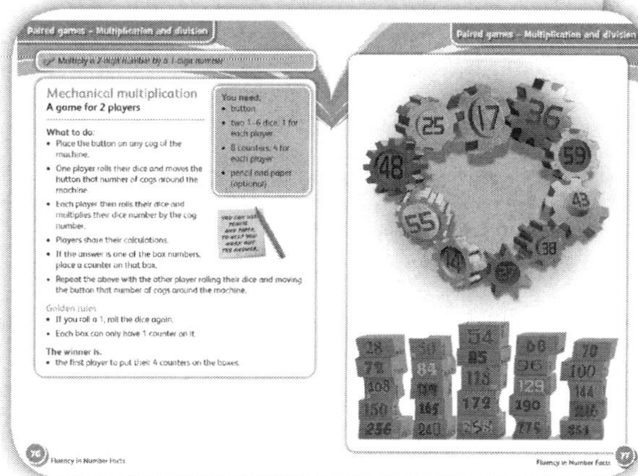

- button (per pair)
- two 1–6 dice: 1 for each player (per pair)
- 8 counters: 4 for each player (per pair)
- pencil and paper (optional) (per pair)

Note

- Provide less able children with pencil and paper to help them work out the answers.

Variations

- Children play the game in groups of three. You need 12 counters: four for each player.

or Calculate mathematical statements for division using known multiplication tables

(**Note:** It is advised that this variation is only played by more able children.)

You need:

- 1–6 dice
- about 20 counters

Take turns to:

- roll the dice, for example, 4
- find a box number that is divisible by the dice number, for example, 84, say the calculation and place a counter on that box.

Golden rules:

- If you roll a 1, roll the dice again.
- If you can't find a box with a number on it divisible by your dice number, miss that turn.
- Each box can only have one counter on it.

The winner is:

- the first player to put the fifth counter on a stack of five boxes (a stack can be completed in any order).

Hunting Yeti

Objective

- Calculate mathematical statements for division using known multiplication tables

Pupil resources

- *Fluency in Number Facts: Facts and Games: Years 3 & 4* book pages 78 and 79 (per pair); PDFs:

→ Paired games and activities → Paired games from the *Facts and Games: Years 3 & 4* book

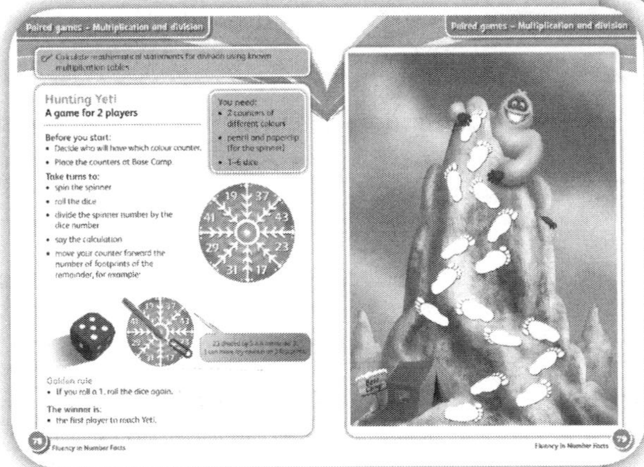

- 2 counters of different colours (per pair)
- pencil and paperclip (for the spinner) (per pair)
- 1–6 dice (per pair)

Notes

- Before the children play the game, ensure that they are familiar with how to use the spinner (see *Facts and Games: Years 3 & 4* book page 80).
- This game involves division with remainders.

Variations

- Children play the game in groups of three, each player using a different colour counter.

or

- Use a 1–12 dice rather than a 1–6 dice (if you roll a 1, roll the dice again). Rather than moving forward the number of footsteps of the remainder, move forward the number of times the dice number divides into the spinner number. For example, if you roll a 6 and spin 31 you move forward 5 footsteps (31 ÷ 6 = 5 r1).

Times-table practice

Objective

- Recall multiplication facts for multiplication tables up to 12 × 12

Pupil resources

- 1–12 dice (per pair)
- 20 counters: 10 counters for each player (per pair)
- container (per pair)

What to do

- Decide which multiplication table you want the children to practise, for example, 8 multiplication table.
- Children take turns to roll the dice.
- Each child multiplies the dice number by 8.
- The first child to call out the correct answer places one of their counters into the container.
- The winner is the first player to place all their counters into the container.

Win the counters

Objective

- Recall multiplication facts for multiplication tables up to 12 × 12

Pupil resources

- 'Hands-on: Multiples of ...' game board (per pair)
- 1–12 dice (per pair)
- 20 counters (per pair)

What to do

- Decide which multiplication table you want the children to practise, for example, 8 multiplication table, and provide them with the appropriate game board, i.e. 'Hands-on multiples of 8' game board.
- Each player puts their index finger on one of the hands at the bottom of the game board.
- One child rolls the dice, for example, 6.
- Both children multiply the dice number by the multiplication table they are practising, for example, 8 multiplication table: 6 × 8 = 48.
- The first player to point to the correct answer on the game board wins a counter.
- The winner is the player with more counters once all 20 counters have been won.

Cover the multiples

Objective

- Recall multiplication facts for multiplication tables up to 12 × 12

Pupil resources

→ Whole-class games and activities → Hands-on game boards

- 'Hands-on: Multiples of ...' game board (per pair)
- 1–12 dice (per pair)
- 20 counters: 10 of one colour, 10 of another colour (per pair)

What to do

- Decide which multiplication table you want the children to practise, for example, 8 multiplication table, and provide them with the appropriate game board, i.e. 'Hands-on multiples of 8' game board.
- Children decide who will have which colour counters.
- Children take turns to:
  - roll the dice, for example, 7
  - multiply the dice number by the multiplication table they are practising, for example, 8 multiplication table, and say the answer, i.e. 56.
- If the answer is correct, they place one of their counters on that number on the game board.
- If the number is already covered, they miss that turn.
- The winner is the player with more counters on the game board once all the numbers have a counter on them.

Stack them up

Objective

- Recall multiplication facts for multiplication tables up to 12 × 12

Pupil resources

→ Whole-class games and activities → Hands-on game boards

- 'Hands-on: Multiples of ...' game board (per pair)
- 1–12 dice (per pair)
- 20 counters: 10 of one colour, 10 of another colour (per pair)

What to do

- Decide which multiplication table you want the children to practise, for example, 8 multiplication table, and provide them with the appropriate game board, i.e. 'Hands-on: Multiples of 8' game board.
- Children decide who will have which colour counters.
- Children take turns to:
  - roll the dice, for example, 6
  - multiply the dice number by the multiplication table they are practising, for example, 8 multiplication table, and say the answer, i.e. 48.
- If their answer is correct, they place one of their counters on that number (but making sure not to cover the number) on the game board.
- If the number already has a counter on it, either with one of their own counters, or one the other player's counters, they place their counter on top of the pile.
- The player whose colour counter is on top 'owns' the pile.
- Children keep going, taking turns, until each player has put their ten counters on the game board.
- Each player then carefully removes all the piles where the top counter is their colour.
- Each player then counts how many counters they have altogether (of both colours).
- The winner is the player with more counters.

Individual activities

Multiplication and division Flip Facts cards

Objective

- Recall multiplication and division facts for multiplication tables up to 12 × 12

Resources

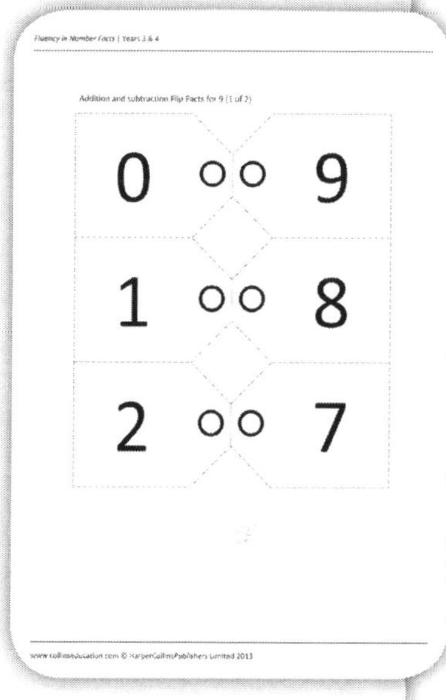

→ Individual activities → Flip Facts cards → Multiplication and division

- 'Multiplication and division Flip Facts cards'
- scissors
- glue
- hole punch
- small piece of string or paper fastener

What to do

- Cut out the cards along the dashed lines.
- Fold each card along the dotted lines to form two-sided cards.
- Glue together the back of each card.
- Punch a hole in the centre of each card.
- Arrange the cards in order with the smallest number on top.
- Fasten the set of cards together with string or a paper fastener.

To practise the multiplication facts for the 8 multiplication table

- Use the 'Multiplication and division Flip Facts cards for 8'.
- Start with the 1 card on top.
- Ask yourself: *1 multiplied by 8 is…?* (8) Turn over the card to check. *2 multiplied by 8 is…?* (16) Turn over the card to check. *3 multiplied by 8 is…?* (24) Turn over the card to check.
- Continue until you reach the card showing 12 and ask: *12 multiplied by 8 is…?* (96).
- Repeat several times, quickening the pace as you go.

(*continued*)

Individual activities

Multiplication and division Flip Facts cards

(continued)

To practise the division facts for the 8 multiplication table

- Use the 'Multiplication and division Flip Facts cards for 8'.
- Start with the 96 card on top.
- Ask yourself: *96 divided by 8 is…?* (12) Turn over the card to check. *88 divided by 8 is…?* (11) Turn over the card to check. *80 divided by 8 is…?* (10) Turn over the card to check.
- Continue until you reach the card showing 8 and ask: *8 divided by 8 is…?* (1)
- Repeat several times, quickening the pace as you go.

- Children spend just five or ten minutes each time, focussing their attention on learning the multiplication and division facts off by heart.

Variation

- Use the 'Multiplication and division Flip Facts cards' for 2, 3, 4, 5, 6, 7, 9, 10, 11 and 12 to practise the other multiplication and division facts for multiplication tables up to 12 × 12.

Number and place value | Addition and subtraction facts | Multiplication and division facts

Sit down, stand up

Objectives

- Recognise the place value of each digit in a 2-, 3- or 4-digit number and a decimal number with up to two decimal places
- Order and compare numbers up to, and beyond 1000, and decimals numbers with up to two decimal places
- Find 10 or 100 more or less than a given number
- Round any number to the nearest 10, 100 or 1000
- Recall and use addition and subtraction facts to 20 fluently, and derive and use related facts up to 100
- Add and subtract numbers mentally, including a 2-digit number and ones, a 2-digit number and tens, two 2-digit numbers, a 3-digit number and ones, a 3-digit number and tens, and a 3-digit number and hundreds
- Recall multiplication and division facts for multiplication tables up to 12 × 12

Teacher resources

- 'Sit down, stand up'

CD → Whole-class games and activities → PowerPoint slides

Pupil resources

- none

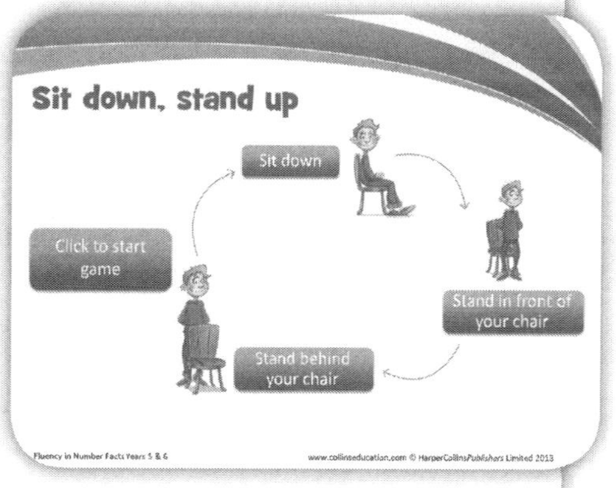

What to do

- Explain to the children that this a game of honesty.
- Display the first 'Sit down, stand up' slide:
  - sit down
  - stand in front of your chair
  - stand behind your chair
- All the children start the game by sitting.
- Ask the class an appropriate question, for example: *What is 7 times 8*?
- Ask a child for the answer, i.e. 56.
- All the children that worked out the correct answer stand up in front of their chair.
- Continue asking questions.
- Each time a child works out the correct answer to a question, they move to a different position following the order on the slide.
- If a child works out an incorrect answer to a question they stay in their current position.
- Continue asking questions until there are some children sitting down, some children standing in front of their chair and other children standing behind their chair.
- Finally, in rapid succession display slides 2 to 7 (which form a continual loop) eventually stopping on one of the slides.
- All the children in the position displayed on the slide are the winners.

Number and place value

Addition and subtraction facts

Multiplication and division facts

Target boards

Objectives

- Recognise the place value of each digit in a 2-, 3- or 4-digit number and a decimal number with up to two decimal places
- Order and compare numbers up to, and beyond 1000, and decimals numbers with up to two decimal places
- Find 10 or 100 more or less than a given number
- Round any number to the nearest 10, 100 or 1000
- Recall and use addition and subtraction facts to 20 fluently, and derive and use related facts up to 100
- Add and subtract numbers mentally, including a 2-digit number and ones, a 2-digit number and tens, two 2-digit numbers, a 3-digit number and ones, a 3-digit number and tens, and a 3-digit number and hundreds
- Recall multiplication and division facts for multiplication tables up to 12 × 12

Teacher resources

- 'Target boards'

Whole-class games and activities → PowerPoint slides

Pupil resources

- none

Target boards

8	=	4	$\frac{1}{2}$	2
96	108	<	32	42
$\frac{1}{4}$	3	–	541	>
+	24	479	×	$\frac{1}{5}$
36	÷	5	10	352

What to do

- Display the first 'Target boards' slide.
- Ask questions similar to the following:
  - *Which number has 4 tens, 1 unit and 5 hundreds?*
  - *Which number is between 350 and 400?*
  - *Which two numbers round to 40?*
  - *Which number is 10 more than 98?*
  - *Which two numbers make a total of 40?*
  - *Which two numbers have a difference of 10?*
  - *Which two numbers when multiplied together equal 24?*
  - *Which two numbers when the larger number is divided by the smaller number have an answer of 4?*
- Ask children to point and say different calculations and expressions using the numbers and symbols on the board, for example: 32 + 10 = 42, ¼ × 32 = 8.

Variations

- Use the second 'Target boards' slide.
- Change the content in either of the target boards.
- Present the children with a target board where some of the boxes are empty. Ask the children to suggest the content for the missing boxes.

Number and place value

Addition and subtraction facts

Multiplication and division facts

Hand me your cards

Objectives

- Find 10 or 100 more or less than a given number (Game 1)
- Recognise the place value of each digit in a 2-, 3- or 4-digit number (Game 2)
- Order and compare numbers beyond 1000 (Game 3)
- Recall and use addition and subtraction facts to 20 fluently, and derive and use related facts up to 100 / Add numbers mentally, including adding three 1-digit numbers (Game 4)
- Add and subtract numbers mentally, including a 2-digit number and ones, a 2-digit number and tens and two 2-digit numbers (Game 5)
- Add and subtract numbers mentally, including a 3-digit number and ones, a 3-digit number and tens and a 3-digit number and hundreds (Game 6)
- Recall multiplication and division facts for the 2, 5 and 10 multiplication tables (Game 7)
- Recall multiplication and division facts for the 2, 3, 4, 5, 8 and 10 multiplication tables (Game 8)
- Recall multiplication and division facts for multiplication tables up to 12 × 12 (Game 9)

Teacher resources

- ‘Hand me your cards’ Teacher’s call card

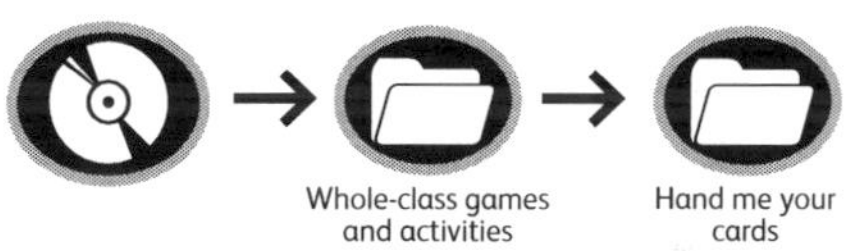

Pupil resources

- ‘Hand me your cards’ (the white and grey answer cards, ideally printed onto card)

What to do

- Choose the appropriate game for the objective(s) you want the children to practise and consolidate (see above).
- Arrange the class into four teams.
- Separately shuffle and distribute the white and grey answer cards. Each team must have nine answer cards – either all white cards or all grey answer cards. Depending on the number of children in the class, some children may have more than one card. Cards with the Challenge 1 icon denote the answer to an easier question. Cards with the Challenge 3 icon denote the answer to a more difficult question.
- Read out the ‘What to say’ questions from the Teacher’s call card (but not the answers!). Read the questions from the top to the bottom of each column, asking all the questions in the left-hand column first, then all the questions in the right-hand column. Note that there are two answer cards for each number, to ensure there is competition to ‘be the first’ to call out the answer.

(continued)

- The first child who has the correct answer on their card, and who calls out this answer, hands their card to the teacher. Team members may assist each other, but only the child that is holding the card can call out the answer.
- Once a child has handed in his/her card(s), they may still assist their team members with the remaining cards. As before, however, he/she is not allowed to call out the answer to the teacher – only the child that is holding the card can call it out.
- Continue asking the questions from the Teacher's call card.
- The winner is the first team with all their answer cards handed in.
- Continue to play the game to see which teams come second and third.

Variations

- Arrange the class into different number of teams:
  - two teams, giving each team 18 cards
  - three teams, giving each team 12 cards (**Note:** One team will have six white answer cards and six grey answer cards)
  - six teams, giving each team six cards.
- Read the questions from the bottom to the top of each column, asking the questions in the left-hand column first, then the questions in the right-hand column. Or ask the questions in the right-hand column first.
- Put the answer cards in the middle of the table so the group can help each other from the start.

Number and place value

Addition and subtraction facts

Multiplication and division facts

Loop cards

Objectives

- Find 10 or 100 more or less than a given number (Game 1)
- Recognise the place value of each digit in a 2-, 3- or 4-digit number (Game 2)
- Order and compare numbers beyond 1000 (Game 3)
- Recall and use addition and subtraction facts to 20 fluently, and derive and use related facts up to 100 / Add numbers mentally, including adding three 1-digit numbers (Game 4)
- Add and subtract numbers mentally, including a 2-digit number and ones, a 2-digit number and tens and two 2-digit numbers (Game 5)
- Add and subtract numbers mentally, including a 3-digit number and ones, a 3-digit number and tens and a 3-digit number and hundreds (Game 6)
- Recall multiplication and division facts for the 2, 5 and 10 multiplication tables (Game 7)
- Recall multiplication and division facts for the 2, 3, 4, 5, 8 and 10 multiplication tables (Game 8)
- Recall multiplication and division facts for multiplication tables up to 12 × 12 (Game 9)

Teacher resources

- none

Pupil resources

- 'Loop cards' (ideally printed onto card)

→ Whole-class games and activities → Loop cards

What to do

- Choose the appropriate game for the objective(s) you want the children to practise and consolidate (see above).
- Shuffle the cards and hand them out to the children. Every card must be used, so if necessary give some children more than one card. Cards with the Challenge 1 icon denote the answer to an easier question. Cards with the Challenge 3 icon denote the answer to a more difficult question.
- Decide who will start the game (the game can begin with any card).
- The first player reads aloud the text on the right-hand side of the card, for example: *Who has 13 plus 7?*
- The rest of the children work out the answer, and the child who has the correct answer on the left-hand side of their card reads it out, for example: *I have 20.* If the answer is correct, that player then reads the text on the right-hand side of their card, for example: *Who has 9 subtract 5?*
- The game continues in this way.
- The game ends when the child who started the game reads out the answer on the left-hand side of their card.

Variation

- To encourage a brisk pace and increase fluency, use a timer and display the 'time to beat'.

Number and place value

Addition and subtraction facts

Multiplication and division facts

Around the room

Objectives

- Count in multiples of 1, 2, 3, 4, 5, 6, 7, 8, 9, 10, 11, 12, 25, 50, 100 and 1000 from any number, forward or backward
- Recognise the place value of each digit in a 2-, 3- or 4-digit number and a decimal number with up to two decimal places
- Order and compare numbers up to, and beyond 1000, and decimals numbers with up to two decimal places
- Find 10 or 100 more or less than a given number
- Round any number to the nearest 10, 100 or 1000
- Recall and use addition and subtraction facts to 20 fluently, and derive and use related facts up to 100
- Add and subtract numbers mentally, including a 2-digit number and ones, a 2-digit number and tens, two 2-digit numbers, a 3-digit number and ones, a 3-digit number and tens, and a 3-digit number and hundreds
- Recall multiplication and division facts for multiplication tables up to 12 × 12

Teacher resources

- none

Pupil resources

- none

What to do

- Children either sit in a circle or at their tables as long as there is a logical 'path' from one child/table to the next.
- Ask one child to go and stand behind the child who is sitting next to them.
- Ask an appropriate question to these two children, for example: *What is the next number in this pattern: 200, 225, 250, 275, 300…? What is the value of the 6 in 4651? Which is larger: 569 or 596? What is 100 more than 345? What is 76 rounded to the nearest multiple of 10? What is 450 add 30? What is 9 multiplied by 12?*
- If the child who is standing calls out the correct answer first, they move and stand behind the next child.
- If the child that is sitting calls out the correct answer first, they stand up and go behind the next child. The child that was just standing sits in the place of the child they were just standing behind.
- The game continues in this way around the room.
- When you have gone around the class say: *All change!* and children go back to their original positions.

Number and place value

Addition and subtraction facts

Multiplication and division facts

One name left

Objectives

- Count in multiples of 1, 2, 3, 4, 5, 6, 7, 8, 9, 10, 11, 12, 25, 50, 100 and 1000 from any number, forward or backward
- Recognise the place value of each digit in a 2-, 3- or 4-digit number and a decimal number with up to two decimal places
- Order and compare numbers up to, and beyond 1000, and decimals numbers with up to two decimal places
- Find 10 or 100 more or less than a given number
- Round any number to the nearest 10, 100 or 1000
- Recall and use addition and subtraction facts to 20 fluently, and derive and use related facts up to 100
- Add and subtract numbers mentally, including a 2-digit number and ones, a 2-digit number and tens, two 2-digit numbers, a 3-digit number and ones, a 3-digit number and tens, and a 3-digit number and hundreds
- Recall multiplication and division facts for multiplication tables up to 12 × 12

Teacher resources

- small box or container

Pupil resources

- small slip of paper or card (per child)
- pencil (per child)

What to do

- Ask the children to write their name on the small slip of paper or card and fold it in half.
- Collect the slips and put them into the box or container.
- Choose two names from the box.
- Ask these two children to stand.
- Ask an appropriate question to these two children, for example: *What is the next number in this pattern: 600, 550, 500, 450…? What is the value of the 8 in 587? Which is smaller: 5968 or 5698? What is 10 less than 4201? What is 687 rounded to the nearest multiple of 100? What is 45 add 12? What is 6 multiplied by 7?*
- For the child who answers correctly first, put their slip of paper into a 'still in' pile. For the child who answers incorrectly, or is beaten on speed by the other child, put their card in an 'out' pile.
- Continuing choosing two names from the box and asking a question.
- When all the names have been chosen from the box, put the children's names that are in the 'still in' pile back into the box.
- Continue the game as before, choosing two names, asking a question and putting the names into 'still in' and 'out' piles.
- Continue the game until only two children, then finally one child is left.

Whole-class games and activities

Number and place value

Addition and subtraction facts

Multiplication and division facts

Whispers

Objectives

- Find 10 or 100 more or less than a given number
- Recall and use addition and subtraction facts to 20 fluently, and derive and use related facts up to 100
- Add and subtract numbers mentally, including a 2-digit number and ones, a 2-digit number and tens, two 2-digit numbers, a 3-digit number and ones, a 3-digit number and tens, and a 3-digit number and hundreds
- Recall multiplication and division facts for multiplication tables up to 12 × 12

Teacher resources

- small slip of paper or card with an appropriate question written on it, for example: 320 + 10 = , 12 + 6 = , 18 – 13 = , 6 × 4 = , 42 ÷ 7 = …

Pupil resources

- none

What to do

- Arrange the class into two or three teams. Ideally, there should be the same number of children in each team.
- Each team stands or sits in a line.
- Secretly show the first child in each team the slip of paper or card showing an appropriate question written on it, for example: 12 + 6 = .
- When the first child in each team has seen the slip of paper say *Go!*
- The first child then works out the answer to the question and thinks of a different question that has the same answer, for example: 20 – 2. They then whisper this calculation to the second child in the line.
- The second child works out the answer, thinks of a different question with the same answer and whispers this calculation to the third child in the line.
- The activity continues as described above.
- When the last child in each team has worked out the answer to the question they are given, they call out the answer. Does the last child's answer match the original question on the slip of paper? If so, this is a winning team.

Variation

- An easier version is to show the first child in each team a number, which teams then whisper to each other.

Number and place value

Addition and subtraction facts

Multiplication and division facts

Folding numbers

Objectives

- Count in multiples of 1, 2, 3, 4, 5, 6, 7, 8, 9, 10, 11, 12, 25, 50, 100 and 1000 from any number, forward or backward
- Recognise the place value of each digit in a 2-, 3- or 4-digit number
- Order and compare numbers up to, and beyond 1000
- Find 10 or 100 more or less than a given number
- Round any number to the nearest 10, 100 or 1000
- Recall and use addition and subtraction facts to 20 fluently, and derive and use related facts up to 100
- Add and subtract numbers mentally, including a 2-digit number and ones, a 2-digit number and tens, two 2-digit numbers, a 3-digit number and ones, a 3-digit number and tens, and a 3-digit number and hundreds
- Recall multiplication and division facts for multiplication tables up to 12 × 12

Teacher resources

- none

Pupil resources

- *The first time you do this activity:* coloured pencils, crayons, and/or felt-tips, sheet of A4 paper (per child and yourself)

Note to the teacher

This activity is not just about children answering mathematical questions. More importantly, it is about encouraging children to *ask* mathematical questions.

What to do – The first time you do this activity

- Provide each child, and yourself, with a sheet of A4 paper and each group with some coloured pencils, crayons and/or felt-tips.
- Demonstrate and ask the children to:
  - place their sheet of paper in the landscape position on the table in front of them
  - write their name in large writing in the middle of the sheet of paper.
- Demonstrate and ask the children to:

Easier version:

  - fold their sheet of paper in half, top to bottom (it doesn't matter whether the writing is on the inside or the outside of the fold)
  - fold their sheet of paper a second time, side to side
  - fold their sheet of paper a third time, top to bottom.

More challenging version:

  - fold their sheet of paper a fourth time, side to side.

(continued)

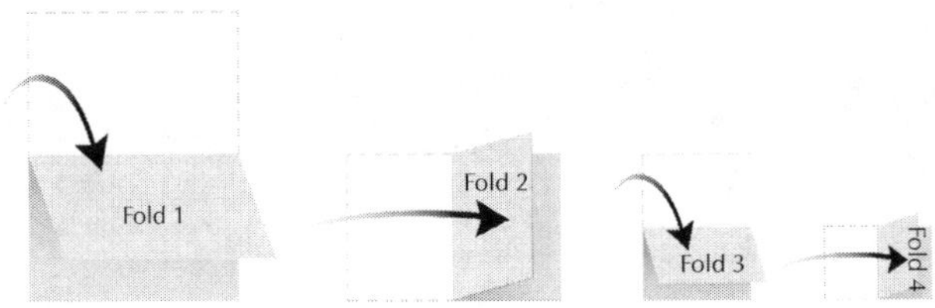

(More challenging version only)

- Demonstrate and ask the children to open out their sheet of paper to the blank side (not the side that has their name written on it). For the easier version there should be eight small rectangles; for the more challenging version there should 16 small rectangles.

Easier version:

- Demonstrate and ask the children to use the coloured pencils, crayons, and/or felt-tips to write neatly, in large writing, each of the numbers 1 to 8, in any order, one number in each small rectangle, for example:

3	5	7	2
8	1	4	6

More challenging version:

- Demonstrate and ask the children to write, in large writing, each of the digits 0 to 9, in any order, one number in each small rectangle. Then in the six remaining empty rectangles, to repeat any six of the numbers, for example:

9		6	2
5	1		
		3	8
4	7	0	

→

9	8	6	2
5	1	9	4
2	6	3	8
4	7	0	5

- Once all the children have done this, ask them to look carefully at the numbers on their sheet.
- Demonstrate to the children how the sheet of paper can be folded to show different 1-digit, 2-digit and 3-digit numbers.

5

4	7

9
3

6	3	8

1
6
7

- Next, ask the children to fold their sheet of paper to show you the number 6.
- Repeat several times asking questions similar to the following until the children are confident in folding their sheet of paper in different ways to display different 1-digit, 2-digit and 3-digit numbers.
  - *Show me a number greater than 182.*
  - *Show me any 3-digit even number.*
  - *Show me an odd number less than 800.*
- Once children are confident in using their 'Folding numbers' sheet, demonstrate the following to the class, asking a confident child to come out to the front to be your partner:
  - Look at the child's 'Folding numbers' sheet and ask them a question similar to those above where the answer can be displayed on their 'Folding numbers' sheet.
  - Once the child has done this successfully, ask them to look carefully at your 'Folding numbers' sheet and to ask you a question where the answer can be displayed on your 'Folding numbers' sheet.
  - Repeat if necessary, being sure to demonstrate more open-ended types of questions to the class.
- Once children are familiar with this, arrange them into pairs.
- Tell the children to take turns in asking each other questions where the answer can be displayed on their partner's 'Folding numbers' sheet. Remind the children that they need to think carefully about what questions to ask, as their partner must be able to show the answer on their 'Folding numbers' sheet.
- After a sufficient length of time, bring the class back together again and discuss with the children the range of questions that they asked. It is important to elicit from the children the difference between a 'poor' question, for example: *Can you show me the number 145?*, and a 'good' question, for example: *Can you show me a number between 120 and 150?*
- Keep the 'Folding numbers' sheets for when you revisit the activity.

What to do – Revisiting the activity

- Ask the children to look at their 'Folding numbers' sheets again.
- Ask pairs to take turns in asking each other questions where the answer can be displayed on their partner's 'Folding numbers' sheet. Remind the children that they need to think carefully about what questions to ask, as their partner must be able to show the answer on their 'Folding numbers' sheet.
- After a sufficient length of time, bring the class back together again and briefly discuss the activity with the children.
- Keep the 'Folding numbers' sheets for the next time you revisit the activity.

Whole-class, group or individual activities

Number and place value

Addition and subtraction facts

Multiplication and division facts

Written activities

Objectives

- Order and compare numbers up to, and beyond 1000, and decimal numbers with up to two decimal places
- Find 10 or 100 more or less than a given number
- Recall and use addition and subtraction facts to 20 fluently, and derive and use related facts up to 100
- Add and subtract numbers mentally, including a 2-digit number and ones, a 2-digit number and tens, two 2-digit numbers, a 3-digit number and ones, a 3-digit number and tens, and a 3-digit number and hundreds
- Recall multiplication and division facts for multiplication tables up to 12 × 12

Teacher resources

→ Written activities

- scissors

Pupil resources

- Written activities sheet (per child)
- pencil (per child)

Introduction

Fluency in Number Facts: Years 3 & 4 includes a set of Written Activities, presented as templates. They are aimed at providing children with further practice and consolidation and also at offering teachers a means of assessing individual children's proficiency in number. They can be used with the whole class, specific groups or individual children.

Although designed to be reproduced onto sheets of A4 paper, many of the templates show the same type of activity presented three times with the following icons used to allow for differentiation: Challenge 1 (easy), Challenge 2 (average) and Challenge 3 (challenging). The intention is that once the teacher has filled in and copied the template that these are then cut into smaller pieces of paper for the children to complete. However, even for those templates that do not include these differentiation icons, these Written activities can also be adapted easily to meet a range of abilities. It is important therefore that these Written activities are viewed as generic worksheets that teachers fill in and adapt in order to meet the different needs and abilities of their children.

Whole-class, group or individual activities

It is envisaged that, whether it be one of the full A4 activities (for example, '16 calculations', '49 calculations' or '100 calculations') or one of the activities that are presented to the children on a smaller piece of paper (for example, 'Across and up', 'Calculation boxes' or 'Dice calculations'), each Written activity should take no longer than ten minutes for the children to complete. Alternatively, to encourage speed and recall, set the children to work, and as they finish the activity they raise their hand and you tell them how long it took them to complete it.

It is recommended that children do the same type of activity (perhaps even involving the same numbers) on two or three consecutive days. This way, the majority of children will see themselves making progress over the two or three days, thus providing greater encouragement and self-motivation.

What to do

- Choose an appropriate Written activity for the whole class, specific groups or individual children, taking careful consideration of the different needs and abilities of the children.
- Fill in the template on screen, then name this version and save it to use again later on. Alternatively, print one copy of the template and fill it in by hand. Detailed guidance regarding possible differentiated content (Challenge 1 Challenge 2 Challenge 3) to use for each of the templates is given below on pages 150–169.
- Once filled in, photocopy as many copies as is required for the number of children you want to complete the Written activity. If required, cut the sheets into two or three smaller strips of paper.
- Distribute the activities to the children taking care to provide each child with the appropriate differentiated version of the activity. Also ensure that each child has a sharpened pencil!
- If it is the first time that children are doing one of the Written activities, spend time explaining how to do the activity. If appropriate, display the saved template on the interactive whiteboard (IWB) to help with the explanation.
- Allow the children approximately ten minutes to complete the activity or set the activity as a timed exercise.
- Once the children have finished, immediately mark the activity. You may want to mark the activity with the children's help, asking children to mark their own sheet or swapping and marking someone else's sheet.
- Be sure to discuss the results of the activity with the children, asking them which questions they found easy, which they found more difficult, and also referring to specific questions, asking them how they worked out the answer. This should provide some excellent data to help identify common errors or misconceptions that children may have. You can then either follow on with some brief impromptu teaching, assisting children to overcome the errors or misconceptions or, alternatively, keep this information in mind for some further teaching at a later date.
- And finally…remember to repeat the same type of activity (perhaps even involving the same numbers) on two or three consecutive days.

Whole-class, group or individual activities

Order the numbers

Number and place value

Notes for the teacher

- Children need to be familiar with the traditional 1–100 number square in order to complete this activity successfully.
- The second Challenge 1 example on page 151 as well as the Challenge 2 and Challenge 3 examples, are all sections from number squares other than a 1–100 number square. Children also need to be familiar with these types of number squares in order to complete these grids successfully.

Challenge 1 101–200 number square

101	102	103	104	105	106	107	108	109	110
111	112	113	114	115	116	117	118	119	120
121	122	123	124	125	126	127	128	129	130
131	132	133	134	135	136	137	138	139	140
141	142	143	144	145	146	147	148	149	150
151	152	153	154	155	156	157	158	159	160
161	162	163	164	165	166	167	168	169	170
171	172	173	174	175	176	177	178	179	180
181	182	183	184	185	186	187	188	189	190
191	192	193	194	195	196	197	198	199	200

Challenge 2 10–1000 multiples of 10 number square

10	20	30	40	50	60	70	80	90	100
110	120	130	140	150	160	170	180	190	200
210	220	230	240	250	260	270	280	290	300
310	320	330	340	350	360	370	380	390	400
410	420	430	440	450	460	470	480	490	500
510	520	530	540	550	560	570	580	590	600
610	620	630	640	650	660	670	680	690	700
710	720	730	740	750	760	770	780	790	800
810	820	830	840	850	860	870	880	890	900
910	920	930	940	950	960	970	980	990	1000

Challenge 2 0.1–10 number square

0.1	0.2	0.3	0.4	0.5	0.6	0.7	0.8	0.9	1
1.1	1.2	1.3	1.4	1.5	1.6	1.7	1.8	1.9	2
2.1	2.2	2.3	2.4	2.5	2.6	2.7	2.8	2.9	3
3.1	3.2	3.3	3.4	3.5	3.6	3.7	3.8	3.9	4
4.1	4.2	4.3	4.4	4.5	4.6	4.7	4.8	4.9	5
5.1	5.2	5.3	5.4	5.5	5.6	5.7	5.8	5.9	6
6.1	6.2	6.3	6.4	6.5	6.6	6.7	6.8	6.9	7
7.1	7.2	7.3	7.4	7.5	7.6	7.7	7.8	7.9	8
8.1	8.2	8.3	8.4	8.5	8.6	8.7	8.8	8.9	9
9.1	9.2	9.3	9.4	9.5	9.6	9.7	9.8	9.9	10

Challenge 3 0.01–1 number square

0.01	0.02	0.03	0.04	0.05	0.06	0.07	0.08	0.09	0.1
0.11	0.12	0.13	0.14	0.15	0.16	0.17	0.18	0.19	0.2
0.21	0.22	0.23	0.24	0.25	0.26	0.27	0.28	0.29	0.3
0.31	0.32	0.33	0.34	0.35	0.36	0.37	0.38	0.39	0.4
0.41	0.42	0.43	0.44	0.45	0.46	0.47	0.48	0.49	0.5
0.51	0.52	0.53	0.54	0.55	0.56	0.57	0.58	0.59	0.6
0.61	0.62	0.63	0.64	0.65	0.66	0.67	0.68	0.69	0.7
0.71	0.72	0.73	0.74	0.75	0.76	0.77	0.78	0.79	0.8
0.81	0.82	0.83	0.84	0.85	0.86	0.87	0.88	0.89	0.9
0.91	0.92	0.93	0.94	0.95	0.96	0.97	0.98	0.99	1

Challenge 3 1–100 number square (different sequence)

1	2	3	4	5	6	7	8	9	10
20	19	18	17	16	15	14	13	12	11
21	22	23	24	25	26	27	28	29	30
40	39	38	37	36	35	34	33	32	31
41	42	43	44	45	46	47	48	49	50
60	59	58	57	56	55	54	53	52	51
61	62	63	64	65	66	67	68	69	70
80	79	78	77	76	75	74	73	72	71
81	82	83	84	85	86	87	88	89	90
100	99	98	97	96	95	94	93	92	91

- For each grid, write four or five numbers, making sure that you write the numbers in the correct positions as located on the appropriate number square.

Notes for the children

- Ensure children understand that each of the grids is a different section from a specific number square. Some of the numbers have been given, and they need to work out which numbers belong in the empty squares.

Whole-class, group or individual activities

Example of differentiation content

Challenge 1

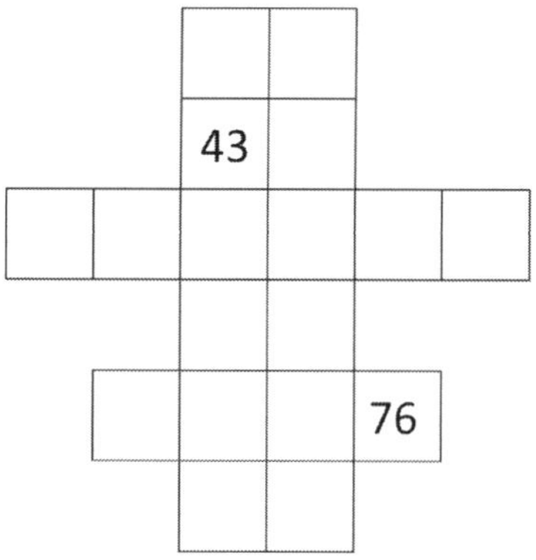

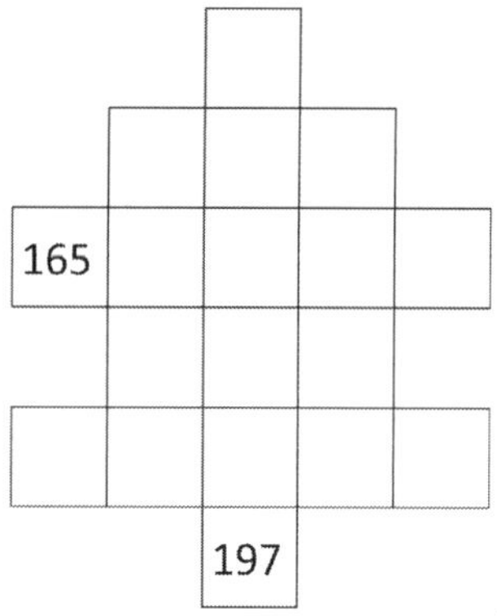

Variations

- If necessary, provide children with the appropriate number square to consult.
- Provide the children with more numbers already on the grid.

Challenge 2

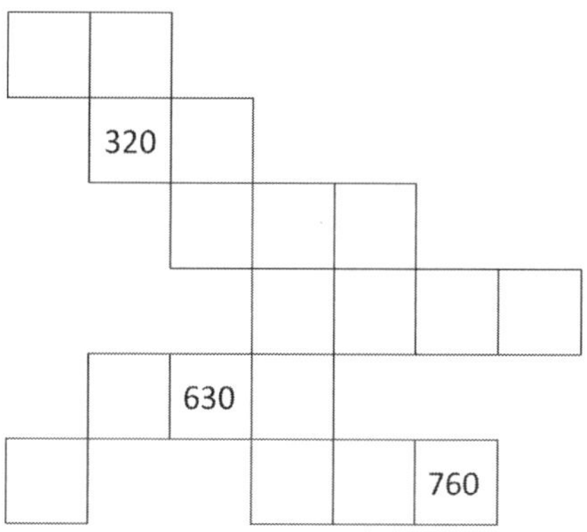

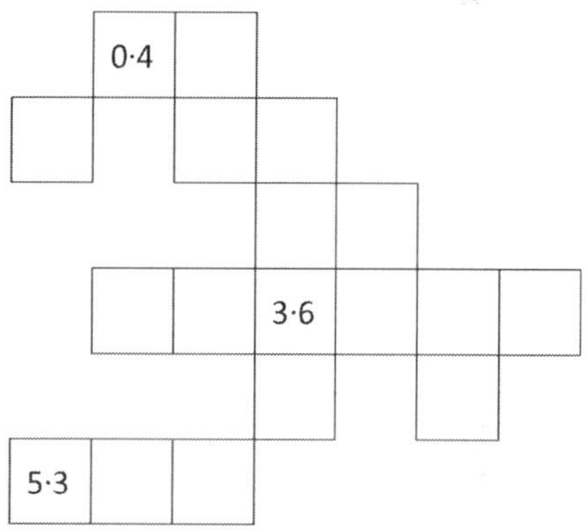

Challenge 3

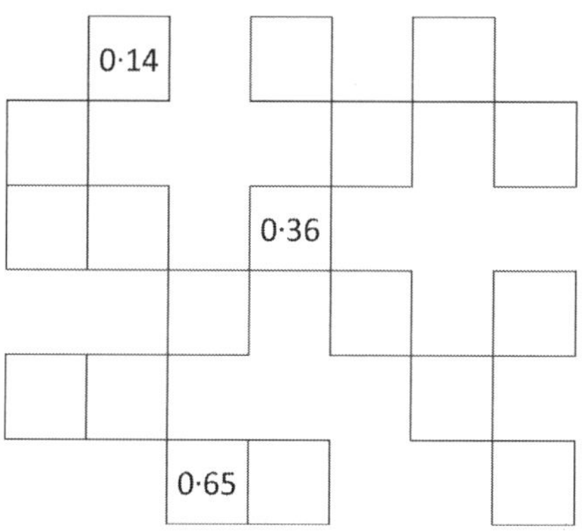

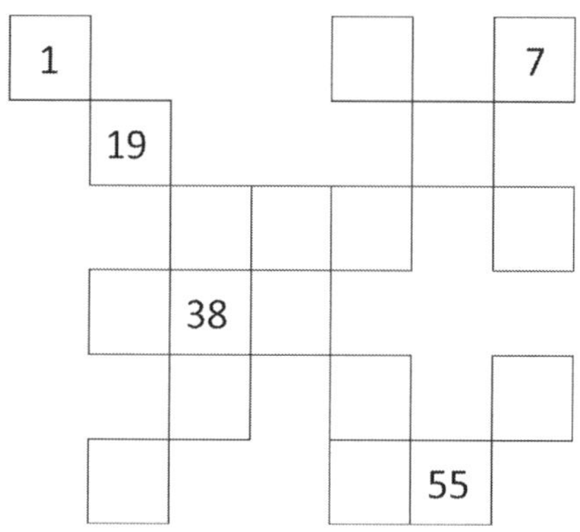

Variations

- Provide the children with fewer numbers already on the grid.
- Provide the children with one of the grids with no numbers on it and ask them to write four numbers on it to make their own 'Order the numbers' grid for a friend to solve.

Whole-class, group or individual activities

Across and up

Addition and subtraction

Notes for the teacher

- This activity is ideal for practising and consolidating the concepts of 1, 10 or 100 more or less.
- For each grid write:
  - a number in the grey box
  - an operation (addition or subtraction symbol followed by a number) on each of the arrows
  - two or three answers in the other boxes on the grid.
- When children have completed the grids, discuss with them any patterns and relationships they notice.

Notes for the children

- Ensure children understand that to complete each grid they start with the number in the grey box and to this number they perform the operations given on the arrows, writing the answers in the appropriate boxes on the grid. They continue across and up the grid performing subsequent operations on the previous numbers written on the boxes, for example:

↑ +5

30	38	46	54
25	33	41	49
20	28	36	44
15	23	31	39

→ +8

Example of differentiation content

Variations

Challenge 1

↑ +2

			22
3			
1	6		

→ + 5

↑ − 3

		10	
17			
20	18		

→ − 2

- Ensure that all answers are less than 100.
- Provide the children with more answers already on each grid.

Whole-class, group or individual activities

Challenge 2

↑ + 5 → + 8

		46	
25			
15	23		

↑ − 6 → − 9

			42
75			
87		69	

Challenge 3

↑ + 4 → − 6

		48	
			34
48			

↑ − 23 → + 12

45			
		92	
91			

Variations

- Provide the children with fewer (or no) answers already on each grid.
- Include calculations that involve adding or subtracting a 2-digit number and ones, a 2-digit number and tens, two 2-digit numbers, a 3-digit number and ones, a 3-digit number and tens or a 3-digit number and hundreds.
- Provide the children with grids with operations written on them, but no numbers in the grey boxes. The children write in their own numbers in the grey boxes and then complete the grids.

Whole-class, group or individual activities

Calculations grid (small)

Calculations grid (large)

Addition and subtraction

Multiplication

Notes for the teacher

- There are two versions of this activity. The three examples given below are for the 'Calculations grid (small)' version. However, the same principles apply to the 'Calculations grid (large)' version.
- For each grid write:
  - the addition, subtraction or multiplication symbol in the grey box in the top left-hand corner of the grid
  - numbers in each of the boxes in the top row and the left-hand column of the grid.
  - two or three of the answers on the grid.
- Note that for the Challenge 3 example on page 155, teachers need to complete the grid and then carefully delete some of the answers and numbers in the top row and left-hand column, ensuring that the numbers remaining are sufficient for the children to fill in all the missing numbers on the grid. This version helps children develop their understanding of the inverse relationship between addition and subtraction, and multiplication and division.
- When children have completed the grids, discuss with them any patterns and relationships they notice.

Notes for the children

- Ensure children understand that to complete each grid they start with the number in the left-hand column of the grid, perform the operation given in the grey box then add, subtract or multiply the number in the top row, writing the answer in the appropriate box on the grid.
- Although it makes no difference for grids involving addition or multiplication (commutative law), for subtraction grids, it is important that children get into the habit of always starting with the numbers down the left-hand column rather than the numbers in the top row.

−	6	2	9	4
56	50	54	47	52
42	36	40	33	38
83	77	81	74	79
78	72	76	69	74

Whole-class, group or individual activities

Example of differentiation content

Challenge 1

+	8	13	5	11
3	11			
2				
6				17
8		21		

Variations

- Ensure that all answers are less than 100 or involve adding or subtracting combinations of 1-digit and 2-digit numbers.
- Provide the children with more answers already on each grid.

Challenge 2

–	6	2	9	4
56	50			
42				
83				
78			69	

Challenge 3

+		62	19	
23	57			
		103		
			67	
75				155

Variations

- Provide the children with fewer (or no) answers already on each grid.
- Include calculations that involve adding or subtracting a 2-digit number and ones, a 2-digit number and tens, two 2-digit numbers, a 3-digit number and ones, a 3-digit number and tens or a 3-digit number and hundreds.
- Include calculations that involve multiplying multiples of 10 by 1-digit numbers, for example, 40 × 6.

Whole-class, group or individual activities

Calculation boxes

Addition

Multiplication

Notes for the teacher

- For each grid write:
  - four numbers in the boxes as shown in the Challenge 1 and Challenge 2 examples on page 157
  - the addition or multiplication symbol in the circle at the top.
- Note that for the Challenge 3 example, teachers need to complete the grid and then carefully delete some of the numbers, ensuring that the numbers remaining are sufficient for the children to fill in all the missing numbers on the grid. This version helps children develop their understanding of the inverse relationship between addition and subtraction, and multiplication and division.
- Also note that for 'Calculation boxes' involving multiplication, that at this stage it is advised to write only numbers less than 7 in the four boxes.
- When children have completed the grids, discuss with them any patterns and relationships they notice.

Notes for the children

- Ensure children understand that to complete each grid they:
  - add (or multiply) pairs of numbers in each row, for example, 23 + 14 = 37 and 31 + 52 = 83, writing the answers in the appropriate spaces
  - add (or multiply) pairs of numbers in each column, for example, 23 + 31 = 54 and 14 + 52 = 66, writing the answers in the appropriate spaces;
  - add (or multiply) the two answers in the right-hand column, i.e. 37 + 83 = 120 and write this answer in the grey box.
- If they are correct, this is also the answer to the sum (or product) of the two numbers in the bottom row, i.e. 54 + 66 = 120.
- Note that children can complete the final part of the activity by adding (or multiplying) the two answers in the bottom row first, writing this answer in the grey box, and then adding (or multiplying) the two answers in the right-hand column to check.

	+	
23	14	37
31	52	83
54	66	120

Whole-class, group or individual activities

Example of differentiation content

Challenge 1

(+)

14	8	
6	10	
		(grey)

Variations

- Ensure that the final total in the grey box is less than 100.
- Provide the children with the final total in the grey box.

Challenge 2

(+)

23	14	
31	52	
		(grey)

Challenge 3

(+)

35		
	18	44
	41	(grey)

Variations

- Include calculations that involve adding a 2-digit number and ones, a 2-digit number and tens, two 2-digit numbers, a 3-digit number and ones, a 3-digit number and tens or a 3-digit number and hundreds.
- For 'Calculation boxes' involving multiplication include examples similar to the following. This version helps children develop their understanding of the inverse relationship between multiplication and division.

(×)

	6	30
3		
	12	(grey)

Whole-class, group or individual activities

Calculation strips

Addition and subtraction

Multiplication and division

Notes for the teacher

- For each strip write:
  - an operation (addition, subtraction, multiplication or division symbol followed by a number) in the circle
  - a number in each of the boxes down the left-hand side of the strip
  - one or two answers down the right-hand side of the strip.
- The star at the bottom of each strip can either be used for the children to write their score out of 10, or if you are timing the activity, the time it took them to complete it.
- Note that for the Challenge 3 example, teachers need to complete the strip and then delete one number from either the left- or right-hand side of the strip. This version helps children develop their understanding of the inverse relationship between addition and subtraction, or multiplication and division.
- Also note that for 'Calculation strips' involving division that, depending on what numbers you use, children may have answers with remainders.
- When children have completed the strips, discuss with them any patterns and relationships they notice.

Notes for the children

- Ensure children understand that to complete each strip, they perform the operation given in the circle on each of the ten numbers down the left-hand side of the strip, writing each answer in the box to the right.

+16

13	29
87	103
41	57

Example of differentiation content

Challenge 1

×4

2	
12	
5	
9	36
11	
4	
7	
3	
8	
6	

☆

Variations

- Ensure that all answers are less than 100.
- Provide the children with several answers down the right-hand side of the strip.

Whole-class, group or individual activities

Challenge 2

+ 16

13	
87	
41	
29	
65	
92	108
38	
46	
54	
76	

☆

Challenge 3

− 23

51	
29	6
	10
	19
94	
67	
	55
69	
	23
85	

☆

Variations

- Don't provide the children with any answers down the right-hand side of the strip.
- Include calculations that involve adding or subtracting a 2-digit number and ones, a 2-digit number and tens, two 2-digit numbers, a 3-digit number and ones, a 3-digit number and tens or a 3-digit number and hundreds.
- Include calculations that involve the multiplication tables up to 12 × 12 or multiplying multiples of 10 by 1-digit numbers, for example, 40 × 6.

Whole-class, group or individual activities

Calculation walls

Addition and subtraction

Notes for the teacher

- For each wall write:
  - three numbers in the 'bricks' as shown in the Challenge 1 and Challenge 2 examples below and on page 161.
  - the operation (+ or –) in the circle at the top.
- Note the following:
  - For the Challenge 3 example, teachers need to complete the wall and then carefully delete some of the numbers, ensuring that the numbers remaining are sufficient for the children to fill in all the missing numbers on the wall. This version helps children develop their understanding of the inverse relationship between addition and subtraction.
  - For 'Calculation walls' involving subtraction, children need to see subtraction as *finding the difference.*
- When children have completed the walls, discuss with them any patterns and relationships they notice.

Notes for the children

- Ensure children understand that to complete each wall they:
  - add (subtract) adjacent pairs of numbers in the bottom row, for example, 45 + 27 = 72 and 27 + 58 = 85, writing the answers in the 'bricks' immediately above each pair of numbers
  - add (subtract) adjacent pairs of numbers in the remaining row(s), for example, 72 + 85 = 157, writing the answer(s) in the 'brick(s)' immediately above this pair / each pairs of numbers
  - write the final answer in the 'brick' at the top of each wall.

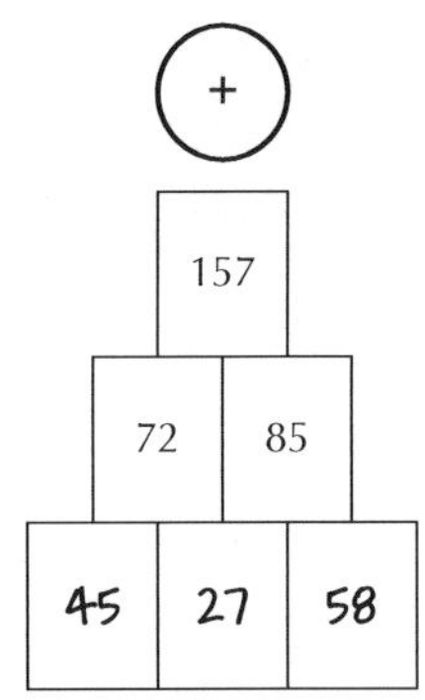

Example of differentiation content

Challenge 1

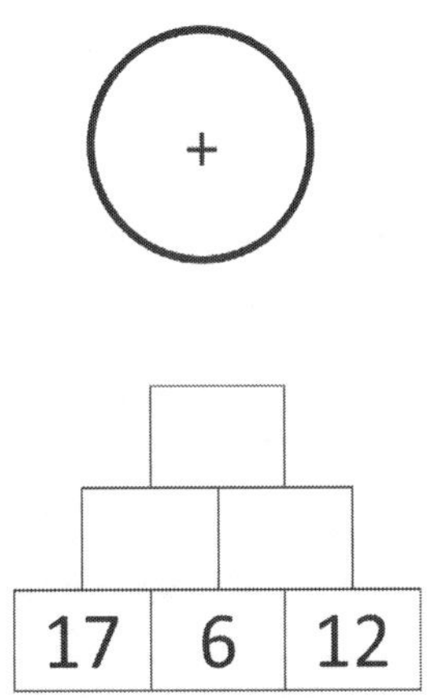

Variations

- Ensure that answers in the top 'brick' are less than 100.
- Provide the children with the final total in the top 'brick'.

Whole-class, group or individual activities

Challenge 2

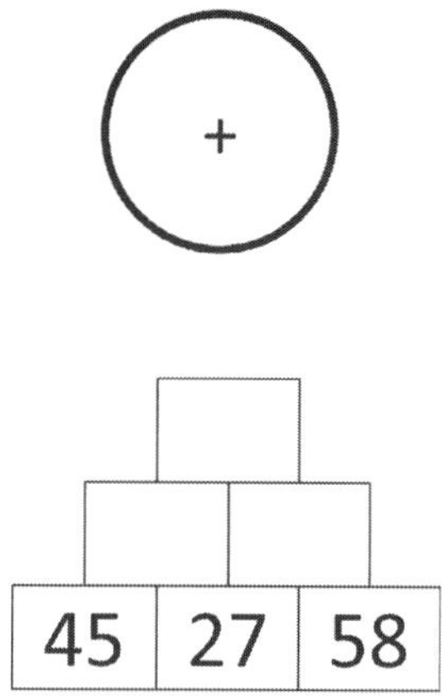

Challenge 3

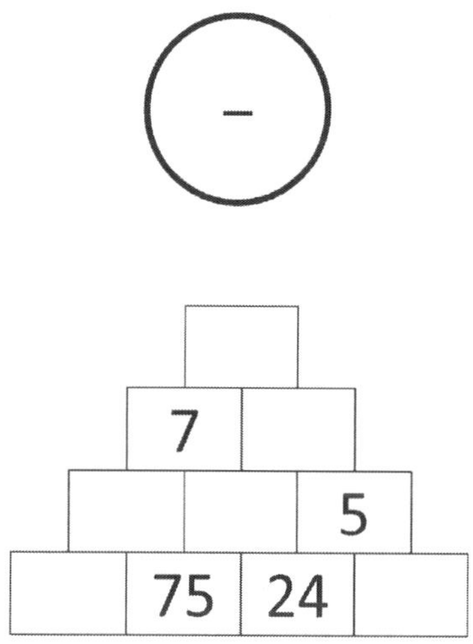

Variations

- Include calculations that involve adding or subtracting a 2-digit number and ones, a 2-digit number and tens, two 2-digit numbers, a 3-digit number and ones, a 3-digit number and tens or a 3-digit number and hundreds.
- Where appropriate, discuss with the children how some 'Calculation walls' involving subtraction can have different solutions, for example:

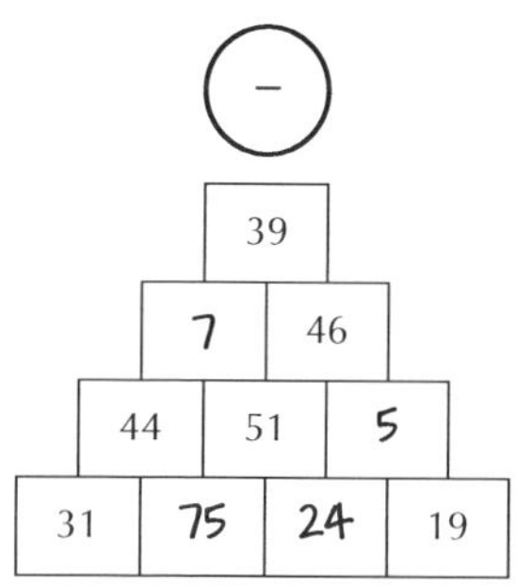

or

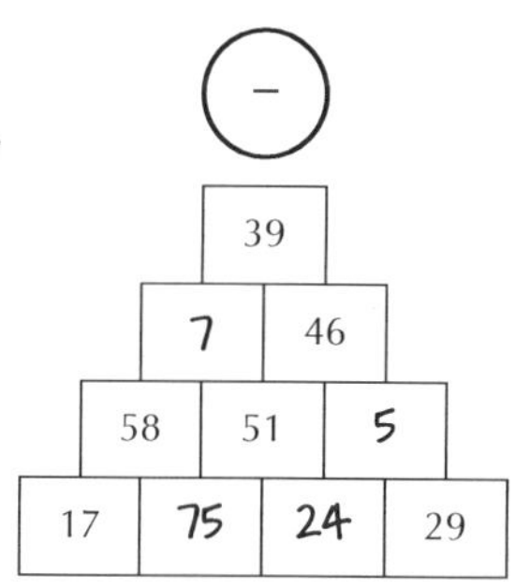

Whole-class, group or individual activities

Number chains

Addition and subtraction

Additional resources

- 1–6, 0–9, 1–12 or 1–20 dice (per child)

Notes for the teacher

- For each chain write a number in the grey box.
- This activity can be differentiated not only by the number you write in the grey box, but also by the dice you give the children to use.
- For 'Number chains' involving subtraction ensure that the final answer in the circle will not be a negative number.

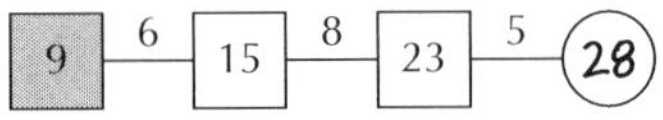

Notes for the children

- Children roll the dice, write the number rolled on the line to the right of the grey box, add (subtract) the dice number to the number in the grey box and write the answer in the first white box.
- The chain continues in this way, with the child rolling the dice, writing the number rolled on the line, adding (subtracting) the dice number to (or from) the number in the previous white box and writing the answer in the next white box.
- Each chain finishes when the child writes the final answer in the circle.

Example of differentiation content

Challenge 1

Challenge 2

Challenge 3

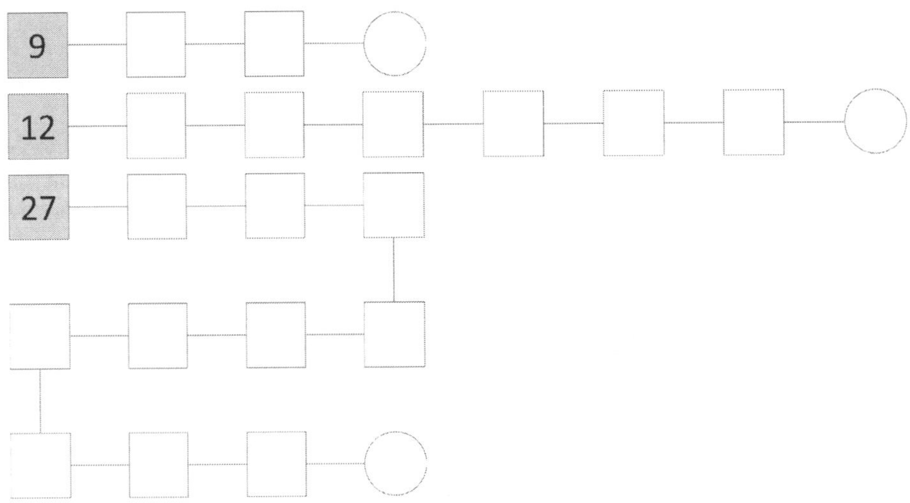

Challenge 1 Challenge 2 Challenge 3

Variations

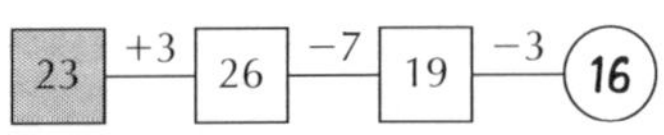

- Write a 2-digit number in the grey boxes and provide the children with a number dice and a six-sided addition and subtraction symbol dice. Children roll both dice and perform the operation generated. If the children reach a point along the chain where they cannot do the calculation, for example, the answer will give a negative number, they roll both dice again.

Whole-class, group or individual activities

Add and subtract
Add and multiply
Subtract and multiply

Addition and subtraction
Multiplication and division

Notes for the teacher

- There are three versions of this activity. The three examples given below are for the 'Add and subtract' table, however the same principles apply to all three versions.
- These activities are introducing children, in an informal way, to the concept of algebra.
- For each table write:
  - a number in each of the eight boxes below the circle ○
  - a number in each of the eight boxes below the square □.
- Ensure that when using the 'Add and subtract', and 'Subtract and multiply' versions, for each row, you write the larger number in the circle column and the smaller number in the square column.
- The star to the right of each table can either be used for the children to write their score out of 16, or if you are timing the activity, the time it took them to complete it.
- Note that for the Challenge 3 example, teachers need to complete the table and then delete two numbers from each row of the table. This version helps children develop their understanding of the inverse relationship between addition and subtraction, or multiplication and division. Also note that the example given on page 164 may prove difficult for many children. It is important that before presenting such a table that you spend time discussing it with the children.
- When children have completed the table, discuss with them any patterns and relationships they notice.

Notes for the children

- Ensure children understand that to complete each table, they perform the operation given in the top row of the third and fourth columns in the table, writing each answer in the appropriate box.

○	□	○ + □	○ − □
27	14	41	13
45	21	66	24
38	16	54	22
63	39	102	24

(continued)

Whole-class, group or individual activities

Example of differentiation content

Challenge 1

○	□	○ + □	○ − □
14	6		
17	9		
12	4		
10	7		
16	8		
11	2		
15	5		
19	3		

Variations

- Ensure that all answers are less than 100.
- Provide the children with several of the answers written in the table.

Challenge 2

○	□	○ + □	○ − □
27	14		
45	21		
38	16		
63	39		
19	11		
56	25		
24	17		
72	40		

Challenge 3

○	□	○ + □	○ − □
58	30		
64			35
	47		38
	16	83	
92		150	
36		49	
	35		26
		67	19

Variations

- Include calculations that involve adding or subtracting a 2-digit number and ones, a 2-digit number and tens, two 2-digit numbers, a 3-digit number and ones, a 3-digit number and tens or a 3-digit number and hundreds.
- Include calculations that involve the multiplication tables up to 12 × 12 or multiplying multiples of 10 by 1-digit numbers, for example, 40 × 6.

Whole-class, group or individual activities

Dice calculations (addition)
Dice calculations (subtraction)
Dice calculations (multiplication)
Dice calculations (division)

Addition and subtraction
Multiplication and division

Additional resources

- two 1–6, 0–9, 1–12 or 1–20 dice, or any combination of two dice (per child)

Notes for the teacher

- There are four versions of this activity – one for each of the four operations. With some exceptions (see below), the same principles apply to all four versions.
- The dice you give the children differentiate this activity.

Notes for the children

- Children roll both dice, writing one number in the square and one in the triangle. They then perform the operation and write the answer in the circle.
- Note the following:
  - For 'Dice calculations (subtraction)' children must write the larger number in the square and the smaller number in the triangle.
  - 'Dice calculations (multiplication)' may not be appropriate for most children in Year 3 as given the random nature of this activity, depending on the dice used, the multiplication calculations that children generate will be ones that they are yet to learn, i.e. for two 1–6 dice: multiplication facts for the 6 multiplication table; for two 0–9 dice: multiplication facts for the 6, 7 and 9 multiplication tables and for two 1–12 dice: multiplication facts for the 6, 7, 9, 11 and 12 multiplication tables (see Variations below for an alternative).
  - For 'Dice calculations (division)' children must write the larger number in the square and the smaller number in the triangle. However, this version may not be appropriate for some children in Lower Key Stage 2 as given the random nature of this activity, most of the division calculations that children will generate will result in the answer having a remainder.

Variations

- For 'Dice calculations (addition)':

(**Note:** This variation is ideal for practising and consolidating the addition facts to 20 and adding a 2-digit number and ones, and a 3-digit number and ones.)

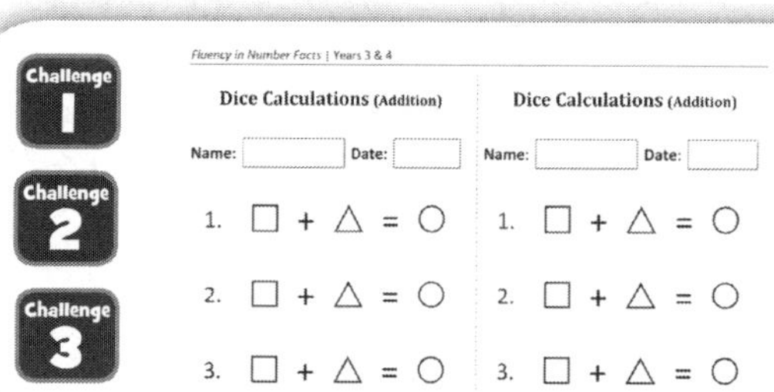

(continued)

- Write a number in each of the ten squares. Provide each child with only one die (or two 1–6 or two 0–9 dice to generate 2-digit numbers). Children roll the die, write the number in the triangle, add the two numbers together and write the answer in the circle.
- Write a number in each of the ten triangles. Provide each child with only one die (or two 1–6 or two 0–9 dice to generate 2-digit numbers). Children roll the die, write the number in the square, add the two numbers together and write the answer in the circle.
- Write a number in each of the ten circles. Provide each child with only one die. Children roll the die and write the number in the square. They then work out what number they need to add to the number in the square to make the total in the circle. They write this number in the triangle. Note that the numbers you write in each of the circles must be larger than the largest number it is possible to roll on the die. Also note that this variation is ideal for practising and consolidating pairs of numbers that make a given total, such as 10, 20 or 100.
- Write a number in each of the ten circles. Provide each child with only one die. Children roll the die and write the number in the triangle. They then work out what number they need to add to the number in the triangle to make the total in the circle. They write this number in the square. Note that the numbers you write in each of the circles must be larger than the largest number it is possible to roll on the die. Also note that this variation is ideal for practising and consolidating pairs of numbers that make a given total such as 10, 20 or 100.

- For 'Dice calculations (subtraction)':

(**Note:** This variation is ideal for practising and consolidating the subtraction facts to 20 and subtracting a 2-digit number and ones, and a 3-digit number and ones.)

- Write a number in each of the ten squares. Provide each child with only one die. Children roll the die, write the number in the triangle, find the difference between the two numbers and write the answer in the circle. Note that the numbers you write in each of the squares must be larger than the largest number it is possible to roll on the die.
- Write a 1-digit number in each of the ten triangles. Provide each child with either two 1–6 or two 0–9 dice. Children roll the dice to generate a 2-digit number, write this number in the square, find the difference between the two numbers and write the answer in the circle.
- Write a number in each of the ten circles. Provide each child with only one die. Children roll the die and write the number in the triangle. They then work out the minuend and write this number in the square.
- Write a 1-digit number in each of the ten circles. Provide each child with either two 1–6 or two 0–9 dice. Children roll the dice to generate a 2-digit number, write this number in the square. They then work out the subtrahend and write this number in the triangle.

- For 'Dice calculations (multiplication)':

(**Note:** This variation is ideal for practising and consolidating the multiplication facts for multiplication tables up to 12 × 12.)

- Write one of the numbers 2–12 in each of the ten squares. Provide each child with one 1–12 die. Children roll the die, write the number in the triangle, multiply the two numbers together and write the product in the circle.
- Write one of the numbers 2–12 in each of the ten triangles. Provide each child with one 1–12 die. Children roll the die, write the number in the square, multiply the two numbers together and write the product in the circle.

Challenge 3

- Rolling two 0–9 dice will generate all of the 2-digit numbers.
- For 'Dice calculations (multiplication)' write 2-digit numbers or multiples of 10 or 100 in the squares or triangles and provide the child with a 1–6 dice, 0–9 dice or 1–12 dice.

Whole-class, group or individual activities

16 / 49 / 100 calculations (1-digit numbers)
16 / 49 / 100 calculations (numbers 1–12)
16 / 49 / 100 calculations (2-digit numbers)
16 / 49 / 100 calculations (3-digit numbers)
16 / 49 / 100 calculations (multiples of 10)
16 calculations (multiples of 100)
49 / 100 calculations (multiples of 10 and 100)

Addition and subtraction
Multiplication and division

Notes for the teacher

- There are 18 versions of this activity:
  - six versions each requiring the children to perform 16 calculations
  - six versions each requiring the children to perform 49 calculations
  - six versions each requiring the children to perform 100 calculations.
- The same principles apply to all versions.
- It is recommended that, except for the most able children, at Lower Key Stage 2 you use the six versions that require the children to perform 49 calculations.
- For each grid write an operation (addition, subtraction or multiplication symbol followed by a number) in the circle.
- The operation you write in the circle differentiates this activity.
- The star at the bottom of each grid can either be used for the children to write their score, or if you are timing the activity, the time it took them to complete it.
- When children have completed the grid, discuss with them any patterns and relationships they notice.

(*continued*)

Whole-class, group or individual activities

Notes for the children

- Ensure children understand that to complete each grid, they perform the operation given in the circle on the number written in the top left-hand corner of each box, writing each answer in the appropriate box.

+18

7 25	9 27	4 22	8 26
3 21	6 24	2 20	1 19
8 26	4 22	7 25	9 27
9 27	3 21	5 23	7 25

- Note that for activities involving subtraction, for example, (– 30) ensure children subtract the number in the circle from the number written in the top left-hand corner of each box.

−30

654 624	191 161	383 353	947 917
876 846	435 405	207 177	508 478
753 723	546 516	168 138	600 570
412 382	734 704	962 932	489 459

Challenge 1

Challenge 2

Challenge 3

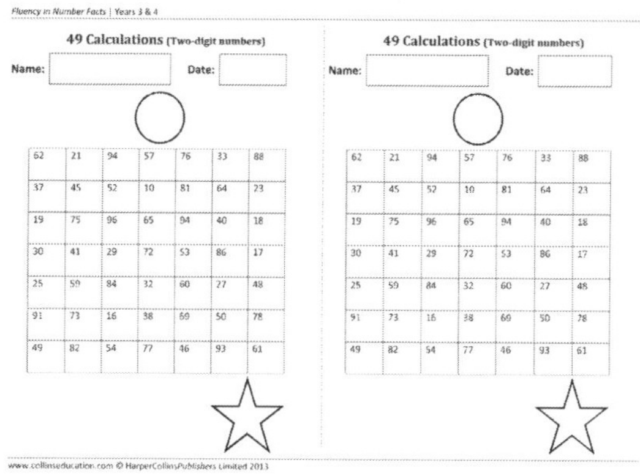

Fluency in Number Facts | Years 3 & 4

49 Calculations (Two-digit numbers)

Name: Date:

62	21	94	57	76	33	88
37	45	52	10	81	64	23
19	75	96	65	94	40	18
30	41	29	72	53	86	17
25	59	84	32	60	27	48
91	73	16	38	69	50	78
49	82	54	77	46	93	61

49 Calculations (Two-digit numbers)

Name: Date:

62	21	94	57	76	33	88
37	45	52	10	81	64	23
19	75	96	65	94	40	18
30	41	29	72	53	86	17
25	59	84	32	60	27	48
91	73	16	38	69	50	78
49	82	54	77	46	93	61

www.collinseducation.com © HarperCollinsPublishers Limited 2013

Variations

- Below is a list of suggestions as to possible operations to write. However, this list must not in any way be seen as the limits that are possible with these activities.
  - 1-digit numbers: (+ 1), (+ 2), (+ 3), (+ 4), (+ 5)… ; (− 1); (× 2), (× 3), (× 4)… (× 12)
  - numbers 1–12: (+ 1), (+ 2), (+ 3), (+ 4), (+ 5)… ; (− 1); (× 2), (× 3), (× 4)… (× 12)
  - 2-digit numbers: (+ 1), (+ 2), (+ 3), (+ 4), (+ 5)… ; (+ 10), (+ 20), (+ 30), (+ 40)… (+ 100); (− 1), (− 2), (− 3), (− 4), (− 5)… (− 13)
  - 3-digit numbers: (+ 1), (+ 2), (+3), (+4), (+ 5)… ; (+ 10), (+ 20), (+ 30), (+ 40)… (+ 100); (− 1), (− 2), (− 3), (− 4), (− 5)… (− 106); (− 10), (− 20), (− 30), (− 40)… (− 100)
  - multiples of 10: (+ 1), (+ 2), (+ 3), (+ 4), (+ 5)… ; (+ 10), (+ 20), (+ 30), (+ 40)… (+ 100); (− 1), (− 2), (− 3), (− 4), (− 5)… (− 10); (× 2), (× 3), (× 4)… (× 12)
  - multiples of 100 (16 calculations version only): (+ 1), (+ 2), (+ 3), (+ 4), (+ 5)… ; (+ 10), (+ 20), (+ 30), (+ 40)… (+ 100); (− 1), (− 2), (− 3), (− 4), (− 5)… (− 100); (− 10), (− 20), (− 30), (− 40)… (− 100)
  - multiples of 10 and 100 (49 and 100 calculations versions only): (+ 1), (+ 2), (+ 3), (+ 4), (+ 5)… ; (+ 10), (+ 20), (+ 30), (+ 40)… (+ 100); (+ 100), (+ 200), (+ 300), (+ 400)… (+ 1000); (−1), (− 2), (−3), (− 4), (− 5)… (− 10)

Challenge 1

- Provide children with the six versions that require them to perform 16 calculations.

Challenge 3

- Provide children with the six versions that require them to perform 100 calculations.

Whole-class, group or individual activities

Addition and subtraction facts

Multiplication and division facts

Objectives

- Recall and use addition and subtraction facts to 20 fluently, and derive and use related facts up to 100
- Add and subtract numbers mentally, including a 2-digit number and ones, a 2-digit number and tens, two 2-digit numbers, a 3-digit number and ones, a 3-digit number and tens, and a 3-digit number and hundreds
- Recall multiplication and division facts for multiplication tables up to 12 × 12

Teacher resources

CD → Mental fluency challenges

- scissors

Pupil resources

- 'Mental fluency challenge' (per child)
- pencil (per child)

Introduction

Fluency in Number Facts: Years 3 & 4 includes 36 graded 'Mental fluency challenges':

- 18 for Year 3: CD → Mental fluency challenges → Year 3
- 18 for Year 4: CD → Mental fluency challenges → Year 4

These challenges are aimed at providing children with further practice and consolidation and also at offering teachers a means of assessing individual children's proficiency in the mental recall of number facts. They can be used with the whole class, specific groups or individual children.

Each challenge covers the key addition, subtraction, multiplication and division number facts that children need to be able to recall instantly by the end of Lower Key Stage 2.

Careful consideration has been given to the progression of the Lower Key Stage 2 curriculum, and for each year group the 18 challenges have been arranged into three different ability levels, with six exercises at each level: Challenge 1 easy, Challenge 2 average and Challenge 3 challenging.

(continued)

It is recommended that children do the same exercise on two or three consecutive days. This way, the majority of children will see themselves making progress over the two or three days, thus providing greater encouragement and self-motivation.

It is envisaged that these exercises could be given to the children either where they take as long as they need to answer all 15 questions, or as a timed exercise (for example: *I want you to answer as many of these questions as you can in eight minutes. Ready? Go!*). Alternatively, to encourage speed and recall, set the children to work and as they finish the exercise they raise their hand and you tell them how long it took them to complete it.

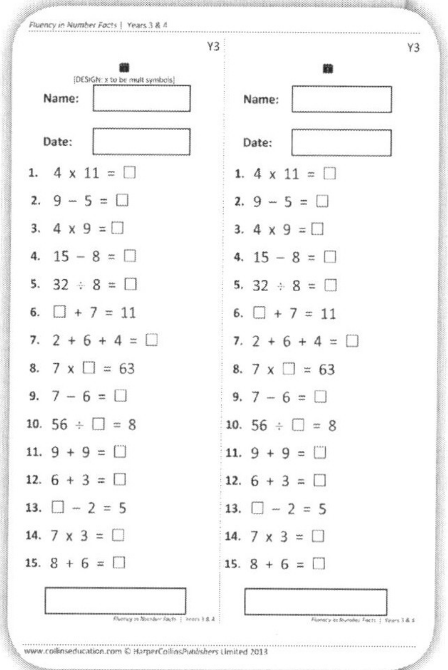
Fluency in Number Facts | Years 3 & 4

Y3	Y3
Name:	Name:
Date:	Date:
1. 4 x 11 = □	1. 4 x 11 = □
2. 9 − 5 = □	2. 9 − 5 = □
3. 4 x 9 = □	3. 4 x 9 = □
4. 15 − 8 = □	4. 15 − 8 = □
5. 32 ÷ 8 = □	5. 32 ÷ 8 = □
6. □ + 7 = 11	6. □ + 7 = 11
7. 2 + 6 + 4 = □	7. 2 + 6 + 4 = □
8. 7 x □ = 63	8. 7 x □ = 63
9. 7 − 6 = □	9. 7 − 6 = □
10. 56 ÷ □ = 8	10. 56 ÷ □ = 8
11. 9 + 9 = □	11. 9 + 9 = □
12. 6 + 3 = □	12. 6 + 3 = □
13. □ − 2 = 5	13. □ − 2 = 5
14. 7 x 3 = □	14. 7 x 3 = □
15. 8 + 6 = □	15. 8 + 6 = □

www.collinseducation.com © HarperCollinsPublishers Limited 2013

Both PDF and WORD versions of the 'Mental fluency challenges' are provided.

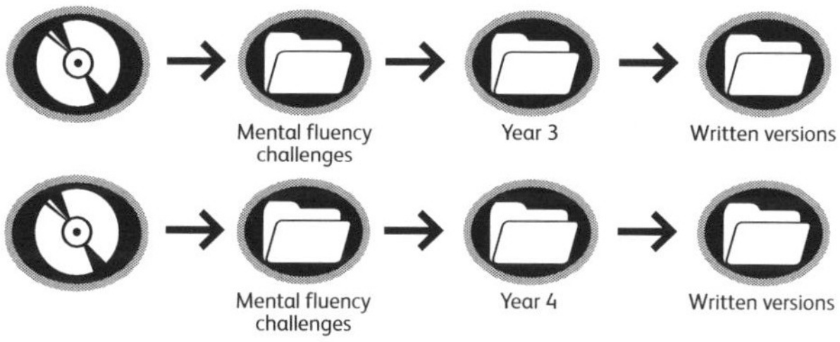

The WORD version is provided so that individual schools or classes can modify the content of the challenges to better suit the needs of their children. However, it is important to be aware that, if changes are made to the content, the continuity and progression of the challenges will be affected.

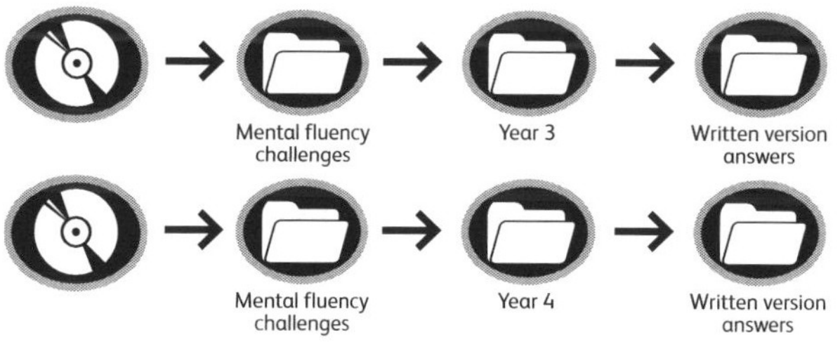

The answers to each of the challenges are provided as individual PDF files. Teachers may want to use these to display to the children when marking and discussing the challenges.

(*continued*)

(continued)

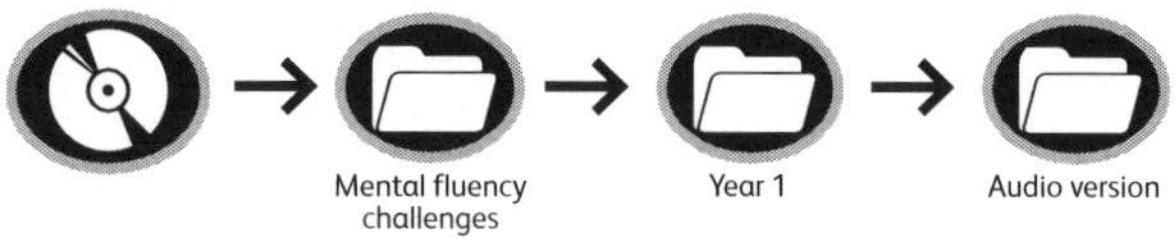

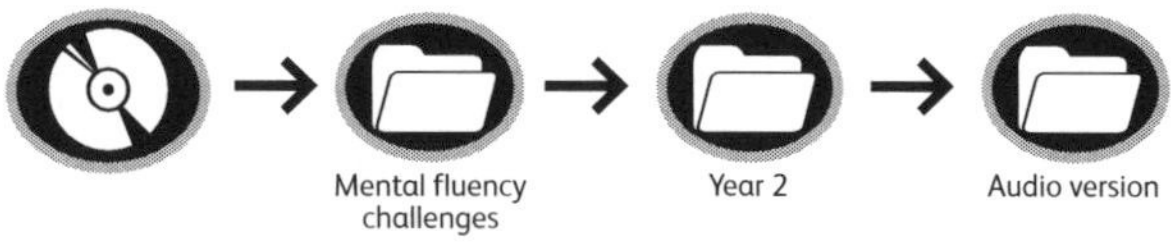

As well as the WORD and PDF versions of the 'Mental fluency challenges', there is also an audio file of each exercise.

A 'Mental fluency challenge answer sheet' is also provided for children to use to record their answers when using the auditory version of the challenges.

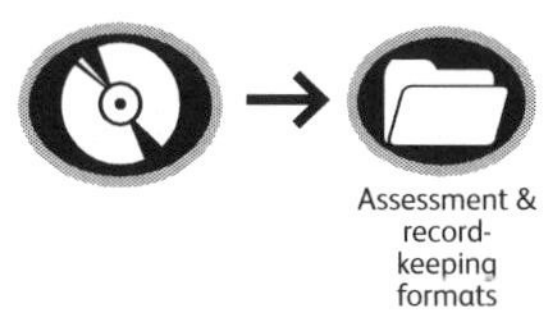

To assist with keeping a record of the different 'Mental fluency challenges' that individual children complete throughout the course of a year, a 'Record of mental fluency challenges chart' for Year 3 and Year 4 is also provided. These charts can also be used to record children's scores.

What to do

- Choose an appropriate exercise for the whole class, specific groups or individual children, taking careful consideration of the different needs and abilities of the children. If undertaking the activity with the whole class, you will probably use an exercise from two or three of the different levels: Challenge 1 easy, Challenge 2 average or Challenge 3 challenging.
- If using the WORD/PDF version, distribute the exercise(s) to the children. If using the audio version, ensure that each child has a copy of the 'Mental fluency challenge answer sheet'. Also ensure that each child has a sharpened pencil!
- Allow the children sufficient time to complete the exercise or set the exercise as a timed activity.
- Once the children have completed the exercise, immediately mark the exercise(s), using the relevant PDF answers sheet(s). You may want to mark the exercise(s) with the children's help, asking children to mark their own exercise or swapping and marking someone else's exercise.
- Be sure to discuss the results of the exercise(s) with the children, asking them which questions they found easy, which they found more difficult, and also referring to specific questions, asking them how they worked out the answer. This should provide some excellent data to help identify common errors or misconceptions that children may have. You can then either follow on with some brief impromptu teaching, assisting children to overcome the errors or misconceptions or, alternatively, keep this information in mind for some further teaching at a later date.
- You may want to use the appropriate 'Record of mental fluency challenges chart' to record the exercise that individual children have completed. You may also want to use the chart to record their score.
- And finally...remember to repeat the same exercise on two or three consecutive days.

Paired games and activities

Addition and subtraction facts

Multiplication and division facts

Objectives

- Recall and use addition and subtraction facts to 20 fluently, and derive and use related facts up to 100
- Add and subtract numbers mentally, including a 2-digit number and ones, a 2-digit number and tens, two 2-digit numbers, a 3-digit number and ones, a 3-digit number and tens, and a 3-digit number and hundreds
- Recall multiplication and division facts for multiplication tables up to 12 × 12

Teacher resources

→ Paired games and activities → Paired calculation cards

- 'Paired calculation cards' (ideally printed onto card)

Pupil resources

- 'Paired calculations card' (per pair)

Introduction

Fluency in Number Facts: Years 3 & 4 includes 36 graded 'Paired calculations cards':

- 18 for Year 3: → Paired games and activities → Paired calculation cards → Year 3
- 18 for Year 4: → Paired games and activities → Paired calculation cards → Year 4

Each card covers the key addition, subtraction, multiplication and division number facts that children need to be able to recall instantly by the end of Lower Key Stage 2.

Careful consideration has been given to the progression of the Lower Key Stage 2 curriculum, and for each year group the 18 cards have been arranged into three different ability levels, with six cards at each level: Challenge 1 easy, Challenge 2 average and Challenge 3 difficult.

It is recommended that pairs of children use the same card on two or three consecutive days. This way, the majority of children will see themselves making progress over the two or three days, thus providing greater encouragement and self-motivation.

(*continued*)

Assessment & record-keeping formats

To assist with keeping a record of the different 'Paired calculations cards' that individual children complete throughout the course of a year, a 'Record of paired calculations cards chart' for Year 3 and Year 4 is also provided.

What to do

- Arrange the children into pairs of similar ability.
- Provide each pair with an appropriate card, taking careful consideration of the different needs and abilities of the children: Challenge 1 easy, Challenge 2 average or Challenge 3 difficult.
- Each pair positions the card between them, with one child having a clear view of Side A and the other child a clear view of Side B.
- Children take turns to ask their partner the 15 questions on their side of the card. Ensure the children realise that they do not say the answer in the grey box. You may also need to demonstrate to the children how to phrase questions such as 12 + [?] = 30, i.e. *Twelve add what other number equals 30,* and [?] – 8 = 26, i.e. *What number, minus 8, equals 26.*
- As each child says an answer, their partner responds saying whether the answer is correct or not.
- Once each child has asked their partner the 15 questions on their side of the card, the children turn the card around and repeat.
- When pairs have finished be sure to discuss the results with the children, asking them which questions they found easy, which they found more difficult, and also referring to specific questions, asking them how they worked out the answer. This will probably provide some excellent data in helping identify common errors or misconceptions that children may have, which you can then either follow on with some brief impromptu teaching, assisting children to overcome the errors or misconceptions, or alternatively keeping this information in mind for some further teaching at a later date.
- You may want to use the appropriate 'Record of paired calculations cards chart' to record the card that pairs of children have completed.
- And finally…remember to ask pairs of children to use the same card on two or three consecutive days.

Addition and subtraction facts

Multiplication and division facts

Objectives

- Recall and use addition and subtraction facts to 20 fluently, and derive and use related facts up to 100
- Add and subtract numbers mentally, including a 2-digit number and ones, a 2-digit number and tens, two 2-digit numbers, a 3-digit number and ones, a 3-digit number and tens, and a 3-digit number and hundreds
- Recall multiplication and division facts for multiplication tables up to 12 × 12

Teacher resources

→ Individual activities → Function machine strips

- 'Function machine strips' (ideally printed onto card)
- scissors

Pupil resources

- 'Function machine strip' (per child)
- 'Function machine' ('My Maths Function Machine', B&W version or colour version) printed onto card (per child)

Introduction

Fluency in Number Facts: Years 3 & 4 includes 36 graded 'Function machine strips':

- 18 for Year 3: → Individual activities → Function machine strips → Year 3
- 18 for Year 4: → Individual activities → Function machine strips → Year 4

Each 'Function machine strip' covers the key addition, subtraction, multiplication and division number facts that children need to be able to recall instantly by the end of Lower Key Stage 2.

Careful consideration has been given to the progression of the Lower Key Stage 2 curriculum, and for each year group the 18 strips have been arranged into three different ability levels, with six strips at each level: Challenge 1 easy, Challenge 2 average and Challenge 3 difficult.

It is recommended that children use the same strip on several consecutive days – perhaps even for a whole week. This way, the majority of children will see themselves making progress, thus providing greater encouragement and self-motivation.

(*continued*)

It is recommended that before children do the 'Function machine strip' activity for the first time, that you provide each child with a copy of the 'Function machine' ('My Maths Function Machine') which is printed onto card for the children to personalise.

Assessment & record-keeping formats

To assist with keeping a record of the different 'Function machine strips' that individual children complete throughout the course of a year, a 'Record of Function machine strips chart 'for Year 3 and Year 4 is also provided.

What to do

- Provide each child with an appropriate strip, taking careful consideration of the different needs and abilities of the children: Challenge 1 easy, Challenge 2 average or Challenge 3 challenging.
- Children carefully feed the strip through their Function machine, only revealing one calculation at a time.
- The child works out the answer and them moves the strip on slightly to reveal the answer.
- Children continue in this way until they get to the end of the strip and the tenth answer is revealed.
- Encourage the children to use the same strip several times in one session – aiming to make fewer errors and/or complete the strip in a shorter period of time.
- When individual children have finished, you may want to ask them which questions they found easy, which they found more difficult, and also referring to specific questions, asking them how they worked out the answer. This should provide some excellent data in helping identify common errors or misconceptions that children may have, which you can then either follow on with some brief impromptu teaching, assisting children to overcome the errors or misconceptions, or alternatively keeping this information in mind for some further teaching at a later date.
- You may want to use the appropriate 'Record of Function machine strips chart' to record the strips that individual children have completed.
- And finally...remember to ask the children to use the same strip on several consecutive days.